Popular Christianity in India

SUNY series in Hindu Studies
Wendy Doniger, editor

POPULAR CHRISTIANITY IN INDIA

RITING BETWEEN THE LINES

EDITED BY

SELVA J. RAJ
AND
CORINNE G. DEMPSEY

STATE UNIVERSITY OF NEW YORK PRESS

Published by
State University of New York Press, Albany

Cover photo: used by permission. The Chariot Docks by Dick Waghorne.

For information, address State University of New York Press,
90 State Street, Suite 700, Albany, N.Y., 12207

Production by Diane Ganeles
Marketing by Michael Campochiaro

Library of Congress Cataloging-in-Publication Data

Popular Christianity in India : riting between the lines / edited by Selva J. Raj and
Corinne G. Dempsey.
    p. cm. — (SUNY series in Hindu studies)
    Includes index.
    ISBN 0-7914-5519-X (alk. paper) — ISBN 0-7914-5520-3 (pbk. : alk. paper)
    1. Christianity—India.   I. Raj, Selva J.   II. Dempsey, Corinne G.   III. Series.

BR1155.P67 2002
275.4—dc21   2001057788

10 9 8 7 6 5 4 3 2 1

To the memory of
the saints in our families who inspired us:
A. S. Joachim, K. S. Arulanandam, S. J.,
Henry and Hilda Courtney, and Mae Dempsey

Contents

Acknowledgments

This volume on popular Christianity in India was born when Selva floated the idea to Corinne at the conclusion of a session we organized for the annual meeting of the American Academy of Religion (AAR) in San Francisco, 1997. Three of the presenters from this meeting have contributed to this volume and others joined in what appeared initially to be a formidable undertaking. Many colleagues and friends have helped to realize our goal without whose support and assistance this volume would not have been possible. Most noteworthy among them is Wendy Doniger who was committed to seeing this collection in print. She not only provided her characteristic encouragement and unflagging support throughout the preparation of the manuscript but graciously agreed to write a fitting foreword. Vasudha Narayanan, who served as the respondent at the AAR session, offered to write a response essay. We are thankful for her encouragement and faith in the volume's potential value. Our special thanks to each of our contributors for their patience and understanding as the volume took shape. Frank Clooney, Joyce Flueckiger, William Harman, Rachel McDermott, Lance Nelson, Karen Pechilis-Prentiss, Paula Richman, Whitney Sanford, Thomas Thangaraj, and Paul Younger, who supported our venture in various ways, deserve special thanks. We thank the many friends and colleagues who are too numerous to mention for their valuable insights and hearty support.

The University of Chicago Press has given us permission to include two articles from History of Religions 39, no. 2 (1999): Corinne Dempsey's "Lessons in Miracles from Kerala, South India: Stories of Three 'Christian' Saints" (150–76) and Joanne Punzo Waghorne's "Chariots of the Gods: Riding the Line Between Hindu and Christian" (96–116). Selva Raj's "The Ganges, the Jordan, and the Mountain: The Three Strands of Santal Popular Catholicism" originally appeared in Doxology: A Journal of Worship 16 (1999): 17–39. His "Transgressing Boundaries, Transcending Turner: The Pilgrimage Tradition at the Shrine of St. John de Britto" first appeared in the Journal of Ritual Studies 16, no. 1 (2002): 4–18. We are grateful to Nancy Ellegate, Senior Acquisitions Editor at the State University Press of New York, for her practical advice and remarkable patience in the preparation of this manuscript. Our thanks are also due to the editorial staff at SUNY Press, especially Diane Ganeles, Senior Production Editor, for their skill and assistance, as well as the anonymous reviewers for helping us to improve the volume further. We are grateful to Albion College for two research grants in support of this work: a Hewlett-Mellon grant from the Faculty Development Committee and a research grant from the Center for Interdisciplinary Studies in Ethnic, Gender, and Global Studies. Of course the essays in this volume would not be possible without the generosity of countless Indian Christians who shared with us their invaluable perspectives and opened us to new ways of thinking. Finally, we offer special thanks to Nick Garigliano, Bindu Madhok, and George Strander for sharing in the highs and lows of editing this volume.

SELVA J. RAJ
CORINNE G. DEMPSEY

Foreword:
The View from the Other Side:
Postpostcolonialism, Religious Syncretism, and Class Conflict

This is an important moment, in both Indian history and American scholarship, to open up the issue of the assimilation of Christianity in India. Scholarship dances to the music of history. The history of Christianity in India has recently opened up to a whole new way of thinking that has not, until now, reached the page, though it may very well have occurred to a number of people who had no access to a printing press, or even to a diary.

For most of the twentieth century, scholars of South Asian religions, on the one hand, and Christian theologians and church leaders, on the other, largely ignored the popular manifestations of Christianity in India, though for very different reasons. Many historians of religions were European or American Christians, whose only slightly displaced missiological drive traditionally focused on exotic and "pagan" religions, the dramatically other Others such as Hinduism, Jainism, and Buddhism. An unfortunate remnant of the missionary and colonial legacy was the never-acknowledged assumption that Christianity was a metatradition immune to and beyond the purview of the empirical methodology of the history of religions. On the other hand, when the history of Christianity in India was taken as an object of study at all, it was viewed, like history in general, from the standpoint of power, from the top down: from the records, and hence inevitably the point of view of the conquerors, in this case the missionaries. This approach regarded the context in which Indian Christianity grew—the world of Hinduism and Islam—as nothing but a problem that Christianity solved, a question to which Christianity was the answer. As Corinne Dempsey notes, the academic community, so heavily influenced by European Christianity, is only now revising its self-understanding of its position as peripheral Other in south India. Protestant scholars in the nineteenth century, adding an anti-Catholic bias to the more general Christian bias, produced an agenda that has continued to pollute the scholarship on comparison even in our day (Smith 1990). The unspoken Protestant bias in religious studies has tended to drive all studies back to "the beginning," ultimately to the Veda, ignoring the long process of history that came after the Veda, a history in which Europeans played an important role.

Precolonial, imperialist history recorded only one half of the story of this interaction, the missionary-eye-view, like someone listening to a person talking on a telephone, unable to hear the responses of the person on the other end of the line. Postcolonial history began to listen in on the call, to hear the voice on the other end of the line. The postcolonial revolution in scholarship, following right on the heels of the political liberation of India in 1947, questioned the motives and ideologies of the conquerors; and, in the shadow of Michel Foucault and Edward Said (Said 1979), it viewed religion in general as nothing but a thinly veiled arm of political power, in this case imperial power. The postcolonial critique concentrated on political aspects of the European domination of India, and scholars of religion rightly responded largely by paying more attention to the political aspects of the construction of religion.

That, however, too, was just half of the story; it failed to analyze the religious aspects of the political construction of India. What might be called postpostcolonialism, a movement reflected in the later writings of Edward Said (Said 1993), rebelled against the first rebels, attempting to rescue the colonized from the still insulting position of victims to which early postcolonialism had consigned them. It sought to excavate and restore the integrity of voices of resistance, and it found them, sometimes preserved in obscure sources that had been overlooked, sometimes embedded like a fifth column within the records of their oppressors. As a more political and less scholarly movement, this resistance has taken on a new face in our day, in the form of violence directed by Hindus (largely incited by right-wing Hindu fundamentalists) against Indian Christians, violence that has been luridly documented in the Western press. Who, now, are the victims and who the resistors?

The British left their props and scripts on stage in India, but most of the actual players exited. By contrast, the Christians are still there, in the form of people who converted from Hinduism or Islam or are descended from such converts. They are also there in the form of people who were born in Europe and went to India as missionaries or are descended from people who did not leave the stage in 1947 (a set movingly evoked by Paul Scott in *Staying On* [Scott 1977]), and we now know that these people are us, at least to the extent that, as postcolonialism has taught us, all European scholars are implicated to some extent in the history of the European presence in India. We can still hear the voices of all of these people now.

The present volume represents a postpostcolonial historiography, one that views the Indians who were subject to Christian missions neither simply as victims nor simply as resistors (against Hinduism or Islam, as was once argued of those who did convert, or against the Christians, said of those who did not convert), but rather as active agents. Not content merely to hear their responses to a call initiated by the British, these scholars are now listening for calls made by the Indians themselves, calls directed not merely to the British but to one another. This is the converts'-eye-view, the view from (in terms of political power) the bottom up. During the last two decades of the twentieth century, Ph.D. students in the history of religions began to do fieldwork that investigates popular manifestations of Christianity in non-Western regions in general and South Asia in particular. In broadening its scholarly focus and readjusting its methodological lens, the history of religions has opened up a new subfield within the discipline that is bringing fresh data to public discourse and scholarly scrutiny. The present collection of essays signals this new movement, interpreting a rich compendium of empirical data through methodologies that acknowledge the complexity of popular Indian Christianity and the complicated identities of Indian Christians, while challenging facile distinctions between Hindu and Christian.

The new consciousness also makes it possible now to consider not only the negative but the positive—or, at least potentially positive—aspects of imperialism, an aspect perhaps easier to see in religion than in politics. Dempsey tells the tale of a boy captured by demons, a boy who had a European vicar (or bishop) on his side. The bishop is constructed as "foreign" (Persian, an ethnicity with positive valences for the Syrian church). This story has resonances in other stories that tell of other foreigners, perhaps Europeans, who fought against demons in India. Stella Kramrisch wrote, years ago, of "white-skinned foreigners said to have come in the thirteenth century from Anatolia and Syria and to have killed the tyrant Punvaro. He had cut off the hands of the architect who had built the city of Patan so that he might not construct anything like it again. The seventy-two horsemen took the fort and killed the chief. . . . These apocalyptic horsemen transmute the fear generated by Muslim invasions into India into a liberating legend in which the evil power does not come from outside but is local, embodied in the tyrant Punvaro" (Kramrisch 1968, 55). Even today, villagers in Kutch make statues of the seventy-two horses and offer sweet rice to the horsemen and ask them for boons (Narayan 1999).

Nowadays we would go on to ask who constructed this myth, and who perpetuated it; and we must not forget that the British found it very useful to tell, on many occasions, other variations on the theme of "the British saving Hindus from Muslims." But there are also many tellings of the story of Punvaro that have a more clearly Hindu provenance, and in Chennai (Madras) today, Hindus do say that the British, especially the early East India Company, liberated Hindus in south India from Muslim control and played not merely a neutral but a positive role in establishing an evenhanded attitude to all religions in its new territory (Waghorne 1999). The story of Punvaro is subversion turned on its head, as it were, subversion inverted, subversion from the top down: it speaks of false consciousness, of mythology imposed from the top down, and of the assimilation of the values of the conquerors by those who are conquered. It views the demon-killing invaders as demons, too, but as benign demons (a well-known category in Hinduism [Doniger 1975, 281–89]) who brought something of value, the gift from another world (Doniger 1999). Demons teach the gods about resurrection in a story told in the *Mahabharata*, in which the gods send the son of their guru Brihaspati to learn the secret of revival from Shukra, guru of the demons (*Mahabharata* 1.71–2; O'Flaherty 1975, 281–89). Being demonized is not always such a bad thing. If the Europeans, hawking their secret of resurrection, are demons, they may well be that sort of demon, the sort that can do you some good—too.

These essays speak of Indian attempts to achieve a new kind of both religious and political dignity through some sort of combination of the religion of their birth and the Christianity of their choice. Never ignoring the destructive aspects of conversion that have been so well documented by those postcolonial scholars who depicted Hindus as victims, and that surely must be supplying at least part of the energy fueling the anti-Christian attacks that are going on in India today, the authors of this volume go on to consider the manner in which many Hindus who came in contact with Christianity, whether as converts or merely as neighbors, found ways to benefit from the contact. These ways took very different forms depending upon a number of factors, such as the moment in history, the part of India, the form of Christianity, and the gender and class of the potential converts.

Of the ten essays in this volume, two deal with history and the other eight primarily with contemporary fieldwork, often historically contextualized. Geographically, the majority of the essays present fieldwork in south India, six from Tamil Nadu and one from Kerala; the other three deal with Delhi, Benares, and the general area of Bihar, West Bengal, and Orissa. This geographical bias is a direct reflection of the fact that the majority of Indian Christians live in south India; and the predominance of Catholics in this area is reflected in the predominance of essays in this volume dealing with Catholics, while only three deal with Protestants and one with the Syrian Church. Eliza Kent notes that the Protestants, less sensual than the Catholics (or Hindus, I would add), afford far less examples of explicit "syncretism" and shun Hindu-Muslim "superstition," perhaps (I would suggest) through an anti-Catholic bias. (Such a bias, as Lata Mani has well argued, fueled the British emphasis on "Scripture"—the *Laws of Manu*—over oral tradition—the rulings of local Indian judges—in their legislation regulating the burning of widows [Mani 1998, 99]). The three essays on Protestantism, by Eliza

Kent, John Webster, and Zoe Sherinian, also deal more explicitly with gender issues, Kent with women's literacy, Webster by noting that, in the absence of *zenana* work, no Dalit women were converted, and Sherinian with female images of god. Dempsey also tells the stories of two women saints, and Richard MacPhail writes about a female medium. The other essays deal primarily with men or with people of unspecified gender.

The issue of class is more complex. Intersecting with the top-down or bottom-up point of view of colonizer vs. colonized, missionary vs. convert, is the more complex question of the class from which converts were drawn. Hotly debated from the time of the earliest successful missionary, de Nobili, the question of elite vs. lower class converts has almost always been studied, like everything else in Indian religion, from the standpoint of the missionaries: what were the advantages of proselytizing among one class or the other? But some of the present essays deal not merely with lower-class Hindus but with tribal people like the Santals, entirely outside the Hindu caste system, and with the Dalits, formerly known as Untouchables, consigned to a limbo inside the Hindu world but excluded from its official social hierarchy. Sherinian, analyzing a Dalit theologian's use of a Tamil version of the Lord's Prayer, grapples with the problematic assertion that Christianity offers Dalits a promise of freedom (from Hindu persecution); elsewhere, Kent has demonstrated just how problematic this assertion is when it is applied to women, who found that, in many cases, they had leapt from the frying pan of Hindu misogyny into the fire of Protestant sexism (Kent 1999). John Webster writes, in this volume, of the conversion of the Chamars, a particular caste of Dalits, who probably perceived Christianity as a "panth," or non-Vedic religious path.

More generally, these essays focus on lower classes in contrast with an assumed elite, on vernacular and oral culture in contrast with assumed Sanskritic literati, above all on lay people in contrast with a professional priesthood. The emphasis on popular religions reflects not only the influence of anthropology upon the history of religions but the increasing presence of new religious movements as an object of study within the discipline, a discipline which, partly in reaction against the construction of "the Veda" by right-wing political factions in India, has begun to seek the heart of Hinduism elsewhere.

There is a still more fundamental (if I may use the expression) way that this volume tears the lens out of the hand of traditional European scholarship about religion in India. That scholarship has heretofore consisted overwhelmingly of the study of Indian religions (Hinduism, Buddhism, Indian Islam) by Christians, occasionally by Jews (Doniger 1994). The Christian bias is stronger in some scholars than in others, but the point of view has proved inevitable. The Christian-Hindu comparison, always implicit in Western scholarship, now comes out of the closet and makes Christianity an object, as well as a subject, of comparison. This switch of lens is yet another gift of the

postcolonial, as well as postmodern, revolution, which has taught us that the
cultures that we are comparing have compared, too, that they are subjects,
like us, as well as the objects of our study. One of the first historians of
religions, Herodotus, compared his ancient Greeks with the Persians and the
Egyptians; a number of recent studies have documented the attitudes of the
ancient Chinese, Hindus, and others toward the Others on their borders (White
1991). From the advent of Christianity, however, the scholarly enterprise of
comparison was heavily colored by mission, often a deeply submerged agenda.
We now know, for instance, how the early Christians strove to understand,
and to justify, the stunning resemblances between their religion and that of
the pagans they so despised. Justin insisted, "It is not we who think like the
others, but all of them who imitate us in what they say," and Clement of
Alexandria accused the (ancient!) Greeks of stealing from the Christians
(Pépin 1991, 659b). This Christian comparative apologetic, in a twisted form,
was the driving force behind that great nineteenth-century comparatist, Sir
James George Frazer, too: what to do about the similarities between Christianity and "paganism" (Ackerman 1987, 95 and 189). This history of the
ways in which Others have compared their own Others shows not only that
our colonialism was not the first colonialism, but that comparison has long
been an imperial enterprise (Doniger 1998).

These essays give us access—in the form of works cited and spoken
words quoted—to the thoughts and words of natives of India, not of Europe
or America, who are doing the comparison, to comparatists who never read
Eliade. In a sense, these native informants are also syncretists who don't
use the "s" word. Several of the scholars in this volume challenge or reject
the concept of syncretism because it entangles us in the problem of essen-
tialism: to say that Hinduism combines, in a syncretistic fashion, with
Christianity is to imply that each religion is a fixed entity that mixes with
the other to form a new entity, as red mixed with blue produces purple. The
problem, of course, is that religions have fuzzy edges and multiple parts;
their interaction is more like mixing the palette of a Monet with the palette
of a Rembrandt. There is Something in India that is neither Muslim nor
Christian but that some of our authors hesitate to call "Hinduism." Dempsey
notes that "ahistorical constructions of overly tidy categories—for example,
'Hinduism' (or 'Christianity')—have created situations where religious tension and violence erupt. . . . particularly . . . when such lived expressions
reflect affiliations and identities that defy politically contrived rigidities."
Joanne Waghorne suggests that, instead of Hinduism, we might speak of a
"shared religious sensibility," and she notes that kings would designate
themselves as Shaiva or Vaishnava, or as Muslim, but not as Hindu. This
is all true, but none of these essays can manage without the term "Hinduism," with or without scare quotes; a good balance is struck by Waghorne's

wise confession at the end (still using the dastardly term): "I could not distinguish easily whether the devotees were in fact Christian or Hindu, and somehow in the atmosphere of the moment, this identification seems not to matter." Without assuming any clear red-vs.-blue distinction between religions, however, it is both possible and useful to determine aspects of a particular religious moment that are Christian (the Cross, the Lord's Prayer, the Eucharist), aspects that are Hindu (the Shiva-linga, the Vedic mantra, the slaughter of a goat), and aspects that are shared (the rosary, the chanting of a prayer, the [symbolic] sacrifice of a lamb or a goat).

Within these broadly shared goals and assumptions, the authors of these essays offer us a number of more specific insights into the most pressing problem of the day: religious conflict. In some areas, but not, alas, in others, anti-Christian rhetoric has diminished, as Indian Christians have become assimilated, generating a different, more peaceful rhetoric in which Europeans, rather than Christians, are the Others. What is it that makes one rhetoric rather than another prevail in a particular place? Waghorne asks what it is about a chariot that can be shared by Hindus and Christians, when other religious factors cannot be shared; she speaks of a shared public space, a "civil theology," and asks, "Why are some styles of worship so readily shared with official and semi-official sanction, while others are not?" She notes that Mary appears to her Hindu devotees in the form of a goddess and to her Christian worshippers as the Holy Mother, and that it was permissible to the Hindus when J. Jayalalitha represented herself as the goddess Durga (not the sort of image most American politicians would court—biting off the head of a buffalo—but tastes differ), but that it was *not* acceptable to the Christians when she appeared as Virgin Mary. So, too, Schmalz's Keralite Syrian is troubled when one of his own converts uses Jesus' name as a mantra. There are limits to this sort of assimilation.

Selva Raj acknowledges the conflict between Hindus and Christians but sees positive, fruitful aspects of the more specific conflict between Indian lay Christians and the Church in Rome, a contrast he sees in terms of a tension between popular and elite religion. He offers a new model for dialogue— ritual dialogue—and advises concentrating on ritual rather than on theology. Waghorne, too, notes that a shared ritual does not necessarily imply a shared theology. Myth, rather than its cousin, theology, has dominated the study of Indian religion for a long time; now its heyday is over, and both anthropologists and scholars of religion have brought new insights to our understanding of the third cousin, ritual. Margaret Meibhom, too, writes of the creation of religious identity without demonizing the other, through interaction with others past and present, to find and/or create past and present selves. These essays demonstrate the rich rewards that attention to ritual offers to anyone interested in religious interaction between Christians and Hindus.

Categories, rather than specific items, of religious excellence become cross-cultural; Syrian Christians who eat pork revere the Jewish woman who died rather than eat pork. Mathew Schmalz introduces us to a Keralite Syrian Catholic healer who is revered in the Hindu mode and employs Hindu tropes. Richard MacPhail, like Selva Raj, writes of Tamil symbols used to represent Christian sacred power outside the institutions of the Church, and, like Schmalz, tells the story of a converted sinner. Implicit in all of these essays is the relationship between not only Hindus and Christians, the main subject of this volume, and Hindus and Muslims, widely studied elsewhere, but Christians and Muslims. Islam is the silent partner here, the invisible third side of what is not just a dialogue between friends or lovers or rivals (Hindus and Christians) but a *ménage à trois* (Hindus, Christians, and Muslims). The third partner in this triangle, too, poses limits to its willingness to assimilate, like the limits transgressed by Durga as Mary and by the Jesus mantra. The emperor Akbar delighted the Jesuits who came to convert him by assuring them that he had indeed become a Christian—and then infuriated them by continuing to worship as a Muslim and, in many ways, a Hindu. This was not what the Jesuits had in mind at all, and is yet another incident that reveals how Europeans regarded the boundaries between religions as being impregnable, where Indians saw them as rather porous. The Islamic third side of this vital triangle still remains to be integrated into a study of this nature, and I would hope that such a study would benefit from the clarity of vision and concern for social justice demonstrated by the essays in this volume.

WENDY DONIGER
UNIVERSITY OF CHICAGO

References

Ackerman, Robert. 1987. *J. G. Frazer: His Life and Work*. Cambridge: Cambridge University Press.

Doniger, Wendy. 1975. *The Origins of Evil in Hindu Mythology*. Berkeley: University of California Press.

———. 1994. "The Love and Hate of Hinduism in the Work of Jewish Scholars." In *Between Jerusalem and Benares: Comparative Studies in Judaism and Hinduism*, ed. Hananya Goodman, 15–22. Albany: State University of New York Press.

———. 1998. *The Implied Spider: Politics and Theology in Myth*. The 1996–7 ACLS/AAR Lectures. New York: Columbia University Press.

———. 1999. "Presidential Address: 'I Have Scinde': Flogging a Dead (White Male Orientalist) Horse." *Journal of Asian Studies* 58, no. 4, November: 940–60.

Kent, Eliza F. 1999. "Tamil Bible Women and the Zenana Missions of Colonial South India." *History of Religions* 39, no. 2 (November): 117–49.

Kramrisch, Stella. 1968. *Unknown India: Ritual Art in Tribe and Village*. Philadelphia: Philadelphia Museum of Art.

Mahabharata. Critical Edition. Poona: Bhandarkar Oriental Research Institute, 1933–69.

Mani, Lata. 1998. *Contentious Traditions: The Debate on Sati in Colonial India*. Berkeley: University of California Press.

Narayan, Kirin. 1999. Personal communication, February 22.

O'Flaherty, Wendy Doniger. 1975. *Hindu Myths*. Harmondsworth: Penguin Books.

Pépin, Jean. 1991. "Christian Judgements on the Analogies between Christianity and Pagan Mythology." In *Mythologies*, English edition of Yves Bonnefoy's *Dictionnaire des Mythologies*, prepared under the direction of Wendy Doniger. Chicago: University of Chicago Press. 2 vols. Vol. 2: 655–65.

Said, Edward W. 1979. *Orientalism*. New York: Vintage Books.

———. 1993. *Culture and Imperialism*. New York: Vintage Books.

Scott, Paul. 1977. *Staying On*. London: William Heinemann.

Smith, Jonathan Z. 1990. *Drudgery Divine: On the Comparison of Early Christianities and the Religions of Late Antiquity*. Chicago: University of Chicago Press.

Waghorne, Joanne. 1999. "Chariots of the God/s: Riding the Line between Hindu and Christian." *History of Religions* 39, no. 2 (November): 95–116.

White, David Gordon. 1991. *Myths of the Dog-Man*. Chicago: University of Chicago Press.

CHAPTER 1

Introduction:
Between, Behind, and Beyond the Lines

Selva J. Raj
and
Corinne G. Dempsey

Indian Christianity may well be as old as Jesus Christ himself. Church tradition and legend trace the beginnings of Indian Christianity to the evangelical works of St. Thomas—one of the twelve disciples of Jesus—who arrived in southwest India in 52 C.E. According to the 1991 census of India, nearly 19.6 million Indians or 2.3 percent of the country's population claim to be Christians (Heitzman and Worden 1996, 170). Though spread throughout the country, major concentrations of Christians are found in the south Indian states of Kerala and Tamil Nadu, the western state of Goa, and the tribal belt of Bihar and Assam. In comparison with other minority religious groups, such as Sikhs, Buddhists, and Jains, who constitute 1.9 percent, 0.8 percent, and 0.4 percent of the total Indian population respectively, the numerical and institutional strength of Indian Christians is significant (119–20). While there is ample—even abundant—scholarly interest in non-Christian religious traditions of India, the heritage and strength of Indian Christianity is little reflected in scholarly literature. This book represents an attempt at bringing some balance to this equation.

Another way in which this volume attempts to provide balance is in its presentation of Christianity from a "popular" perspective, one that stands outside institutional prescription. Most studies of Christianity in India, until recently, have focused on the historical, colonial, missiological, and theological dimensions, leaving out the experiences and expressions of the people on the ground. An important corrective offered by popular expressions and practices is that they challenge commonly constructed distinctions and power relations between Hindu and Christian, elite and local, East and West, and

1

indigenous and foreign. The volume's subtitle, *Riting Between the Lines*, evokes this challenge.

Popular Indian Christianity indeed takes us to "messy" terrain in which religious identities, borders, and authority are not concrete and absolute, but often fluid and subject to negotiation. Yet this "mess" seems only discernable from the backdrop of institutional, universalizing formulations of identity, boundary, and authority, not from the perspective of the practitioner. A common reaction to this perceived discrepancy has been to relegate popular Christian traditions to the realm of aberration or sideshow. Yet we feel it is important to take seriously the ways in which local traditions offer coherence and meaning to practitioners in ways that complement and, in some significant instances, supplant institutional modes. By retrieving popular practice as a vital and viable part of the Christian package, this volume adds depth and breadth to our understanding of Christianity as a whole and wrests ourselves from possible inclinations to treat it (or its denominations) as an agreed-upon, centralized, monolith.

Distinguishing local Christianities from institutional prescriptions, often giving rise to intrareligious tensions and promoting interreligious solidarity, is the tendency for the former to formulate leadership, ritual, and meaning based on immediate, earthly concerns such as health, wealth, and human dignity.[1] In some instances, these concerns reflect devotees' seemingly precarious position as Indian Christians: as natives who adhere to an ostensibly foreign system, and as Christians who practice amid a Hindu culture. More often than not, local practices work to validate such seemingly "mixed" identities, giving them cultural continuity and coherence. Grassroots Christians experience in these practices, as Michael Amaladoss puts it, "the roots of their own identity as a people. They show that religion is for the people, not vice versa" (1999, 272). This attention to earthly concerns and enactment of complex identities partially explain the tenacity and resilience of local practices in the face of institutional disdain and constraint.

The volume is arranged in three sections that reflect broad themes having to do with issues of identity, healing, and alternative models of leadership reflected by popular religious practices. Although these themes drive the formation of the volume's three sections, they play out throughout the entire volume to differing degrees. The first section, "Festivals and Rituals: Forging Hybrid Christian Identities," illustrates the role of public religious expressions and tackles the issue of identity most directly. Joanne Waghorne describes chariot processions during Tamil Christian festivals as expressing and celebrating layers of shared Hindu-Christian practice and symbolism, historically and currently promoted by devotees in spite of clerical disapproval. While virtually identical in design, Hindu and Christian chariots artistically mark crucial differences as well; such practices stake boundaries between traditions but do so differently than institutionally mandated. Selva Raj's first essay likewise notes how north Indian Santal Catholics articulate their layered tribal, Hindu, and Christian allegiances through their enactment of ritual. Raj argues that ritual's reflection of complex identities and relationships offers an important type of interreligious dialogue, one that organically emerges from the lived experiences of the laity. In her discussion of the Velankanni shrine in Tamil Nadu, Margaret Meibohm demonstrates how some Indian Christians perform pilgrimage as a means for integrating disparate aspects of their complex identities. Focusing on Mumbai (Bombay) Christians, predominantly westernized urbanites, Meibohm argues that their annual participation in the Velankanni festival helps them to integrate and assert the indigenous, Indian side of themselves and their tradition. In this section's final essay, Selva Raj describes shared practices at the St. John de Britto shrine in Tamil Nadu. He argues that shrine activities, enlivened by both Hindu and Christian devotees and largely removed from clerical expectation, create a liminal space that transcends religious distinction. De Britto not only offers healing and fertility to his pilgrim devotees, but a welcome transgression that proves redemptive.

It is important to note that ethnographic data in these essays suggest that the process of identity formation does not entail the demonization or domination of others—both indigenous and foreign—but rather their juxtaposition and merging. As such, public festivals and rituals are a resource for creating complex, vibrant expressions of Indian Christian identity. In addition, ritual performances like these also serve as vehicles and mediums for dialogue between Indian Christians and their Hindu neighbors, a model that radically differs in form and efficacy from those adopted by institutional religion and its leadership. This "dialogue on the streets," implied by the essays, is indeed a dialogue of rituals, a dialogue in action, and an ecumenism of the laity.

The second set of essays, "Saints and Wonderworkers: Healing Disease and Division," focuses on the role of healing in local Christian contexts to illustrate the tensions between lay spirituality and institutional prescription. In Corinne Dempsey's study of three Christian saint shrines in Kerala, she notes how one "saint" garners his powers from demons; another's claim to fame is the healing of a Muslim boy; and a third "Christian" saint is, in fact, Jewish. Drawing pilgrims of all faiths to these shrines are the saints' reputations for miracles, not particular religious allegiances; local religious delineations are more tied to efficacy than to creed. Richard MacPhail describes a Tamil Catholic woman, Philomena, who acts as a medium between her burgeoning clientele and the Virgin Mary. Her typically Indian mediumship and its supporting rituals mesh religious distinctions and provide access to saints and the spirit

world. Philomena's healing practice and charisma, free from priestly intervention, challenge traditional authority structures in such a way that they
provoke disdain and censorship from local church leaders. Mathew Schmalz
introduces us to a self-appointed Catholic charismatic healer, Jude, who works
in north India with clients of all religious backgrounds. Schmalz points out
Jude's ingenious strategies and improvisations that blend north Indian Hindu
conceptions and perceptions into Christian discourses on healing. Jude's practice simultaneously preserves his Christian identity and guarantees his ministerial power.

The volume's final section, "Visionaries and Missionaries: Redefining
Religious Authority," examines alternative forms of leadership within the
realm of Protestant Christian practice. Distinct from Catholicism and Orthodox Christianity, Protestant traditions typically steer away from religious
syncretism and thus do not test the parameters of hybrid affiliations. This
does not mean, however, that local Indian Protestant traditions do not pose
their own kind of challenge to structures set by religious elites and foreign
missionaries. Eliza Kent writes about a Tamil lay woman, Muttammal, who
restructures the gendered and classed power relations of the Church of South
India (CSI) to enhance her own spiritual powers and authority. Using the
highly valued "text" as her vehicle, assimilating its meaning to the local
landscape and culture, and using it in ways that highlight her skills, Muttammal
ministers to a nonliterate population for whom her style and message have
particular meaning and power. In John Webster's essay, he argues that the
shaping of Christianity in India, typically seen through the eyes of missionaries, can be understood differently when viewed in light of the lived experiences of Indian Christian converts. Comparing missionary strategies in Delhi,
1859–1884, he notes how British Baptist leaders strategically promoted low-
caste Chamar members' abilities to form and build the Delhi Church. As
clergy quickly discovered, Chamar-led open-air *basti* (settlement) services,
involving lively singing and dancing, had a far greater impact on the growing
Church than did staid Sunday services or intellectualized bazaar preaching.
Zoe Sherinian concludes this section with the music and theology of CSI
priest-composer, James Theophilus Appavoo. Under his visionary leadership,
Dalit (oppressed) Christians in Tamil Nadu attempt to redefine traditional
power relations. Deliberately non-Western and nonelite, Appavoo's choice of
musical style signifies a break from and resistance against established religious and social power structures. Drawing upon realities embedded in the
lives of Dalit Christians, Appavoo aims, through music and liturgical innovation, to help them reclaim their voice and sense of dignity. The central
themes in this collection of essays have been artfully captured and eloquently
framed in Wendy Doniger's Foreword and Vasudha Narayanan's Afterword.
In her Foreword, Doniger, who has developed a new interest in the study of

popular Christianity in India, sets the stage by positioning the volume within the context of contemporary post-colonial critique. In her Afterword, Narayanan reflects on the essays from the perspective of a Hindu scholar and highlights three distinct types of Hindu responses to the diverse Christianities in India.

As these essays demonstrate, popular Christianity in India is neither homogenous nor uniform but essentially plural and diverse, formed by era, region, caste identity, and local earthly and spiritual need. In significant ways this plurality reflects the pluriform cultural, ethnic, linguistic, and religious landscape of India. It is therefore both legitimate and appropriate to speak of many popular Christianities in India. As such, these essays not only broaden and alter the scope of Christianity, but challenge normative scholarly and religious understandings. This is reminiscent of recent debate over the category "Hinduism." In part, the debate stems from the fact that "Hinduism" is a somewhat contrived term, originally applied by outsiders to denote indigenous religious practices in India.[2] More related to the issue at hand, Hinduism is a problematic term because it is not a centralized entity containing universally agreed upon texts, teachings, and traditions. In the interest of accuracy as well as in an effort to avoid privileging any particular brand of Hinduism as authoritative (typically Sanskritic or Brahmanical), some scholars have taken to referring to the tradition in the plural as "Hinduisms" or "Hindu traditions."[3] In light of the essays in this volume, if we are to acknowledge intrareligious diversity through a plural label, it seems consistent to think about Christianity/ies in the plural as well. On the other hand, it would be equally consistent to use the singular when referring to any major religious tradition, as long as we understand that all contain diversity in spite of moments when they appear, or wish to appear, unified and centralized. In either case, and most importantly, to concern ourselves with Hinduism's multiplicity up against a taken-for-granted Christian singularity is misleading at best.

Scholars have recently had much to say about the ways Christianity has been used as the measuring stick against which missionaries and European- and North-American trained scholars identified and gave value to—or devalued—"religion" outside the Christian domain (Asad, Balagangadhara). While this phenomenon stems largely from nineteenth- and early-twentieth century colonial chauvinism, with its antiritualistic, belief-centered bent, it nonetheless continues to influence the field of religion and the comparative study of religion today (Smith 1987, 100). As a result, non-Western others have traditionally been viewed through lenses that understand Christianity—and therefore the category "religion" more generally—as textually oriented, based on belief and doctrine rather than practice. To fit the mold, Hinduism, for example, has largely been constructed through its relationship to ancient and elite texts that may have little meaning for the majority who today think of themselves as Hindu.[4] This is true of Indian Christianity as well. It is quite telling that those scholars of religion who study popular traditions have typically limited themselves, until very recently, to non-Christian expressions. The study of popular Christianity has largely been the domain of anthropology.

One way to remedy this bias is to develop an alternative measuring stick, to expand the categories that drive the enterprise of labeling and comparison to include non-Western and nonelite constructions, including those that inform popular Christianities. A means for this kind of reformulation, implicitly expressed throughout this volume, is to change the fodder from which we engage our study. When we physically move the location of comparative religious studies to the ground and, in the case of India, to shared terrain, then fodder for comparison and intra- as well as interrreligious dialogue becomes organic events that emerge from human needs and lived experiences. When viewed from this new terrain, the question as to whether or not a practice, event, person, or community is or claims to be Christian or Hindu (for example) may be difficult if not impossible to answer. Yet this is precisely why such a shift is important. When the center is decentered, the lines once drawn may no longer apply. Perhaps it's time for some new lines.

Notes

1. Wendy Doniger O'Flaherty writes about how ritual provides a response to human suffering whereas, in the face of such real life issues, religious philosophy seems inadequate (1976: 9).

2. This is an important point to consider when thinking about the history of religious traditions and of colonialism in India. Indeed, some have chosen to use the term "Sanatana Dharma" in place of Hinduism when describing their own religious practices and beliefs. Yet, in many ways, "Hinduism" does indeed exist, adopted by a good many contemporary Indians and others in a variety of ways. Responding to what many feel to be an ideological dilemma, T. N. Madan insists that "it is futile and rather pedantic to insist on the artificial character of modern Hinduism, as if all reality were not socially constructed" (179).

3. The tentative way scholars of religion use the term Hinduism is comically portrayed by Donald Lopez, who says that scholars of Hinduism can be distinguished from experts on other religions "by their overdeveloped pectoral muscles, grown large from tracing quotation marks in the air whenever they have mentioned 'Hinduism' for over the past ten years" (832). For further discussion of this issue, see Larson and Frykenberg.

4. Max Müller himself was disappointed with many of the Hindu rituals he witnessed in India. He encouraged students of Hinduism to study the ancient texts in order that they might distinguish "between what was the doctrine of the founders and their immediate disciples, and what were the afterthoughts and, generally, the corruptions of later ages" (20).

References

Amaladoss, Michael. 1999. "Toward a New Ecumenism: Churches of the People." In *Popular Catholicism in World Church*, eds. Thomas Bamat and Jean-Paul Wiest, 272–301. New York: Orbis Books.

Asad, Talal. 1993. *Genealogies of Religion: Discipline and Power in Christianity and Islam*. Baltimore: Johns Hopkins University Press.

Balagangadhara, S. N. 1994. *"The Heathen in His Blindness. . ." : Asia, the West, and the Dynamic of Religion*. Leiden: E. J. Brill.

Frykenberg, Robert E. 1989. "The Emergence of Modern 'Hinduism' as a Concept and as an Institution: A Reappraisal with Special Reference to South India." In *Hinduism Reconsidered*, ed. Gunther D. Sontheimer and Hermann Kulke, 29–49. New Delhi: Manohar Publications.

Heitzman, James, and Robert R. Worden, eds. 1996. *India: A Country Study*. Washington, D.C.: Federal Research Division of the Library of Congress.

Larson, Gerald. 1995. *India's Agony Over Religion*. Albany: State University of New York Press.

Madan, T. N. 1998. *Modern Myths and Locked Minds: Secularism and Fundamentalism in India*. Delhi: Oxford University Press.

Müller, F. Max. 1972 [1870]. Introduction to "The Science of Religion: Four Lectures Delivered at the Royal Institution in February and May, 1870." Varanasi: Bharata Manisha.

O'Flaherty, Wendy Doniger. 1976. *The Origins of Evil in Hindu Mythology*. Berkeley and Los Angeles: University of California Press.

Smith, Jonathan Z. 1987. *To Take Place: Toward Theory in Ritual*. Chicago: University of Chicago Press.

PART I

～

Festivals and Rituals:
Forging Hybrid Christian Identities

CHAPTER 2

Chariots of the God/s:
Riding the Line Between Hindu and Christian

Joanne Punzo Waghorne[1]

The Christianity of Madura under the Jesuits was indeed disguised
idolatry. Except that the image of the Virgin Mary was worshipped
in the temples and paraded upon the cars, there was little change in
the old ceremonies and processions of Hindooism. There was the
same noise of trumpets and taum-taums and kettledrums, there was
the same blaze of rockets and Roman candles and blue lights, there
were the same dancers, with the same marks of sandal-wood and
vermilion on their naked bodies (Kaye 1859, 33).

Things are moving in the state of Tamil Nadu at the southern tip of
India. New Indian-made cars zip along the crowded streets of Chennai (formerly called Madras), and even the old "cars" of the God/s, great wooden *tēr*
(chariot) are being refitted with new braking systems and steel rims or totally
rebuilt for a new age of travel. This renewed interest in the very old practices
of the chariot procession is as much a part of the Roman Catholic communities in Tamil Nadu as the Hindu. These highly public statements of devotion are now, as they have been in the past, events that on the one hand mark
and make a claim to territory, God/s circle the streets of "their realm," but on
the other hand exhibit God/s in public on the uncertain periphery of their
domains. Everyone is invited to come together in these public streets at the
borders where all worlds meet. Thus the very site of the procession is a
shared *public* space, where no single deity or religious tradition can claim
clear title. The revival of the long-neglected chariot processions may mark a
willingness of many religious people within Tamil Nadu to begin to negotiate
a renewed civil religious idiom—in the face of other movements within India
to fix discourse into the narrow road of Hindu nationalism.

11

The nineteenth-century missionary description of the early Roman Catholic missions in Tamil Nadu quoted above, if relieved of its negative rhetoric, could describe practices today from the great chariot festival at the old church at Avur in a rural area of Pudukkottai District to the urban processions in Chennai of Our Lady of Velankanni in the suburb of Besant Nagar. In Avur, the week after Easter, a brightly painted wooden image of the Risen Christ rides in state on a magnificent wooden *tēr* along the streets of this very small village with a very long history of Christian missionary activity. In Avur

Figure 2.1: The massive chariot in Avur blows dust into the streets of the small village.

hundreds of devotees, many of whom are Hindu, pull on two massive chains attached to the front of this three-storied wooden chariot with man-high wheels (figure 2.1). Atop the ornate wooden plinth, poles support a canopy of rich cloth that shades the Risen Christ in the hot April sun. The wooden *tēr* and the stone platform-tower with spiral steps to reach the thirty-foot-high plinth closely resembles the *tēr* and tower at the nearby temple for the Goddess Mariyamman, whose chariot festival occurs in the same month. In Besant Nagar, thousands assemble to watch the elegantly carved image of Mary in a white and gold sari ride in her ornate wooden palanquin along the beach road of this prosperous urban neighborhood. Again Mary's holy form is draped in a rich silk sari, and she wears elegant gold jewelry much like the goddesses of the nearby Mahalakshmi Temple. A busy passageway with vendors selling images of the Virgin Mary and Mahalakshmi—produced in much the same style—connects the newly constructed church to this new temple not a block away. A quick glance would indeed make it appear as if nothing but the names and forms of the deities separated the chariot procession at the Hindu temples from the festivals at the Christian churches.

Both of the Christian events have expanded in recent years. The days are gone when such practices came under the ban of a papal bull or even the frowns of secularist governments. The priest at Avur made it clear that the chariot festival was celebrated with dispensation from Rome and that the present *tēr* dated from 1802. The pastor at the new church for Our Lady of Velankanni in Chennai expressed pride that the festival celebrating the birthday of the Blessed Virgin Mary drew increasing numbers of devotees from all religious groups. This rapprochement between Hindu and Christian styles of worship had the public sanction of the former Chief Minister Jayalalitha. In Manapparai, a small town near Tiruchirappalli, a banner on a grand chariot belonging to Saint Thomas Church pictured the chief minister, hands folded in veneration, and proclaimed her help in the inauguration of this "holy chariot."

The building and renovation of Christian chariots in contemporary Tamil Nadu cannot be separated from new public interest in the rebuilding of grand chariots for all *kōyil*—the common Tamil term for temple or church. By 1989 the magazine *Frontline* reported the new fervor for reestablishing chariot festivals at temples where the wooden cars had been left to deteriorate for years (Sthapati 1989, 76–79). Another article notes, "The pomp and splendour and pageantry of the car culture has an appeal to Christians and Muslims also . . . a Hindu institution, the car festival through the centuries has influenced other religionists too thus serving as a symbol of 'unity in diversity' " (Kalidos 1989, 69–75). In a major temple like Tyagesa in Tiruvarur the chariot was renovated at a cost of 600,000 rupees and in places as far flung as Nedungudi in Pudukkottai, a now wealthy restaurant owner in Singapore finally fulfilled a vow to rebuild the wooden car in his famous local temple (see Gandhi 1983, 824–25).[2] Building or renovating a *tēr* is a very expensive undertaking. These multistoried structures rise over thirty feet high. A team of carvers works, often in public view, for months to intricately carve the multiple, wooden panels that finally are jointed together with elaborate corner braces layer upon layer, first the plinth then three, six, or more layers. Iron-smiths then join giant wooden wheels to the metal axle. The wooden bas-relief panels are designed to educate the public on the history of the Lord or Lady who will ride in this grand vehicle. The building of a *tēr* gives any religious institution a very public voice within a town or city. Whether by private support or public funds both Christians and Hindus transfigure their devotion into wood and steel and move onto the streets in what has long been the ultimate act of public display, the chariot festival (see Michell 1992, 29–52).[3]

The sharing of style of worship has its points of confluence but also its limits. The former chief minister of the state of Tamil Nadu,[4] J. Jayalalitha, educated in convent schools, seemed as willing to support the growth of Catholic festivals as Hindu. She remained in the good graces of her Christian constituents until a partisan marked her forty-seventh birthday with a poster depicting her as the Virgin Mary, displayed all over Chennai next to another poster of the chief lady as the Hindu Goddess Durga (figure 2.2). At this point, in a very apt phrase, all hell broke loose in the Christian community but not in the Hindu. The United Christian Council joined the Archbishop of Madurai Diocese in calling for "reparation prayers" throughout the state for the "blasphemous" act *(The Hindu* 10 March 1995, 4). Why are some styles of worship so readily shared with official and semiofficial sanction, while others are not? What is it about the chariot festival, in particular, that makes its form so flexible, so readily adopted by Christians and others and so much a part of the contemporary revival of public religion in Tamil Nadu?

At issue here is the nature of shared forms of public ritual. Early missionaries, mostly Protestant and eventually Catholic as well, had great difficulty understanding how a shared form of ritual did not imply a shared theology and hence a Christianity that was nothing more than Hinduism by another name. Public rituals indeed share a common religious idiom. But this public language cannot be reduced to a simple conjecture that Christians succumb to their "Hindu" environment—the conclusion of the most influential modern discussion on "intermingling patterns of culture" of Christians in south India (Diehl 1965,175–80). In south India, what the nineteenth century so easily called "Hinduism" did not dominate until the twelfth century. Before that, the religious landscape of Tamil country was peopled by Buddhists, Jains, and the many devotees of the gods Shiva and Vishnu. The devotees of Shiva and Vishnu never saw themselves as coreligionists under a common umbrella of "Hinduism." Later Muslims and Christians joined the mix. All contended

Figure 2.2: The poster that shocked Roman Catholics hangs in the streets of Chennai.

with each other. Yet, all were undergirded by a much older sense of divine power that remains alive today.[5] This undergarment of religion/s in Tamil Nadu remains hidden by its outer layers. Not simply Hindu, for want of another term, I would call it a *shared religious sensibility* that makes all dialogue and debate intelligible and possible. The critics of the adoption of "Hindu" forms to further Christian piety failed to realize the sharing of a common idiom like the *tēr,* rather than blurring the distinctions between the gods who ride these divine chariots, serves to stress difference—but of a very special kind that we still fail to see. There must be a common idiom for dialogue, an accepted grammar in which to pose debate. Yet at the same time, this common public religious idiom, if it is to function commonly, does not negate difference. It matters very much that Mary, dressed in a sari but in Her color of white and gold, rides atop the palanquin, and not the Goddess Parvati. It matters that the Risen Christ is pulled through the streets and not Lord Shiva. The argument for this chapter will rely on visual details of two Christian chariot processions that I witnessed and Dick Waghorne photographed, at Our Lady of Velankanni in a prosperous middle-class neighborhood in suburban Chennai and at a very old church in the poor Christian village of Avur in rural Pudukkottai District, 200 miles south of the metropolis.

The Chariot at the Intersection of Ecclesiastic Authority and Popular Devotion in Tamil Nadu: A Century of Debate

The Shrine of Puṇita Periya Nāyaki Mātā (Holy Great Protecting Mother), a large impressive Roman Catholic church, seems out of place in the tiny village of Avur. Dating from 1747, the church was constructed on the plan of an earlier church built in 1697 by the Jesuit missionary, Father Ventantius Bouchet, who founded the small Christian settlement with a basilica worthy of the major center of Catholicism that he envisioned for Avur (Gandhi 1983, 792–96). Although the Jesuits had the support of the various Hindu rulers of the area, especially the rajas of Pudukkottai, the money for the mission and the church came from local Christians and from France. Bouchet went on from Avur to become the superior of the mission of the Carnatic and was in Rome during the serious wave of controversy over the "Malabar rites"(Neill 1985, 77). This controversy arose due to the special accommodation that the Jesuits of the nearby Madurai Mission had made with their high-caste converts to retain many practices in dress and celebrations after their baptisms. Although the Jesuits had been vindicated in permitting the practices during the seventeenth century, Avur never grew to fill Bouchet's dream in the eighteenth. The mission was crippled in its development by the later infamous papal suppression of the Jesuits. The mission in Avur passed from one Catholic jurisdiction to another, often with considerable dissension (Aiyar 1916, 399–402).

The papal bull of 1744 ended the Jesuit policies of "accommodation" that the brilliant Italian nobleman-turned-priest, Robert de Nobili, initiated just before Bouchet's time. De Nobili scandalized later generations of missionaries and many of his own contemporaries by adopting the saffron robes, begging bowl, and bamboo staff of a Hindu *sannyāsī,* a mendicant. De Nobili began his mission in the city of Madurai in 1606 and within a few years settled in a small thatched hut near the famous Meenakshi Temple. He quickly realized that no high-caste Hindu would convert to a religion that at that time was associated with the Parangi (foreigners)—an unflattering term for the meat-eating, unwashed, and thus virtually untouchable Portuguese masters of Goa. The former Roman nobleman began to refine his behavior to fit the customs of the elite of Madurai. In addition to dressing as a *sannyāsī,* he adopted a strict vegetarian diet, observed all the rules for cleanliness that marked a man of the upper castes, spoke and wrote elegant court Tamil, and styled himself as a Roman raja, a member of the ruling class. Later he penned several discourses, still extant, in Tamil and Sanskrit, arguing Christian theology through classical Hindu texts. De Nobili permitted his Brahmin converts to continue wearing their sacred thread, with a small cross attached, and other bodily signs, as was the fashion for men of their high standing. Throughout his long efforts to accommodate his lifestyle and his teachings to the Indian cultural environment around him, de Nobili struggled with serious accusations of near heresy from both the Brahmin theologians of Madurai and many members of his own church. The Brahmins eventually exonerated him of all charges of atheism (Cronin 1959, 92–103), but the Portuguese authorities in Goa and his fellow clerics condemned his methods. Finally, after a long struggle, Pope Gregory XV issued the bull *Romanae Sedis Antistites* in 1623, sanctioning de Nobili's policy of allowing high-caste Hindus to retain signs of their status (Cronin 1959, 221–30; Neill 1985, 31). De Nobili's close kinship with the pope and other high authorities in Rome may have saved the day for the Jesuits but the battle over linking "Hindu" practices to the rites of the Church continued into the eighteenth century when a new pope finally reversed the earlier decision. The encyclical *Omnium Sollicitudinum,* condemning accommodation to Hindu practice, remained in effect until the mid-twentieth century (Neill 1985, 79).

The central place that Robert de Nobili holds in the historiography of Catholic missions in southern India disguises some real paradoxes. Why, if the Jesuits were disbanded and the Malabar rites eventually condemned, has the church at Avur celebrated the chariot festival since 1766, well after the fatal papal bull? Why was the tiny church able to construct a grand wooden chariot in 1802 to replace the earlier, less permanent bamboo structure?[6] In a perceptive study of popular cults among Muslims as well as Christians during the seventeenth century in Tamil Nadu, Susan Bayly paints a very different picture of Christianity in the religious environment of the times. Her tableau is filled with *sannyāsīs* and various holy men and women revered as healers and teachers who claimed to derive their power from the Catholic saints and the Virgin Mary. Few of these were affiliated with or sanctioned by ecclesiastic authorities, and many derived their Christian imagery from the maritime communities who had converted earlier under Portuguese rule but quickly developed their own Christian rites and pantheon (Bayly 1992, 321–40). While the itinerant wonder-workers spread devotion to Christian figures, the Parava caste, the most prominent of the fishing and trading communities, built its own churches and initiated festivals in and near Tuticorin. In 1720, independent of the Church, the community constructed the Golden Car for their patron form of the Virgin Mary, Our Lady of Snows. In 1806 they built a grander chariot that still runs today (Bayly 1992, 343). Both of the chariots at Avur seem to ride closely on the heels of their compadres in Tuticorin but with some important differences. The Avur chariot festivals are derived from the Jesuits, and at this point de Nobili again enters the picture.

This chariot procession in Avur could never be considered renegade nor idolatrous because its lineage is ecclesiastic. The Paravas, although sometimes prosperous traders, were regarded as low-ranking fishermen among the elites that de Nobili converted. The rules of purity that the Italian priest had adopted prevented his association with such men, and he created another body of missionaries, Pandaraswamis, to minister to the lower-ranked castes (Bayly 1992, 392; Cronin 1959, 251–52). Some of these Pandaraswami Jesuits established the car festivals in their permanent missions. The scenario was likely the same for Avur—designed as a serious mission center and always integrated into the larger Catholic Church framework. Indeed, the invitations printed in Tamil for the annual Car Festival from Avur carefully place the history of the festival within a strict Church genealogy. The 1990 invitation even speaks of the Jesuits missionaries as Veda Bhodakar (*vēta pōtakkarkaḷ*), Teachers of (Holy) Wisdom, and uses highly honorific Tamil forms when naming them. In Madurai, de Nobili was given the name Tattuva Bhodakar, Teacher of Reality (Cronin 1959, 127).

The car festival at Christian churches such as Avur cannot be placed on an elementary scale of "accommodation" to popular Hindu practices on the one side and adherence to pure Roman Catholic doctrinal rites on the other. As Bayly makes clear, the real measure of orthodoxy was not in the nature of the practices but in whether these genuflect to the Church or in whether they derive their power from the overarching religious logic of the Tamil countryside, albeit with a nod to the Holy Mother Church. Thus the grand church and festivals of Our Lady of Snows could have been suspect, while the holy *tēr* festival at Avur was not. Important here is the nature of "the religious landscape," which is Bayly's term for the milieu of the times. As mentioned earlier, what we now call Hinduism came late to this area. Prior to the fifth century, another kind of religious sentiment, which centered on the kings and goddesses (see Waghorne 1994), as Bayly reveals in the title to her book, was and still is alive (see Hart 1975, 21–50; Shulman 1980, 138). In addition to this, Buddhism lived on in south India into the fourteenth century, and Jains remained strong. Both venerated renunciative holy men above the gods. The religious melange of Tamil Nadu that focused on renunciants, kings, goddesses—personages not principles—cannot be called "Hindu" in the contemporary sense. When Pope Gregory XV issued *Romanae Sedis Antistites,* allowing converts to wear the thread and other marks "as distinctive signs of their social status, nobility, and of other offices" (Cronin 1959, 229), the Holy Father may well have tapped into the cultural logic of the Tamilians. Such customs and many of the rites adopted by Indian Catholic Christians are in some sense a matter of "civil" practice and hence not "religious"—if we take religion to mean a very specific sect. In this sense these common practices belong to the "civil religion" of Tamil Nadu; a larger definition must remain until this whole story unfolds.

The revival of chariot processions in the modern world with whole-hearted participation by the Roman Catholic community flies in the face of two centuries of Protestant missionary critique of the all-too-easy Catholic accommodation to the "silly observances" and "ghastly superstitions" of the "Hindoos" (Kaye 1859, 33–34). The critiques grew shrill in the mid-nineteenth century when Protestant missionaries and upstanding scholars in Great Britain looked back in horror at the easy accommodations to Hinduism that the early Jesuit missionaries effected in the then infamous Madurai Mission. The religion of the Hindoos now solidified in the minds of the British as "Hinduism" took its heaviest blows during this period from the 1830s to the 1850s in part because of the rising power of the evangelicals on the one side and British utilitarianism on the other—neither had any use for ostentatious displays. The chariot festivals were often singled out as the epitome of all that was idolatrous and dangerous in Hinduism. The English language gained the word "juggernaut" at this time. This term is a corruption of the name of Jaganath, "lord of the universe," the presiding deity of the great temple at Puri in east-central India, whose chariot festival remains a major religious event. From the colonial descriptions of the unwieldy restlessly moving chariot, a juggernaut came to mean "a belief or an institution that elicits blind and destructive devotion to which people are ruthlessly sacrificed; an overwhelming advancing force that crushes or seems to crush everything in its path."[7] Missionaries often linked the chariot processions epitomized by the Puri festival to the outmoded and cruel Hindu religion that subjugated the spiritual and material welfare of the Indian people.

A secondhand description of the chariot festival at Puri from a famous missionary who first visited Puri in 1806 captures the injured sensibilities of the time. Claudius Buchanan, the story goes, "first made the acquaintance of the giant idol known as Juggernaut. With the influence of the salubrious sea breezes of Pooree, he found the monster hiding in high carnival" (Kaye 1859, 33–34). Kaye's full description suggests a lewdness, what we would now call a sadomasochistic impulse, at the heart of the chariot festival. The French Catholic missionary, Abbé J. A. Dubois, in 1816 already connected chariot festivals throughout Tamil country with a general licentiousness. "Decency and modesty are at a discount during car festivals. . . . it is common enough for clandestine lovers, who at other times are subject to vexatious suspicion, to choose the day of the procession for their rendezvous in order to gratify their desires without restraint" (Dubois 1906 [1818], 604). Chariot festivals could never be associated with Christianity. By this time the Church in Britain was safely relieved of much of its own history of public religious processions and church festivals.[8]

In the mid-nineteenth century, the British rulers of India were caught between two principles not easy to balance: their long-standing promise of noninterference with the religious practices of their subject peoples and the equally pressing concern to look after their moral and material well-being. Until the 1840s, the rulers of India, The East India Trading Company, kept up active support of religious festivals in imitation of the Indian rajas whom they superseded. The Company sent marching bands and troops to keep order and guard the valuable jewels on the bronze images used for processions. After rancorous debates in Parliament, all such connections with "idolatry" were forbidden.[9] Much of the rhetoric about the chariot processions at this time was part of this great public debate in Britain over the supposed support of "idolatry" by a "Christian government." Thus a sharp distinction emerged in public rhetoric between a moral and wholesome Christianity and the licentiousness of public religious displays in India. Interestingly, state rituals presumed to be secular were encouraged both at home and in the colonies, especially if they focused attention on the queen-empress and glory of British rule (Waghorne 1994, 31-53). But in the 1870s, Victoria, as the newly declared empress of India, confirmed her government's respect for the religious sentiments of her Indian subjects. Festivals had to be tolerated. This conflict instilled a sense of wariness of festivals in the officers of the Indian Civil Service that continued into the post-Independence Indian Administrative Service.[10] Years of missionary critique of supposed rancorous public display took its toll on the educated elite of an old colonial port city like Madras (now Chennai). Such display continued but often without the open support of the educated elite of society.

The hostility toward religion in general and public displays of religions in particular reached its peak in the state of Tamil Nadu during the 1960s with the election of the first Dravidian-based party, a populist group supporting Tamil language and culture but not the "Hinduism" that they saw as imported from a hostile Aryan north. All of this radically changed with the election of a set of former cinema stars as chief ministers of the state. First M. G. Ramachandran and then his successor J. Jayalalitha reestablished open support of religious festivals as a mark of the grandeur of Tamil culture. The face of M.G.R. (as he is still called) could be seen in a gigantic light sculpture during the great chariot festival at a famous temple in Mylapore in Chennai in 1987. Jayalalitha surpassed her political mentor and former leading man with active support of temples and churches. Thus religious festivals, particularly the chariot procession, now have the favor of the government of Tamil Nadu[11] as well as great popular support from the growing educated middle-classes throughout the state. It's a new day for the public display of religions.

The Chariot Procession at Avur

The pristine shining interior of this beautiful church, which we saw a week before the festival, was dusty and littered with bits of food and other

Figure 2.3: This seeming European-style painting of the crucifixion depicts a landscape that resembles the environment of Avur.

residue from the large numbers of the faithful encamped in the church when we arrived on April 23, 1995, a week after Easter. Inside the church lies an open sepulcher, where the image of the Risen Christ had lain throughout Easter week. The Risen Christ now stands outside at the edge of the stage, where for the two previous nights players performed the Passion and the Resurrection dramas. These were followed by a late night Mass at the church. At the side of the main altar within, miniature images of Mary and Joseph kneel watching the baby Jesus with the small Christmas lights still visible. A mural of the crucified Christ covers most of the wall above a side altar. Christ, deathly pale with bleeding legs and pierced hands, hangs on the cross set in a rocky barren landscape that might be Pudukkottai or Palestine (figure 2.3). The landscape is the only tiny detail that might link this European Christ to his Indian surroundings. At first glance, the church itself gives the appearance of a European structure. But a closer look at the archways and the cornices on the columns reveals an eighteenth-century style of architecture (figure 2.4) that also appears in the old palace of the former rajas of Pudukkottai in the town not twenty miles away (Waghorne 1994, plate 56). This church announces its place in the Indian landscape not

Figure 2.4: The church at Avur seems large for the small village that it anchors.

in broad strokes but in very small architectural details and in the remnants of its many devotees.

We had photographed details of the large wooden *tēr* before all of the paraphernalia of the festival covered it. The style of the *tēr* closely resembles other chariots in the region but again with some significant differences. This chariot has three layers of sculpted wood and not six or seven as is the case with the Hindu forms. Since each layer of the Hindu chariot symbolizes the realm of one of the Hindu gods, I would guess that these layers at Avur refer to the Trinity.[12] The detailed carved images would take a major paper to outline, but all these images reference Christian narratives of the saints and the life of Jesus while adding some decorative features taken from the repertoire of royal symbols in this former princely state (figure 2.5).[13] On the day of the festival the great chariot is fitted with an ornate canopy of printed

Figure 2.5: The carved figures on the chariot combine the cross with the *yali*, a mythical animal used as a sign of royal power. They are a major decorative element on most temple chariots.

cotton cloth. From the roof of this hangs the traditional tombai,[14] cloth columns used for all happy occasions. The tombai, canopy, and all of the cloth that drapes the chariot are all floral with none of the images of lions and other mythical beasts that decorate Hindu *tērs*. As with neighboring chariot festivals for other deities, the divine figure in the main car does not travel alone. A smaller chariot carrying St. Michael the Archangel and a larger chariot with the Virgin Mary precedes the Risen Christ. Mary's *tēr*, painted a sky blue, was decorated with red roses. St. Michael's vehicle also wears blue paint.

Outside, booths selling sweets and trinkets line an area near the chariot route that rounds the four streets of this largely Christian village. The *tēr* begins and ends its journey from a special docking tower in typical Nayak style, identical to the dock at the nearby temple to the goddess Mariyamman (figure 2.6). Both towers likely date from the time of the first church car of 1766. Before the procession, the faithful carry the wooden image of the Risen Christ palanquin-style to the *tēr* with the priest in attendance. The parish priest, Father Maria Francis, describes Christ as wearing "a dhoti" on his waist and an upper cloth of white silk with a gold border draped over both shoulders. In his left hand he carries a flag with a gold cross on a white silk background. The Christ image is the only one dressed by devotees for the festival. His icon body, taken naked from the sepulcher, requires new clothing before he goes out on the streets in triumphal procession. His Tamil devotees dress him in the attire of an elite man—the same formal dress worn by a gentleman entering an orthodox temple or attending a wedding or feast. The Blessed Virgin does not wear a sari in Avur, but her image is carved with the same clothing of pink chemise with a blue mantel found all over Europe. She stands on a slender silver moon with angels peeking out from a base of clouds. This is her traditional Catholic form as Queen of Heaven, and in Avur she wears a crown of bronze with what look like inset rubies. St. Michael wears the garments of a Portuguese warrior of the sixteenth century inscribed onto his wooden body (figure 2.7). The Archangel, Guardian of Heaven, completes a triad of holy figures that parallel three deities processed in Hindu temples in Pudukkottai: Shiva as Lord of the Universe, His consort Parvati as the Mother Protector of the world, and Chaṇṭēśvara as guardian of all of Lord Shiva's heavenly treasures.

The chariot procession speaks of the triumphal rule of the universe by Christ risen, not by Shiva. In Avur, the soulful procession of the body of Jesus that marks Catholic procession in southern Europe does not occur. Here the glorious Risen Christ rides in state in his domain. Interestingly, unlike the Hindu chariot procession, the priest of the *kōyil* here does not ride with his Lord. As the great chariot rolls forward in a cloud of dust, the priest and other dignitaries walk in front of the sweating hundreds of men who pull the Risen Christ. The sun shines very bright in April, and the unwieldy chariot pulls in its own direction. Getting such a mass of near-solid wood around the streets surrounding the church proves

Figure 2.6: The chariot docks near the tower at the church in Avur to receive its divine passenger.

an exhausting task. When the *tēr* docks at its tower, the crowd of those who have served God as his human horses reach a frenzy. A special delegation of the faithful then mounts the stairs. They are ecstatic as they enter the canopy and take the Risen Christ into their arms and move down the stone stairs with him. The faithful wait at the end of the procession for the managers to throw them the marigold flowers that decorate the chariot. Some invert their black umbrellas to catch the blessed flowers. Nothing else is offered or received.

The differences between this Christian festival and the Hindu processions in the district are written in many small details. The very conscious choice of colors and patterns for the cloth draping and the paint on the lesser chariot—pink and blue, floral and not paisley patterns, cloth devoid of any other imagery—reflect Christian colors and form with a history in Catholic Europe. Also notable is the presence of the cross atop the chariots in the place where the finial marking a

Figure 2.7: Saint Michael wears the armor with a cross that resembles the uniforms of 16th century conquistadors

Hindu structure in the shape of a bronze pot would otherwise appear. The chariots and the holy images are draped in roses, marigolds, and jasmine, all flowers that also bedeck Hindu deities. But here there are no lotuses—the flower par excellence of the Hindu gods. All of these signs are meant to be seen and understood in a very Tamil context. Here are the answers to the questions: Who is Lord of the universe? Who is the Queen? Who guards the gates of Heaven?

The Birthday of the Blessed Virgin Mary at Besant Nagar

Besant Nagar stretches along the coast in the south of Chennai. Prosperous middle-class professionals moved to this newly built suburb beginning in the 1970s when taxicabs could not be persuaded to travel so far from the city.

They settled around several fishing villages and displaced others. Now, crowded and considered quite near to the city, the area has attracted residents from various castes and religious backgrounds. The community, named after the Irish Annie Besant, an important woman in the Theosophical Society, has an eclectic flavor like the religious sentiments of its namesake. The large gated grounds of the world headquarters of the society form the northern boundary of the area. Within this compound is the city's best library for those interested in world religions. The oldest sections of the neighborhood stretch along the beach road, which begins to curve inland about two miles from the start. Here at the juncture of the beach road and a street returning to the main route to downtown Chennai, stands the new chapel complex of Our Lady of Velankanni. This is a kind of branch church of a much larger and more famous basilica about 200 miles south on the coast of the Tanjore district. The duplication of famous rural shrines in this urban setting is common. Nearby, in the same neighborhood, residents with help from a benefactor abroad are constructing the Arupadaividu Temple (*arupatai-vītu,* six sites of battlements), which brings together in an abbreviated facsimile shrines of the six holy places where the god Murugan defeated demons. Temples to mark each of these victories by Lord Murugan are scattered in separate rural shrines all over Tamil Nadu. The grand Mahalakshmi temple, one block down the coast from Our Lady, gives devotees the opportunity to visit all of the nine forms of the goddess of wealth and well-being under one roof. Thus Besant Nagar offers the convenience of worshipping a variety of famous divine beings without leaving this comfortable neighborhood.

The Basilica of Our Lady of Health in Velankanni, Tanjore District, like the smaller version in Besant Nagar, draws devotees from "all castes and religious communities" unlike the shrine to Our Lady of Snows in Tuticorin, which remains the powerful central shrine for the fisher-trader caste only. Susan Bayly traces the wide popularity of Velankanni to the struggle of the Roman Catholic hierarchy to "replace the caste-based cult worship practiced by the Paravas with more popular and broadly based religious forms." She points to the paradox that the Catholic missionaries chose to support the cult of Our Lady of Health, a "warrior and a conqueror," whose shrine even official guides claim was once the site of a powerful goddess. Our Lady, legend tells, conquered the goddess after a fierce battle and established herself at the vanquished lady's abode (Bayly 1992, 367–68). Thus the Virgin Lady of Velankanni won a wide following that extends well beyond the Christian community as a healer of illness and a victor over all demonic forces—attributes often associated with the goddess Mariyamman.

The presence of the Roman Catholic hierarchy pervades the festival celebrating the birthday of the Blessed Virgin Mary at the shrine in Besant Nagar. While the rural chariot festival draws only the local clergy, the Archbishop of Madras presides over the festivities here. With crimson vestments, gold and white shawl, and red miter, he celebrates Mass for thousands of worshippers, chanting the service in Tamil. Later, the Archbishop reads prayers in front of the wooden palanquin that is to carry the image of Mary through the streets. Even his vestments match the colors of the sari that drapes the image of the Virgin Mother in front of him. The parish priest, just before the Mass, hears confessions in an outdoor confessional. Nuns sell religious literature. The entire event clearly has the imprimatur of the Church. Yet, the same seeming paradox is here as in Velankanni: there are more signs of Christian-Hindu confluence than I saw in rural Avur. The festival begins, just like ones in nearby Hindu temples, with the raising of the flag—the white and gold of Our Lady of Health. Worshippers, as in a Hindu festival, touch this flagpole and tie the traditional holy strings dipped in turmeric powder around the pole as a pledge to attend the festival to its end. Long lines of devotees wait at the

Figure 2.8: Saffron-robed devotees pray with a rosary as they walk past a stall selling Christian posters.

entrance to the chapel to offer various gifts to Our Lady. Among these are wax candles that are exclusively Christian, but I also see brass trays with a broken coconut, jasmine flowers, and a banana, which is similar to Hindu offerings. Missing from the trays are camphor, betel nut, and red vermilion. Apparitions of Robert de Nobili are here in the forms of saffron-robed mendicants, men and women, carrying rosaries (figure 2.8)! The parish priest told me earlier that he is pleased that Hindus also worship here. I cannot distinguish easily whether the devotees are in fact Christian or Hindu and somehow, in the atmosphere of the moment, this identification seems not to matter.

The architecture of the shrine complex also mixes very traditional Catholic imagery with subtle markings of a wider religious landscape. The complex contains a chapel to Our Lady, a parish house for the clergy and administration, an outdoor shrine to Our Lady of Health, and room to construct a *pandal*, an outdoor tent of massive bamboo poles covered with palm fronds used for annual festivals and weddings. Across the street is a large office building with a massive cross atop where the central administration for the Roman Catholic Church in the city is housed. The chapel mixes motifs that echo a Portuguese heritage with a touch of the Islamic and the modernism of Le Corbusier.[15] The facade, stucco with embedded tiles, has two turrets at the ends of the sloping triangular roof. The steeple rises from the back and looks a bit like a satellite relay station with a cross on top. A loudspeaker is attached but no bell. The outdoor shrine houses a permanent plaster image of the Blessed Virgin. Built as an octagon in the likeness of a crown, the Archangel rests on top. All of the decorative elements, crosses at the top of each point of the crown, are completely Christian. But Mary is enclosed by wrought iron bars in workmanship typical of the area. On her birthday, a delegation of ladies from the church carefully drape her in a beautiful dark blue sari with a pink and green paisley motif woven into the rich silk. They dress her affectionately like a young daughter on her wedding day.

Our Lady of Health in Besant Nagar will not ride a grand chariot for her birthday. Here in an urban environment, Mary rides an ornate wooden palanquin that is carefully carved with interlacing crosses—a diminutive Gothic cathedral. But a closer look reveals that the palanquin is modeled on the chapel next door. Like the chapel, the palanquin has a triangular facade with two turrets on either side. It is as if the very modern chapel were remade in miniature in wood but given a Gothic flare. The palanquin, although thoroughly Christian in its styling, actually follows the broader religious logic of the region far more accurately than the *tēr* at Avur. The chariots of the god are expected to take their form from the *gōpura*, the great gate-tower of the temple that houses the deity.[16] They are "mobile architecture" (Michell 1992, 36).

Again, like neighboring temples, the Besant Nagar complex has a special image of Mary meant for procession only. Also like their Hindu neighbors, the faithful watch as several of their members dress and decorate the

Figure 2.9: Our Lady of Velankanni stands inside her palanquin dressed in a magnificent gold brocade sari.

holy image. Three men chosen from the congregation carry the golden scepter, the processional icon, and the crowns to the waiting palanquin. Another pair of men takes the image of Mary, dressed in a white and gold brocade sari with her infant son in her arms and places a red and gold crown on her hair and another on her son's small head (figure 2.9). The dressers fit the scepter to her hand and one very important devotee has the honor of tying the *tali* around Mary's neck and placing a ruby necklace on the Infant Jesus and his mother. The act of tying the *tali* is filled with rich cultural associations. The *tali,* a pendent hung on a cloth string, is tied at the moment of marriage by the husband or the husband's sister and marks the woman as truly auspicious and fit for motherhood. Thus when the Mother of the World goes out to meet her devotees in Besant Nagar, she wears all the marks of a blessed Tamil mother. To her Hindu devotees she takes the form of a goddess, to her Christian worshippers she is the Holy Mother.

The entire event at this coastal suburban neighborhood is written in mixed metaphors, combining traditional Catholic signs with Hindu emblems of power, all set on the stage of contemporary urban public life. Throughout the festival, devotional music to Mary blares over loudspeakers—the words praise the Mother of the World, but the female voice sounds as if it belongs in the local cinema. The tunes are buoyant; none of the somber tones of Ave Maria fall on this festival. A massive image of Mary formed from strings of lights shines in the night sky. The caption reads in Tamil, *Mariyē vāḻka*, literally "Long Live Mary," but this could also be worded as Ave Maria. Similar light sculptures appear that year for festivals for the Goddess Mariyamman and many other Hindu deities. Chief Minister Jayalalitha is as much up in lights on the streets as she had been on the silver screen. A giant light sculpture of the chief minister illuminates the entrance to the grand Tamil Nadu state fair. In contemporary urban Tamil Nadu, the older public culture that Susan Bayly and others have explicated so well has developed into a new underlying idiom of public life. As the florescent tubes cast their blue-green light on the palanquin of the Blessed Virgin, she seems to float out into a night crowd of adoring fans. The Lady who stands on the moon becomes the star of stars (figure 2.10).

Chariot Processions and Public Rituals—a Dialogue on the Streets

The last two decades have seen a renewed interest in lavish public rituals transformed by new contemporary idioms of public culture in the state of Tamil Nadu. Both religious chariot processions outlined here occurred in a context of other extravaganzas carefully staged by political parties. The last term of the former chief minister Jayalalitha ended literally in a blaze of lights—she lost a crucial election in part because she stood accused of overspending public funds on her lavish displays. She was back in power in the central government as head of her party, the A.I.A.D.M.K (All India Anna Dravida Munnetra Kazhagam). In the last national elections, however, her choice to support the losing Congress Party appeared to have ended her career, but she won a major victory in the assembly elections in 2001 and has returned to power. During 1994–95 she held two major public events that I witnessed, the Eighth International Conference-Seminar of Tamil Studies in the ancient city of Tanjore and the opening of a new waterline in Pudukkottai city. Both of these events were within thirty miles of Avur. Their style of public display clearly set a new standard for grandeur, although many referred to it in less flattering terms. In Pudukkottai hundreds of craftsmen built the facade of a Moghul fort out of wire, paper, and plaster! Inside the tent at the back, a grand stage was set with an image of the Mother of Rivers, the Goddess Kaveri, who stood

Figure 2.10: Our Lady of Velankanni attracts many devotees from diverse communities as she moves into the streets of Besant Nagar.

above a ceremonial faucet that the chief minister opened. The event was meant for the cameras. The entire city of Pudukkottai became a grand stage for massive light sculptures of M.G.R. and his once leading lady, Jayalalitha, in their most famous roles. There were grand archways depicting the former actress as various personages including the Queen of the Nile. The same style of stage setting filled the streets of Tanjore for the Tamil Studies conference. Those of us who lived near the residence of the chief minister in Chennai frequently saw her up in lights at the corner of the road, where she traveled to her office. The idioms of the movie world became part of public display and spilled over to the religious world as well.

The new sense of public spectacle may not completely explain the re-emergence of the chariot festivals after so many years of silence, but it is part of the mix of public life that marks the contemporary scene in Tamil Nadu. In what ways has this new public idiom effected the reconstruction of public *religious* life in Tamil Nadu? Susan Wadley, in her introduction to a new set of essays on the media and the transformation of religion in South Asia, argues that the new information technologies have helped to "bypass the social bottlenecks that have inhibited" the propagation of all-India religious symbols to the masses. She points to the older context of religious imagery that remained enmeshed in very particular social groups. Such images were signs of identity not to a whole society but to a particular group. The new technologies have had a "socially 'disembedding' effect on religious tradi-tions" (Babb and Wadley 1995, 3–4). In the case of the procession of the Virgin Mary in suburban Chennai, the event itself is not mediated through technology but rather shares in an idiom invented for the motion picture, the oldest of the new technologies to influence public culture in Chennai, a world-class capital for moviemaking (see Dickey 1993). The very sounds of the event and the lights, usually reserved for the stars of film and politics, turns the religious procession into a movie theater with a grand difference—the devotees are no longer viewers but equal participants in a drama depicting triumph and power. The chosen few who "star" as Our Lady's valets and near kin may have important roles, but they are not alone in the glory of the hour. And here is the point, where the old tradition of the chariot festival in par-ticular and the newer media-style event share a common link—all such pro-cessions have always required a cast of thousands. The "accommodation" that the Catholic Church makes in twentieth century urban India is not to "Hindu" practice but to the pervasive styles of the mass media.

While the influence of the movie genre is obvious in Besant Nagar, the technologies of the contemporary world do not permeate the scene in the very poor village of Avur, although its inhabitants are no strangers to the cinema or to the glittering political world of Jayalalitha. Here in Avur, the more traditional performance of the chariot festival still plays to a devoted audience. I remem-ber no loudspeakers or blaring music, but it is a grand display nonetheless. Hundreds pull the *tēr*. Hundreds more wait and watch as the chariot nears its goal after long, hot hours of massive human effort. This grand spectacle needs no other props to compete with the image-world of the cinema or match its drama. With a cast of thousands, the chariot procession merges Christianity into the very Indian practice of triumphal royal procession. The deity enthroned in this mobile *kōyil* surveys the streets of the divine royal domain. Participants become servants of God, but in a larger sense God's devotees also become the power that drives his/her process into the world. In an explanation of the chariot procession, the head priest of the famous

Kapaleeswara temple in Chennai spoke of the procession as an exercise in democracy—everyone must pull together to make the wheels of power roll (Waghorne 1992, 27). In Avur, the Risen Christ rules his kingdom on earth but with the combined force of his many devotees. The chariot festival combines signs of royal power with images that speak easily in a democratic world. Here God reigns, inaugurated each year through the sweat of the multitudes.

The long-standing debate over Christians sharing common ritual forms within the larger south Indian religious scene has been settled defacto by an Indian Catholic Church. Freed to use Tamil during the reign of Pope John XXIII, the clergy moved to reclaim its cultural as well as linguistic heritage. A title of a recent book by a contemporary member of the Church in India tells it all: *Indian Christians: Search for Identity and Struggle for Autonomy* (Mundadan 1984). The movement to link India's *sannyāsi* heritage with the Roman Catholic Church's long-standing monastic tradition has become a serious part of the Church in India (Ralston 1987; Thangaraj, 1994). In openly choosing to speak of God in the shared "religious sensibilities" of Tamil Nadu, the Church in India has accepted a new *civil theology*. Here I mean the term more literally as public discourse about divinity than the shared form implies. To envision God triumphant in the world in India is also to accept the presence of a plurality of powerful personages. This is a very contemporary answer to the old charges that by adopting "Hindu forms," Christians were liable to the charge of "idolatry." But in public life in Tamil Nadu, on the streets of the town or the village, God triumphant cannot be the only divine figure in the universe. The very image of victory leaves room for a plurality of gods—indeed they are necessary to assert the glory of one's own. Such a figure is not really foreign to European Catholic imagery. Just as a small dwarf-like body peeps out still from under the feet of the Lord Shiva in his cosmic dance, Mary stands on the snake reminding Christians that the Devil remains—defeated but alive.

Moreover, the chariot processions do not imply that a rivalry and the "victory" between divine personages is necessarily between Hindu and Christian gods. To this day in Boston in the mixed Italian neighborhood of the North End, images of various patron saints and forms of the Virgin Mary particular to the native cities of the now long-migrated Italians are still processed in the streets during the festival day of the saint. These festivals compete with each other for the attention of the public and assert, once again, pride in particular powerful personages. The same is true in Tamil Nadu; the competition for public glory finds all temples and churches in competition. And, Chennai residents have their opinions of the "best" processions or divine figures, something that often changes with time. The language of the chariot procession is expressed through a multiplicity of powers but ultimately glorifies the One who has won the hearts of the devotees—for that day, for that time, for that place. Christians in Besant Nagar and in Avur seem well satisfied with that kind of victory.

Notes

1. Research for this paper was carried out as part of a larger project on new temples in the city of Chennai and its environs and was funded by the American Institute of Indian Studies and the National Endowment for the Humanities. I wish to thank both organizations and the priests at Our Lady of Velankanni Church in Besant Nagar and the church in Avur for their kind cooperation. Photography and initial interviews in Avur were done by my husband Dick Waghorne as was the photography at Besant Nagar.

2. We photographed the process of rebuilding this famous chariot throughout the year 1994–95. The old car was disassembled, and a facsimile of all images were recarved on newly cut wood, and all parts recreated and replaced! Nedungudi is a very small village with a great temple in rural Pudukkottai District.

3. Religious organizations can receive public funds in south India. The Hindu Religious and Charitable Endowment, a Tamil Nadu state government agency, oversees the finances for many Hindu temples that are considered public institutions and thus in need of state support and control. For an overview of the endowment, see Presler 1987.

4. India is organized much like the USA with state governments sharing power with a central government in New Delhi. The chief minister has the powers of an American governor.

5. Norman Cutler provides a good summary on recent scholarship on south India as a multireligious region. See Cutler 1998, 463–75.

6. Earlier chariots in Tamil Nadu may have been built out of bamboo poles and then disassembled. This was likely the case in Avur. See Kalidos 1989, 71.

7. American Heritage Dictionary, version for Microsoft Office and Windows 95.

8. The crusade against such practices was not confined to India. Dubois seems to have joined the growing British rhetoric against "idolatry" that was as much directed against the uneducated at home in Britain as the errant native Christian in India. A prime example of this is the popular 1821 work, *Essay of the Evils of Popular Ignorance,* by John Foster. Foster's new critique of "idolatry" follows much of the logic of social reform with a renewed Christian evangelism. See also my essay, Waghorne 1998, 216–17.

9. Parliamentary Paper no. 66 of session 1845.

10. This is clearly shown in the film version of E. M. Forster's *Passage to India.* I also speak from many years of dealing with I.A.S. officers, many of whom continued to greet the coming of public religious events with mixed feelings at best, sometimes with hostility or subtle embarrassment. This is less true not more than a decade ago and certainly not true for all officers of the central government. Local officials of the Tamil Nadu government tended to be more supportive of such events.

11. Jayalalitha was just sworn in as the chief minister after a significant victory in the polls. She replaced the DMK (Dravida Munnetra Kazhagam) person who had defeated her in the last elections.

12. From an interview with the carvers who were remaking the great chariot at Nedungudi in Pudukkottai district, March 16, 1995. I did not do a close study of the chariot at Avur, which deserves a detailed analysis of its own.

13. Pudukkottai district was once a small independent state ruled by a Hindu Maharaja.

14. There are a number of words here that I do not transliterate but keep in the form that they so commonly appear in English conversation or publications: *tombai, pandal, tali.*

15. This famous architect was commissioned to design a new state capital called Chandigarh in north India. His design revolutionized design in modern India. Most modern houses and office buildings in major cities derive from his work.

16. I was told this during the chariot procession at the nearby Kapaleeswara Temple. My informant pointed out that the *ter* used to have the same number of layers of sculptures as the *kōyil,* but that those layers were damaged. This may not be an accurate story, but it reflects the sentiments in the area on the proper nature of the chariots.

References

Babb, Lawrence A., and Susan S. Wadley, eds. 1995. *Media and the Transformation of Religion in South Asia.* Philadelphia: University of Pennsylvania Press.

Bayly, Susan. 1992. *Saints, Goddesses, and Kings: Muslims and Christians in South Indian Society, 1700–1900.* Cambridge: Cambridge University Press (South Asian Edition).

Cronin, Vicent. 1959. *A Pearl to India: The Life of Robert de Nobili.* New York: E. P. Dutton & Co.

Cutler, Norman. 1998. "South India as a Multi-religious Region." In *India's Worlds and U.S. Scholars, 1947–1997,* eds. Joseph W. Elder and Edward C. Dimock 463–65. New Delhi: Monohar and the American Institute of Indian Studies.

Dickey, Sara. 1993. *Cinema and the Urban Poor in South India.* Cambridge: Cambridge University Press.

Diehl, Carl Gustav. 1965. *Church and Shrine: Intermingling Patterns of Culture in the Lives of Some Christian Groups in South India.* Uppsala: Acta Universitatis Upsaliensis.

Dubois, J. A. 1906 [1818]. *Hindu Manners, Customs and Ceremonies.* Trans. by Henry K. Beauchamps. Oxford: Clarendon Press.

Gandhi, Gopal Krishna. 1983. *Tamilnadu District Gazatteers: Pudukkottai.* Madras: Government of Tamilnadu, 824–25.

Hart, George L. 1975. *The Poems of Ancient Tamil.* Berkeley and Los Angeles: University of California Press.

Kalidos, Raju. 1989. "Chariots of Culture." *Frontline* [India] (July 8–21): 69–75.

Kaye, John William. 1859. *Christianity in India: An Historical Narrative*. London: Smith, Elder & Co.

Michell, George ed. 1992. *Living Wood: Sculptural Traditions of Southern India*. Bombay: Marg Publications.

Mundadan, A. Mathias. 1984. *Indian Christians: Search for Identity and Struggle for Autonomy*. Bangalore: Dharmaram Publications.

Neill, Stephen. 1985. *A History of Christianity in India, 1707–1858*. Cambridge: Cambridge University Press.

Presler, Franklin A. 1987. *Religion Under Bureaucracy: Policy and Administration for Hindu Temples in South India*. Cambridge: Cambridge University Press.

Radhakrishna Aiyar, S. 1916. *A History of the Pudukkottai State*. Pudukkottai: Sri Bihadambal State Press.

Ralston, Helen. 1987. *Christian Ashrams: A New Religious Movement in Contemporary India*. Lewiston, N.Y.: Edwin Mellen Press.

Shulman, David. 1980. *Tamil Temple Myths*. Princeton: Princeton University Press.

Sthapati, Ganapathi V. 1989. "Festival of Fervour." *Frontline* [India] (July 8–21):76–79.

Thangaraj, M. Thomas. 1994. *The Crucified Guru: An Experiment in Cross-cultural Christology*. Nashville, Tenn.: Abingdon Press.

Waghorne, Joanne Punzo. 1999. "The Divine Image in Contemporary South India: The Renaissance of a Once Maligned Tradition." In *Made on Earth, Born in Heaven: Making the Cult Image in the Ancient Mediterranean and Contemporary India,* ed. Michael B. Dick, 211–43. Winona Lake, Ind: Eisenbrauns.

———. 1994. *The Raja's Magic Clothes: Re-Visioning Kingship and Divinity in England's India*. University Park: Pennsylvania State University Press.

———. 1992. "Dressing the Body of God: South Indian Bronze Sculpture in its Temple Setting." With photographs by Dick Waghorne. *Asian Art* Sackler Museum of the Smithsonian Institution. (Summer): 27: 8–33.

CHAPTER 3

The Ganges, The Jordan, and the Mountain:
The Three Strands of Santal Popular Catholicism[1]

Selva J. Raj

Popular Catholicism, which guides and defines the religious life and practices of Catholics in India, constitutes a vibrant and vital strand of Indian Catholicism. Prominent in ritual manifestations, popular Catholicism in India contains several features that distinguish it from Catholicism elsewhere. A noteworthy feature of this popular Catholicism is that the usual distinctions between the Hindu, Muslim, primeval, and Christian traditions, as well as the normative boundaries between official and popular religion, become significantly blurred. The dynamic of Santal popular Catholic religious life, represented in its life-cycle ceremonies, life-crisis rituals, calendrical festivals, and magico-religious practices, provides a textbook case for this phenomenon of blurred boundaries. Taking the funerary tradition as a representative sample, this essay examines the patterns of popular acculturation in Santal Catholicism and the Church hierarchy's responses to it, and proposes a model for dialogue.[2]

Santal Popular Catholicism: A Brief Description

In his demographic description of the Santals, J. Troisi maintains that the Santals are "the largest homogenous scheduled tribe in the country" (Troisi 1978, 24). According to the 1990 census of India, the Santals numbered approximately 4.2 million or 6.18 percent of the nation's total tribal population (Heitzman and Worden 1996, 199–200). The bulk of Santal population is concentrated in the three Indian states of Bihar, West Bengal, and Orissa. A sizeable Santal population is also found in Assam, Tripura, Megalaya, Bangladesh, and Nepal. Though called Santals by others, the Santals refer to

39

themselves as *hor*, meaning "man." The language of the Santals is Santali, a branch of the Munda family of languages. Under the influence of Christian missionaries, the Santals have adopted the Roman script that is in currency to this day. As regards their ethnic or political history, the Santals do not have a recorded history of their own, although they possess a rich oral tradition. The first authoritative written record of Santal history was compiled in Santali by L. O. Skrefsrud from oral transmission and was translated later by P. O. Bodding (Bodding 1946; Bompas 1909).[3]

Santal folklore describes this tribe as a wandering race. Although there is no consensus among either scholars or the Santals themselves about their original habitat, by the mid-eighteenth century large numbers of Santals were found in the Chotanagpur tribal belt, particularly in the Singhbhum district in Bihar.[4] By the end of the eighteenth century, they migrated to the Rajmahal hills in Bihar. Since then the tracts of the Rajmahal hills have been considered the heartland of Santal life. Socially, the Santals possess a well-organized social structure with a clearly defined hierarchy of offices, duties, rights, and privileges. The village council *(panchayat)*, where every properly initiated Santal gains membership, is the village high court, and the village marketplace *(hatia)* is the center of weekly social gatherings and fellowship (Mukherjea 1943; Orans 1965). However, the most important place in every Santal village is the sacred grove *(jahersthan)*, the abode of the five principal spirits of the tribe, where periodic sacrifices and oblations are offered to the resident spirits.[5]

The traditional religion of the Santals revolves around faith in and the desire to establish an intimate relationship with supernatural beings, powers, and spirits *(bonga)* (Troisi 1978, 71). So crucial is this relationship that some scholars describe Santal religion as "bongaism" (Mazumdar 1979, 324–38). Its calendrical rites and magico-religious practices involving sacrifices, oblations, and libations serve as the concrete instruments for maintaining a right relationship and communion with the spirits *(bonga)*. These spirits are believed to guarantee societal stability and personal well-being.[6]

For centuries, the Santals lived in relative cultural isolation and suffered economic exploitation at the hands of local Hindu moneylenders. They came under missionary influence in the mid-nineteenth century. The prevailing social and economic climate of bonded labor, exploitation, and misery were most suitable for Christian missionary activities (Sahay 1986, 69). The Santal rebellion of 1855 was a failed attempt to gain social and economic relief. To the Santals emerging from this failed rebellion, the advent of the missionaries brought some hope. Since its introduction, Christianity has made deep inroads into Santal tribal religion and culture.

Of the various Christian groups, Roman Catholic Christianity has had the most profound impact on the Santals when measured by the bumper crop of converts it has reaped in the last five decades. The subsequent

Christianization of the converts has resulted not only in the superimposition of a foreign ritual system on the indigenous tribal universe but also in the restructuring and redefinition of their social and cultural life. Conversion meant the detribalization and coerced alienation of converts from their indigenous cultural milieu and religious universe. The social, cultural, and geographical segregation of converts from their tribal confreres, evidenced in the development of Catholic settlements *(bustees)* in some villages, where converts have minimal interaction with non-Catholic Santals, was an attempt to extricate the converts from their native cultural milieu. Though converts appreciate the socioeconomic and religious benefits of conversion, many refuse to renounce their tribal heritage or indigenous identity/identities. All of this has given rise to a distinct form of Catholicism.

Prominent in its ritual manifestations, this complex and interactive popular Catholicism represents the confluence of at least *three distinct ritual strands* that I classify as the *Ganges*, the *Jordan*, and the *Mountain*. While they are associated respectively with Hinduism, Christianity, and Santal tribal religion, they are held together in an enduring dialogical relationship of mutual interaction and transformation. Even as converts negotiate the confluence of these strands, the indigenous Mountain functions as the central wellspring of religious imagination and ritual behavior. The ongoing intermingling of these three doctrinally incompatible partners finds concrete representations in a variety of ritual performances including lifecycle ceremonies, crisis interventions, seasonal festivals, and magico-religious practices. The interface of multiple ritual strands enables the convert community not only to assert and satisfy its manifold loyalties, often in defiance of ecclesial instructions, but also to construct a distinct identity for itself that is *authentically tribal, fully Indian,* and *genuinely Christian.*

The Santal Catholic Funerary Tradition:
An Example of Blurred Boundaries

The Santal Catholic funerary tradition, which serves as a concrete illustration of this dynamic, reveals the converts' simultaneous resistance and openness to the pressures of social and religious acculturation (Thomas 1987, 450–58). Its tripartite structure consists of the preburial, burial, and postburial rites, each with its clearly defined goals and appropriate ritual specialists.

Preburial Rites

Though the Santals cremated the dead in the past, today burial is the prevalent practice among all Santals, including Catholics (Campbell 1979, 81-86; Cole 1979, 345–49; Culshaw 1949, 150–60). Both Catholic and non-Christian Santals,

who share the Indian preoccupation with minimizing the ritual pollution resulting from death, exhibit great care and caution in the speedy disposal of
the body. For the most part, the Catholic domestic preburial rites reflect the
persistence of indigenous (Santal, tribal, and/or Hindu) funerary assumptions
and customs. After the body is ceremonially bathed and anointed with oil and
turmeric, the female members of the household pour water into the mouth of
the deceased, place some of his/her personal possessions such as clothes, a
plate, and a vessel on the coffin, and bid farewell with loud lamentations (Troisi
1978, 182).[7] An important aspect of this all-female domestic farewell ceremony
is the placing of coins on the coffin or on the mouth of the deceased, intended
to help defray the cost of the journey to the world of ancestors *(hanapuri)*.
Ordinarily, women do not accompany the body to the burial site.

Burial Rites

The Catholic public burial rites involve two different sets of ceremonies,
an official Catholic liturgy and a modified native tribal liturgy. Frequently, the
Catholic liturgy assumes the form of a simple prayer service and a formal
commendation rite led by the priest or the village catechist. At the conclusion
of the Catholic liturgy, the tribal ceremonies once again gain prominence. The
male members of the village gather at the burial site to bid farewell to the
deceased by offering some coins and a drink of water. The personal belongings
of the deceased are then retrieved and sold. Following this, the village *bailee*
(an official in Santal social hierarchy) cuts a lock of hair from the deceased.
This ceremonial removal of hair ritualizes the Santal assumption that the dead
return to the otherworld in the manner they first came into this world. Hair
shaving by male mourners, a purificatory bath in a nearby river, and a communal meal consisting of puffed rice *(moori)* and rice-beer conclude the public
rites. This riverside fellowship has both practical and psychosocial functions.
Besides averting potential quarrels and bickering over the money retrieved
from the coffin, it also strengthens social and family ties and offers moral and
psychological support to the bereaved members of the family. Unlike traditional Santals who bury the coins with the deceased, some Catholics use these
monies and those procured from the sale of the deceased's personal belongings
for the ensuing rice-beer fellowship. Others use the proceeds to pay for a
memorial Mass for the deceased. The "conversion" of the coin ceremony is
illustrative of the enduring pattern of Catholic modification, whereby the intent
and meaning of a tribal rite are Christianized and given a Catholic flavor.

A striking feature of both the Santal Catholic and Santal preburial and
burial practices concerns the specific roles assigned to men and women.
While women play a prominent role in the preburial domestic ceremonies,
men are the sole actors in the public burial rites and the subsequent public

purificatory rites and the social fellowship. These conventional prescriptions governing proper ritual space for men and women and the prohibitions against women's participation in the public ceremonies reinforce societal assumptions regarding gender roles.

While the above constitutes the general burial tradition of Santal Catholics, the traditional Santal burial practices include other rituals that converts claim to have abandoned. Two such omissions are noteworthy. First, unlike their tribal confreres, ordinarily Santal Catholics do not perform chicken sacrifices at the burial site. The second significant omission is the oil-bath *(telnahan)* ceremony observed five days after the burial. According to Santal tradition, this purificatory rite ensures the freedom of the deceased from malevolent forces and spirits as well as the collective purification of the village community including the village spirits, so that the entire society can return to normality and order. The ceremony gains its name from the purificatory bath undertaken by all mourners after rubbing oil on themselves. In addition to the purificatory bath, the ceremony entails the offering of oil cakes and twigs to the great spirit *(Maran Buru*, literally, "Great Mountain"), the primordial human couple *(Pilchu Haram* and *Pilchu Budhi)* and the departed spirit, and imploring the protection of the spirits for the deceased (Troisi 1978, 193–94). After this ritual oblation two members of the family become possessed by *Maran Buru* and the spirit of the deceased individual, to whom water and rice-beer are offered. This rite provides an opportunity for family members to ascertain the cause of death. At the conclusion of the possession rite, fowls are offered to the attending spirits. A communal meal prepared from the flesh of the animals concludes the oil-bath ceremony. According to my informants, the reason why Santal Catholics do not observe these ceremonies is that these practices have direct reference to spirit worship, which they are expected to renounce. Though most Catholics publicly claim to have abandoned the oil-bath ceremony and its associated rituals, pastoral realities tell a different story.[8]

The Postburial Memorial (Bhandan) Rite

Of all the funeral practices, the postburial memorial rite *(bhandan)*, usually observed on the fortieth day, provides the most compelling case for multiritualism and ritual intermingling. Multiritualism is a religious performance in which the devotee observes more than one set of rituals, often drawn from diverse and disparate (sometimes even contrary) traditions, in order to obtain solutions to a single human or spiritual crisis. Put simply, it is a sort of ritual smorgasbord. Before we examine this dynamic of multiritualism in the Santal Catholic *bhandan* ceremony, a brief overview of the traditional Santal *bhandan* rite would be helpful.

The closest male relatives have their hair shaved and take a purificatory bath. When these preliminary rites are completed, family members and guests, each of whom is obligated to bring a fowl, goat, or pig as sacrificial offering, assemble at the deceased's home for rice-beer fellowship. A possession rite, in which three persons become possessed by the deceased, the village founder, and *Maran Buru* (the Great Spirit) respectively, follows the rice-beer fellowship (Campbell 1979, 85–86). The purpose of the possession rite is to find out whether or not the spirits were satisfied with the funeral ceremonies. The centerpiece of the memorial rite, however, is the *khuttum* ceremony (the ritual slaughter of animals by beating them to death), performed by a village official at the headman's sacred grove *(manjhisthan)*. A portion of the memorial meal consisting of rice, vegetables, and sacrificial meat is offered to the deceased and the presiding spirits of the village, after which the entire community partakes in rice-beer fellowship and a festive meal.

The Catholic version differs from the above traditional pattern in some important ways. Conducted in the home of the deceased instead of the conventional village headman's sacred grove *(manjhisthan)*, the Catholic *bhandan* rites commence with a Catholic prayer service led by the village catechist followed by a series of mortuary rituals—some tribal and some Hindu—including hair-shaving, a purificatory bath, the sacrifice of fowls, a communal meal, drinking, singing, and dancing. Only rarely will a memorial Mass precede these rituals, and I was struck by the convert community's rather nonchalant and matter-of-fact attitude toward the memorial Mass. When asked, many Santal Catholics said that they do not consider the Mass a necessary requirement for the efficacy of the native rite. An important procedural variation in the Catholic version concerns the mode of slaughtering the sacrificial animals. In lieu of the prescribed *khuttum* method, Catholics slaughter the animals by slitting their throats, since the former has in Santal tradition clear associations with spirit worship. Despite its resemblance to the Hindu *sraddha* ceremony and the official Catholic memorial service, the Catholic *bhandan* rite is essentially an indigenous ceremony governed by tribal taboos and prescriptions. For example, Santal Catholics scrupulously adhere to the societal prescription that the *bhandan* rites should be completed before any auspicious events like marriage. However, Santal Catholics exclude, as with the burial rites, the spirit-worship *(bonga-puja)* and the possession rite. To this general pattern there are several exceptions necessitated by existential familial and social realities. Both the laity and the native clergy repeatedly told me that often the content and character of Catholic *bhandan* change with the complexion of the audience. If the majority of the participants are non-Catholic, then the rite becomes less Catholic and more tribal, involving such forbidden practices as spirit-worship *(bonga-puja)*.

Another notable feature of the Catholic *bhandan* ceremony is the ritual prominence accorded to the village catechist, who is the authorized specialist for both the Catholic and tribal parts of the ceremony, and the virtual exclusion of the ordained priest. Ordinarily, the priest does not attend, nor is he invited to attend. Even if he is present to celebrate Mass, which occurs occasionally, he has no ritual function in the tribal ceremonies. After the Mass he retreats into the background and makes way for the catechist. Because of his ritual expertise, his nuanced understanding of Santal religious and cultural traditions, and above all his personal status in the community, the catechist is considered the proper "Catholic" official for these non-Catholic practices, especially the animal slaughter. He is therefore charged with what we might call "liminal symbolism." As a liminal figure himself (he is an intermediary between the priest and the laity, between the tribal society and Catholic religion), the village catechist symbolizes the liminal character of the celebration held on behalf of a liminal figure (the deceased) sponsored by a liminal convert community (Troisi 1978, 194–96).[9] The virtual exclusion of the priest from the *bhandan* ritual context seems to be a symbolic statement of the relationship between the normative center (the hierarchy) and the functional center (the laity), who perceive the former as the peripheral other. The Catholic *bhandan* data suggest that while the Catholic version retains the spirit, structure, and prescriptions of the traditional *bhandan* rite, it is characterized by several procedural and substantive modifications, notably regarding the location, the method, the ritual specialist, and the recipient of the rite.

The Dynamic of Popular Acculturation

The Santal society as a whole is currently caught up in the tidal wave of transition ushered in by the forces of modernization, industrialization, and Christianization (Mahapatra 1986, 1–2; Mittal 1986, 87; Mandelbaum 1970, 613–16). What was once a homogenous tribal group has now evolved into a complex society comprising various subgroups like the Santal Protestant Christians, Santal Catholics, "Hinduized" or Sanskritized Santals, and urban Santals. Their diverse social and religious conditions have generated new lifestyles and, by extension, new dilemmas and obligations.

Though the effects of this transitional condition are evident in every subgroup in the Santal society, they are particularly visible among Santal Catholics. They not only share the transitional condition of the larger Santal society but are also caught up in the dialectic of intercultural and intracultural transitional cycles. Consequently, these Catholics find themselves commuting between several worlds. First, they move back and forth between Santal cultural values such as the pursuit of pleasure *(raska)* and modern values like progress, development, technology, and thriftiness. The case of urban Santal Catholics who seek to preserve their tribal identity in the industrial milieu is a concrete example. Second, they belong to the worlds of traditional religion and the newfound religion (Catholicism), which predicates constant commuting between the native ritual system and the adapted foreign ritual system. Thus the Santal Catholic community finds itself in a cycle of liminality.

On the one hand, the Santal society requires converts not only to respect their parental tradition but also to follow the traditional Santal practices and customs. These tribal practices themselves are profoundly influenced by north Indian tribal religious culture. On the other hand, these converts are obligated to be faithful to the norms, prescriptions, and traditions of the Catholic Church. Additionally, Santal Catholics, who have been under Hindu religious influence for centuries, are also obligated to respect the religious customs and practices of their Hindu neighbors. The speedy disposal of the body, the hair-shaving rites, and the concern for avoidance of pollution are some of the more concrete instances of the Hindu influence on Santal Catholic ritual life. This state of multiliminality resulting from conversion has produced multiple identities and manifold loyalties that in turn have necessitated the phenomenon of multiritualism and ritual intermingling.[10] Thus, the significant moments of an individual Santal Catholic's life are marked by at least two, but frequently several, sets of ritual celebrations as exemplified in the Santal Catholic funerary tradition.

Motives

This phenomenon of interactive ritual systems is the result of the complex interaction or, what Kitagawa calls, the circularity and "seamless synthesis" of social, cultural, political, and religious factors (Kitagawa 1990, 224-25). Some of the compelling motives are: attachment to indigenous practices; an enduring faith in the proven efficacy of tribal practices; social pressure from the non-Christian Santal community, which often includes family members and relatives; domestic concerns like family unity; the desire to cling to the social, economic, cultural and religious benefits flowing from dual identities; and the urge to protect cultural heritage, village hegemony, and tribal identity. In addition, there is a growing awareness among Santal Catholics today that conversion need not necessarily entail the renunciation of time-honored tribal practices and customs.

Fidelity to multiple ritual systems guarantees certain personal, social, and religious benefits and allows for the preservation of several interactive systems within Santal popular Catholicism. This also explains the converts' persistent refusal to renounce their multiple identities. The initiation rites observed by Santal Catholics are instructive here. In addition to the Catholic confirmation rite, Santal Catholics also observe an indigenous initiation rite *(caco chatiar)* that reveals Hindu and tribal features. Celebrated in early adolescence, the *caco chatiar* is a tribal initiation rite mandatory for all Santal young men. On the appointed day, the midwife, who had assisted at his birth, bathes the candidate after which young women anoint him with oil and turmeric. The village moral guardian *(jogmanjhi)* then recites the tribal lore to the initiate beginning with the creation myths, the origins of the tribe, its wanderings, and its present habitat. As the community enters into another round of rice-beer drinking, the *jogmanjhi* declares that by partaking in the rice-beer fellowship, the village society offers its collective approval and validation for the rite. In Santal tribal religion, this rite serves dual functions. First, it grants a Santal youth adult status and full membership in the tribal society with its accompanying rights and obligations. Second, it permits the initiate to have direct access to and establish a personal relationship with the spirits *(bonga)*. Thus the indigenous rite has religious and social dimensions.

Many Catholics repeatedly stated that they observe the *caco chatiar* rite solely for cultural reasons, as it guarantees certain sociocultural benefits unavailable through the official Catholic sacramental structure. They claim to have relinquished the religious dimension of the indigenous rite and replaced it with the official Catholic confirmation rite. According to them, these two sets of initiation rites satisfy two basic yet separate needs or impulses. While one fulfills the canonical requirement for full participation in the sacramental life of the Church, the other satisfies the sociocultural need for adult status and full membership in tribal life. Additionally, the *caco chatiar* rite affords an opportunity for converts to reaffirm, demonstrate, and strengthen their tribal solidarity with non-Christian Santals. The concepts of *dhorom* (Catholic religion) and *samaj* (tribal society) best articulate the converts' dialectical condition and simultaneous dependence on two separate resources.

Threefold Strategies of Popular Acculturation[11]

What strategies do Santal Catholics employ in forging for themselves the union of three doctrinally incompatible religious traditions? How do converts integrate tribal rituals that are sometimes contrary, if not contradictory, to Catholic tenets? How do they cross over what seem to be impermeable boundaries? Are tribal rituals and symbols simply adopted minus their myths, meanings, and beliefs, or is the original meaning of native symbols and rituals altered and given a new meaning to suit a new belief system? As a collective response to the dialectic of change and continuity, Santal Catholic syncretism reflects the convergence of several syncretic patterns. In some instances, indigenous assumptions (Santal, tribal, and/or Hindu) are expressed through Catholic symbols and rites, and vice versa, while in other cases, the indigenous, especially tribal, rites are preserved minus their tribal assumptions that are replaced by Catholic assumptions and beliefs. In still other cases, indigenous rites and symbols survive in the Catholic ritual system after some careful modifications. Finally, indigenous rites may simply coexist with Catholic rites. These various patterns may be broadly classified under the three principal categories of inclusion, supplementation or parallelism, and traditionalization.

INCLUSION

Inclusion implies the incorporation of Catholic elements into tribal rituals and practices and vice versa without major changes in their meaning or significance. It occurs primarily in two contrasting contexts: when the tribal rite is perceived to be or is, in fact, contrary to or incompatible with the Catholic belief system, and when the tribal rite is perceived to be harmless. The inclusion of Catholic elements serves at least two purposes: either it neutralizes, and in some cases nullifies, the potential danger and threat the tribal rite (e.g. *bonga* worship) presents to the integrity of Catholic belief, or it replaces a forbidden component of the native ritual. The substitution of the Catholic prayer service and/or the Mass for the "spirit-worship" *(bonga puja)* during the *bhandan* ceremony as well as during the Flower *(baha)* Festival are two compelling examples (Troisi 1979, 462).[12] Conversely, the incorporation of tribal elements into Catholic rituals provides local character to Catholic life and practice. This pattern is evident in the significance attached to rice-beer fellowship in Santal Catholic mortuary celebrations. The incorporation of the indigenous vermilion ceremony *(sindurdan)* into the Catholic nuptial rite, as well as other traditional Santal festive expressions like tribal dances and singing into official Catholic liturgical contexts, is an additional example of this pattern of inclusion.[13] Three factors seem to have sustained this process of inclusion: a) the steady increase in the number and position of native clergymen, b) the theological appreciation for Santal religiocultural heritage among the nonindigenous clergy, and c) the increasing influence of the theologies of indigenization and inculturation that became popular in the Indian Catholic Church after the Second Vatican Council.

SUPPLEMENTATION OR PARALLELISM

Supplementation or parallelism refers to that strategy wherein indigenous (Santal, tribal, and/or Hindu) and Catholic rites are allowed to coexist more or less in their original form. Though evident in almost all areas of Santal Catholic religious life, this phenomenon is particularly prominent in life-cycle and life crisis contexts, when Santal Catholics observe at least two, but often more, sets of rites whose integrity is neither altered nor compromised. Depending on the context, one set of rites might serve to complement, supplement, or simply duplicate the other set of rites. The Catholic public burial tradition, in which the official Catholic rite is sandwiched between Santal burial rituals, exemplifies this supplementation or parallelism strategy. While Church authorities view the official Catholic rites as primary and the indigenous rites as secondary, there are numerous occasions when the converts regard the indigenous rites as primary and the Catholic rites as secondary. The two-tier marriage system of Santal Catholics is a good example. Ordinarily, most Santal Catholics observe two distinct sets of marriage ceremonies, a church ceremony *(girja bapla)* and a village ceremony *(ato bapla)*. The church ceremony, which satisfies the canonical requirement, is viewed by Church officials as the primary marriage rite. However, Santal Catholics and the traditional Santal society consider the village ceremony and its associated rituals as the central marriage rite. It not only satisfies their tribal, cultural, and psychological sensibilities but also ratifies and completes the church ceremony. Thus, what becomes a supplementary rite at a given moment is determined by a variety of factors including the convert community's catechetical development, its psychological disposition at the time of ritual performance, and the religiocultural demographics of the village.

TRADITIONALIZATION

Traditionalization is the adoption of foreign rituals/symbols *after* their meaning and significance are modified or transformed (Singer 1980, 360). In other words, indigenous (Santal, tribal, and/or Hindu) assumptions are expressed through Catholic symbols and rites, and vice versa. On the one hand, native elements are carefully filtered, "baptized," and Christianized in order to fit into the Catholic belief system, a pattern well exemplified in the coin-rite and the substitution of the Catholic prayer service for the spirit worship in the Catholic *bhandan* service. On the other hand, Catholic and nontribal elements are indigenized and traditionalized in order that they fit into the fundamental tribal worldview. The adoption of the Santal Flower *(baha)* Festival into the Catholic liturgical calendar, as well as the priestly ordination rite discussed in the next section, are instances of the tribalization of Catholic features.

Given this plurality of patterns, how might one classify Santal Catholic syncretism? While typologies of syncretism developed in other similar contexts might provide a helpful backdrop, Santal syncretism should be viewed in terms of its internal dynamic and framework since culture-specific typologies have their inherent constraints and limitations (Colpe 1987, 218–27). Based on our data, I describe the acculturative process in Santal popular Catholicism as *selective syncretism*. This type of syncretism is neither an indiscriminate integration of indigenous elements into the Catholic religious structure, nor is it entirely based on foreign Catholic materials. Instead it is a selective syncretism of features drawn from the indigenous tribal and/or Hindu system and the adopted Catholic system.

Interestingly, this syncretic process has no known founders or culture heros. It does not originate in a single charismatic Santal leader or a collective prophetic leadership or any revolutionary movement.[14] The theologies of indigenization and inculturation that have been gaining momentum in Santal Catholicism are relatively recent. Santal Catholic syncretism seems to be the natural response of the convert community as a whole, a popular process—spontaneous and creative—impelled by the existential considerations of cultural survival and identity in the context of changed religious conditions. This process confirms the widely held view that syncretism is essentially a "folk" phenomenon occurring first in the world of popular practice, which theologians eventually articulate, as secondary reflections, in systematic categories.

The Church Hierarchy's Response to Popular Acculturation

The persistent defiance of normative boundaries and the periodic excursions into forbidden ritual territories, so prominent in Santal popular Catholicism, have been matters of concern for the Church hierarchy. Are these necessarily signs of a dysfunctional Catholicism? Is there a significant perspectival disparity between the laity and the hierarchy? How does ecclesial leadership diagnose and treat this apparent "disease" of popular Catholicism? Despite its pitfalls, the outsider-insider model might be a useful interpretive category to understand the Church hierarchy's response.[15]

In Santal Catholicism, the term "outsider" refers to anyone who, either through cultural origin or social condition, is removed or is perceived to be removed from the world of lay Catholic life and practice. In contrast, the term "insider" refers to one who, irrespective of ethnic or cultural origin, sympathizes with and celebrates popular religiosity. Santal Catholics consider most non-Santals *(dikhu)*[16]—whether foreign or Indian, Hindu, or Christian—and those visibly associated with the Church hierarchy as outsiders. Conversely, not all Santal Catholics are automatically and necessarily insiders. Some of them are actually considered "fallen-away" Santals or native *dikhus* because of their physical absence or cultural alienation. These "fallen away" Santal Catholics have the dual burden of dispelling popular perceptions concerning their cultural status and regaining their tribal identity, a burden that falls particularly on the native clergy rather than on the laity.

Outsiders' Response

A significant majority of the Church leadership, and those who es-
pouse the traditional Catholic theological position, might be classified as
outsiders. Suspicion, disdain, and rejection are the hallmarks of the outsiders' response to the religious practices of the folk. With the exception of a
small minority, most Church leaders tend to regard popular practices as
unhealthy remnants of a primitive religiosity that ought to be steadily weeded
out. Such a negative appraisal has widened the gap between official Catholicism and popular Catholicism. Even the few Church leaders who appreciate the tribal religious heritage are far removed, by virtue of their
office and status, from the existential religious concerns and cultural needs
of the folk. The oft-repeated complaint, "our bishops and priests do not
understand our tradition," is not unfounded. Often, the Church leaders'
negative appraisal is based on misinformation, limited understanding, and
cultural prejudice. This partly explains why Santal Catholics seem to pay
little or no heed to ecclesiastical ordinances.

Insiders' Response

The insiders' group encompasses all those who actively celebrate and
intellectually sympathize with Santal popular religiosity. This group includes
three constitutive subgroups: a) the enlightened legal outsiders who are accepted and treated as practical insiders; b) insiders who, after a period of
cultural alienation and ideological separation, have returned to their religiocultural
roots and regained their insider status; and c) common practitioners who by
birth, faith, and practice are insiders. I classify them as *outside-insiders*, *"born-
again" insiders*, and *fulltime-insiders* respectively.[17] While the first group consists mainly of non-Santal clergy and scholars (Indian and foreign), the native
clergy form the bulk of the second group. By virtue of their social status and
ecclesiastical power, these clergy members often function as public defenders
for their groups. The third subgroup is comprised of lay practitioners.

Outside-Insiders

Though technically outsiders, the outside-insiders act, behave, dress, and
live as insiders. Their evaluation of indigenous religiocultural practices resonates largely with that of the fulltime insiders. To them, the Santal tradition
possesses many positive elements that are not only harmless but also vital for
transplanting the Christian faith into Santal soil. Basing their arguments on
the incarnational and contextual model, they seek to provide a distinct theological identity for Santal Catholicism that is truly reflective of its indigenous

religiocultural heritage. Tribalization or Santalization of Catholic faith and life is the watchword in this camp. Its members seek to achieve this objective through a process of "preservation through purification." Such an attitude is grounded on the assumption that the native practices require religious purification prior to their incorporation into the Catholic religious system. Purificatory efforts are primarily aimed at those aspects of traditional Santal religion that are considered incompatible and/or potentially dangerous to Catholic faith. The remarks of a veteran Jesuit missionary, an archetypal outside-insider, are worth noting: "Santals who convert to Christianity," he asserts, "carry over their traditional beliefs in the *bonga* and *dan* [witchcraft] practices. Our [missionaries'] task is to initiate a process of purification of the systemic impurities endemic in Santal religious and cultural structure."[18]

Though the current perspectives of the outside-insiders mark a positive shift from the negative appraisal of their predecessors, this purification strategy is problematic on at least two counts. First, the criteria of purity and impurity currently employed in the purification process are essentially drawn from Christian and Western sources. There is no agreement between the missionaries and converts about what constitutes pure and impure. More importantly, to date, the agents of this unilateral purification process have been mainly foreign missionaries.

"BORN-AGAIN" INSIDERS

The "born-againers" are those legal insiders who were once divorced from their cultural and mythological universe but eventually returned to their tribal heritage through a second naivete, as it were. They simultaneously resemble and differ from the other insiders. On the one hand, by natural endowments and cultural ties, the "born-againers" have, unlike the outside-insiders, an innate affinity to the insiders' universe. On the other hand, exposure to more cultures (Hindu, Christian, Western, and Muslim), better Catholic religious formation, and higher formal education set them apart from the fulltime insiders. They maintain a certain cultural distance and critical spirit, both of which tend toward greater objectivity. A spirit of resurgence, cultural pride, and renewal of Santal religiosity are characteristics of the "born-againers."

If indigenization or tribalization is the principal focus of the outsider-insiders, retribalization and re-Santalization is the cherished goal for the "born-againers." Its advocates are not content to merely provide a tribal dress or flavor to Santal Catholicism but call for a reconstruction and a new hermeneutic. The creation of native theological categories and the development of an authentic Santal sacramental system that is firmly rooted in and expressed through Santal symbolism are their principal goals. The Santal version of the priestly ordination rite, which markedly differs from the official Catholic rite, is a case in point.

As with all Santal public rituals, the ordination ceremony takes place before the entire village community including non-Christians *(bidin)*.[19] Each household brings traditional gifts such as rice, vegetables, and flowers. The ceremony takes place on a platform *(pinta)* that has been purified with cow dung several days prior to the actual celebration. The consecration of the altar, erected according to Santal ritual prescriptions, involves the sacrifice of a chicken and the sprinkling of blood on the altar. While the clergy is cognizant of this rite, they neither participate nor officiate. On ordination day, the ordinand undergoes a triple tribal purificatory bath in oil, milk, and water administered by a group of village virgins. Following these rituals, both the candidate and the ordaining prelate are dressed in the traditional Santal attire of *dhoti* and shawl. In lieu of the official miter, the bishop wears a turban *(pagadi)*, which is a local symbol for authority and leadership. The processional and offertory rites are replete with native features, including festive drum beating and colorful tribal dancing performed by dozens of young men and women. The laying on of hands by the ordaining prelate remains, as in all Catholic priestly ordination rites, the central rite, but there is a preponderance of tribal features that serve as preparatory and concluding rites. After the ordination ceremony, the village headman *(manjhiharam)*, who often is a non-Christian, places a turban on the newly ordained priest, signifying the latter's public and solemn induction into the village social hierarchy. The newly ordained now assumes the position of the traditional ritual functionary *(naeke)*, leading to a subtle restructuring of the Santal social hierarchy. Though the headman's ceremonial role does not affect the validity of the rite, his presence and token participation have profound social significance. The locus of the ceremony, the consecration of the altar, the triple purificatory bath of the candidate, the native liturgical vestments, the elaborate dancing, and the prominent liturgical role of the village headman *(manjiharam)* are some of the more salient tribal elements in this Santal Catholic ordination rite practiced in some Catholic dioceses.

Through these and similar measures, the "born-againers" challenge the authenticity of normative Catholic interpretations of Santal religiosity and call for a new hermeneutic. Three factors seem to have contributed to this spirit of resurgence: a) the increased access by native priests to positions of power and leadership in the Church hierarchy, b) their nuanced understanding of Santal religiocultural practices, and c) their insider status in the Santal society as well as in the Church hierarchy. Let me cite two concrete instances of this trend toward theological reconstruction. *Maran Buru* is the presiding spirit of the Santal pantheon. Christian missionaries, who saw him as the Santal version of the biblical Satan because he is believed to have taught the primordial human couple the secrets of sex and rice-beer, demanded the formal renunciation of *Maran Buru* and other spirits (*bonga*) as a requirement for baptism. However, today many "born-againers" have made concerted efforts to reverse the demonization of *Maran Buru* and reinstate his importance in Santal religious life. The numerous affectionate references to this genial grandfather of the tribe in Catholic liturgical hymns is a compelling example of reconstruction.

We find a similar effort in the sphere of divination *(ojahism)*. Many native priests are calling for a rethinking of the normative opinion that considers this institution as an unfortunate remnant of a primitive past and inadequate catechesis. The remarks of a Santal priest are instructive: "*Ojahism* is not an evil practice as many tend to believe. We [Santals] regard it as an authentic tribal curative system, a process of healing that has functioned effectively, especially during crisis situations. As a Santal, I can understand and appreciate why our people return to their tribal medicinal system. I look forward to the day when Santal practices will become an integral part of Santal Catholic life."[20]

FULLTIME INSIDERS

The power and vitality of Santal popular Catholicism are most visible in the devotional world of the fulltime insiders. If "born-againers" are the *remythologized*, these fulltime insiders are what Wendy Doniger would call the *mythologized*. A deep attachment to and abiding faith in the efficacy of Santal religiocultural practices, an urge to preserve the native ritual system, and a resistance to change are characteristics of this group. As such, they are the custodians of Santal culture. In addition to these factors, their cultural geography predicates frequent social interactions and religious exchange. Living in close physical and cultural proximity with non-Christian Santals, some of whom might be their relatives, these converts are under intense social pressure to adhere to traditional Santal practices.

These fulltime insiders offer no theological arguments for multiritualism or cross-religious communication, because in their view such arguments do not really matter. To them, the argument from tradition, psychologico-cultural satisfaction, and existential religio-practical needs are good enough. Foremost among these reasons is the urge to obtain personally satisfying solutions to crisis situations making the crossing of ritual and doctrinal boundaries both inevitable and salutary. This means that they regard themselves as Santals first and Catholics only secondarily. Their hyphenated identities and multiple loyalties predicate constant commuting between diverse ritual streams. Left to themselves, these fulltimers exhibit no guilt feelings for embracing the "forbidden." My knowledge of Santal Catholics leads me to believe that whatever sense of guilt they may express is the by-product of clerical indoctrination.

In sum, the story of Santal popular Catholicism is the story of the enduring vitality and resilience of popular religious practices and the dynamic survival of a convert community amidst the challenges and obligations of newfound identities. It is a product of a complex interaction of indigenous (Santal, tribal, and Hindu) and nonindigenous (Catholic) sources that together define its identity. It is neither exclusively popular nor entirely official since Santal popular religious culture and official Catholicism frequently interact in such a way that official Catholicism and Santal popular religion trade roles with each other. In this way they alternate between being peripheral and central.

Ritual: A New Model for Dialogue?

The dynamic of Indian popular Catholicism exemplified in Santal Catholicism demonstrates that an extraordinarily productive locus for efficacious dialogue is the world of rituals rather than the world of theological concepts and categories. Turner (1985) and Driver (1991, 184) have shown the power of ritual to transform the spiritual and social condition of the performer as well as the audience. I suggest that the performance of others' rituals also transforms and that such performances can transform one person's or one group's understanding and attitude toward "the other." In this sense, ritual also functions as a medium for encountering "the other" and a model for dialogue on a profoundly experiential level.

Though Church authorities were persuaded by some maverick Jesuits like Robert de Nobili to recognize the potential value of the ritual model as early as the seventeenth century, the latter's aggressive missionary designs eroded its efficacy. Institutional inculturation, pioneered mainly by foreign missionaries in the wake of the Second Vatican Council, is the most recent ecclesial recognition for the ritual model. However, even this initiative has had only limited appeal among the religious masses because of its inherent elitism on two levels. The first concerns its monastic leaning, mystical emphasis, and philosophical (more precisely Vedantic) orientation from which the vast majority of Indian Catholics consciously distance themselves. The second factor regards the complexion of its members and leaders. At least within Indian Catholicism, institutional inculturation was conceived and nurtured mainly by foreign monks and missionaries in order to relate Catholic faith to the Indian religious scene. Though their Indian successors have embraced this model, its current advocates and sympathizers are all members of the religious elite (priests, nuns, and some bishops). In origin and membership, therefore, institutional inculturation has

predominantly been an elite theological enterprise with little or no involvement of the religious laity.

The data from Santal popular Catholicism suggest that the most efficacious
ritual dialogue occurs in the existential human and spiritual experiences of
the religious folk, in the world of popular inculturation. In Santal Catholicism, *ritual dialogue is the living ecumenism of the laity; it is dialogue in
action.* This popular inculturation, which the religious laity has so effectively
pursued for quite some time, is a metatradition in its own right, not lacking
in logic, rationality, or sophistication. It provides a corrective to the conceptual, elitist, institutional inculturation or institutional dialogue that has been
found wanting, as it tends to be divorced from the existential human and
spiritual experiences of the majority of Indian Catholics. This lay ecumenism
offers an alternative paradigm for religious dialogue. In Hindu sacred geography, the confluence of sacred rivers is valued as the ideal locus for *moksha*,
for encountering the Divine. Similarly, it would appear that in the lives of
Santal Catholics the confluence of ritual streams is the ideal locus for dialogue, for encountering "the other."

Notes

1. Inspiration for this title came from a R. Panikkar article entitled "The
Jordan, the Tiber, and the Ganges: Three Kairological Moments of Christic Self-
Consciousness" (1987). I am grateful to Wendy Doniger, Frank Frick, Bill Harman,
and Corinne Dempsey for their careful comments on an earlier draft.

2. My first contact with Santal Catholics was in the summer of 1971 when I
lived with them in the Catholic villages of Alampur and Rahutara in West Bengal.
Since then I have spent several summers in different Catholic villages in Bihar and
West Bengal. Later a year's residence in Islampur gave me numerous opportunities
to observe and participate in several Santal rituals and festivals. My association with
Santal Catholics was renewed again during my dissertation fieldwork in 1990 in the
dioceses of Dumka in Bihar and Raiganj in West Bengal. The field research itself
included participatory observation of Santal Catholic religiocultural life as well as
formal interviews and informal conversations with a cross section of the Catholic
population, including bishops, priests (Santal and non-Santal), nuns, native catechists,
village leaders, and the laity. The data furnished in this essay are primarily based on
this fieldwork and my familiarity with the group for over two decades.

3. The works of Bodding and Bompas constitute the two most authoritative
sources on Santal history and folklore.

4. The British government officials in India engineered the migration of the
Santals to the Rajmahal hills in order to clear the virgin forests and create human
habitation, since the Santals were renowned for their jungle-clearing skills.

5. The sacred grove is not peculiar to the Santals but a popular feature among the Chotanagpur tribal groups in central India. For a fuller treatment of the sacred grove phenomenon in Chotanagpur, see Roy 1979, 417–22; Sahay 1979, 434–35; Mahapatra 1987, 51–52.

6. The vertical and horizontal dimensions of Santal rituals are well articulated by Gautam (1977) and Culshaw (1949). Emphasizing the vertical dimension, Gautam writes: "The feasts and festivals provide the Santals with a link with the unknown and invisible world of the bongas" (201). Speaking of the horizontal dimension, Culshaw observes, "The main intention of Santal cult of sacrifice is to ensure the stability of the society and the well-being of its members" (88).

7. Of the various accounts on Santal funerary practices, Troisi's account is by far the most comprehensive. I have drawn much insight and information from his account.

8. The disparity between Santal Catholics' public claims and private practices is a recurring performance pattern designed to mislead outsiders, especially Church authorities.

9. Though the deceased is released from the underworld through the *telnahan* ceremony, the departed spirit does not reach its final abode. It is in a liminal condition until the *bhandan* ceremony is observed. Only then does the deceased reach its final destination, that is, the realm of the ancestors.

10. In this essay, I have adopted the Turnerian interpretation of liminality as an autonomous category for people who are betwixt and between.

11. The synthesis-vs.-syncretism debate has been an ongoing methodological concern among scholars of religion. While I recognize the merits of the synthesis argument, the materials presented in this essay lead me to favor syncretism over synthesis.

12. Observed in February-March, the Flower (*baha*) Festival marks the beginning of the spring season. From the religious standpoint, the Santals perceive the beginning of the spring festival as an auspicious moment for "a massive propitiation of the major *bongas* who are asked to keep the village free from any sickness or witchcraft and to preserve the crop and cattle. It [the Flower Festival] is also considered as a fertility feast" (Troisi 1979, 1, 462).

13. During the church ceremony, the groom applies *sindur* (vermilion) to the forehead of the bride through which he seals the marriage contract and attaches her to himself. In the traditional Santal marriage system, the *sindurdan* (literally, the gift of vermilion) is the binding portion of the rite. Though this rite was banned by Church officials in the past as it implies belief in *bongas* and *bonga puja* (spirit-worship), recently some liberal priests have incorporated it into the church ceremony. For a detailed account of Santal Catholic wedding rituals, including *sindurdan* and other examples of the inclusion pattern, see Raj 1994, 318–33.

14. With the exception of the 1855 rebellion and the current Jharkand movement, both of which are primarily sociopolitical movements, there have not been many revolutionary movements in Santal recorded history.

15. I am aware that the outsider-insider distinction is problematic on several levels and use it here only as an operating hermeneutic tool.

16. The term *dikhu*, which is a pejorative reference to non-Santals and outsiders, reveals the Santal fear of outsiders. So deep-seated is this fear that traditional Santal religion has anthropomorphized this fear by creating a specific category of malevolent and hostile spirits called *bahre bonga* (outskirts spirits). Aversion, avoidance, and appeasement are the traditional reactions to these spirits. In the human order, the Santals view all outsiders as malevolent and hostile, at least initially. Conversion has had only limited impact on the elimination or diminution of this fear.

17. In developing this classification, I have drawn much inspiration from W. D. O'Flaherty's insightful typology of scholars of religion whom she classifies as the *mythologized*, *re-mythologized*, and *de-mythologized* (1988, 120).

18. Interview with P. Aquilina, S.J., at Torai, Bihar, on August 25, 1990.

19. Attributed to Hans, S.J., of the Hazaribagh Jesuit Province, this particular ordination rite is observed mainly in the Catholic diocese of Daltonganj, Bihar. Though I have not witnessed this rite, I have heard of its increasing popularity among liberal Church leaders. The following information is based on an eyewitness account provided by B. Murmu, S.J., during an interview in Dumka on August 27, 1990. In a private conversation in early 1991, N. Harland, S.J., who had worked among the Chotanagpur tribal Catholics for over two decades, corroborated this account.

20. Interview with Rev. C. Soren in Dumka on August 27, 1990.

References

Archer, W. G. 1974. *The Hill of Flutes—Life, Love and Poetry in Tribal Life: A Portrait of the Santals*. London: George Allen & Unwin Ltd.

Berling, Judith. 1980. *The Syncretic Religion of Lin Chao-en*. New York: Columbia University Press.

Bodding, Paul. 1942. *Traditions and Institutions of Santals—Horkoren Mare Hapramko Reak Katha*. Leiden: Broggers Boktrykkeri.

Bompas, C. H. 1909. *Folklore of the Santal Parganas*. London: David Nutt.

Campbell, A. 1979. "Death and Cremation Ceremonies among the Santals." In *The Santals: Readings in Tribal Life*, vol. 1, ed. J. Troisi, 81–86. Delhi: Indian Social Institute.

Cole, F. T. 1979. "Santal Ideas of the Future." In *The Santals: Readings in Tribal Life*, vol. 1, ed. J. Troisi, 87–89. New Delhi: Indian Social Institute.

Colpe, Carsten. 1987. "Syncretism." Trans. by M. J. O'Connell. In *The Encyclopedia of Religion*, vol. 14, ed. M. Eliade, 218–27. New York: Macmillan Publishing Company.

Culshaw, W. J. 1949. *Tribal Heritage*. London: Lutterworth Press.

———. 1979. "Some Notes on Bongaism." In *The Santals: Readings in Tribal Life*, vol. 1, ed. J. Troisi, 94–97. Delhi: Indian Social Institute.

Driver, Tom. 1991. *The Magic of Ritual: Our Need for Liberating Rites that Transform Our Lives and Our Communities*. New York: Harper SanFrancisco.

Gautam, M. K. 1977. *In Search of Identity: A Case of Santals of Northern India*. Leiden: np.

Griffiths, Bede. 1982. *The Marriage of East and West: A Sequel to the Golden String*. Springfield, Ill.: Templegate Publishers.

———. 1973. *Vedanta and Christian Faith*. Clearlake, Calif.: Dawn Horse Press.

Heitzman, James, and Robert R. Wovden, eds. 1996. *India: A Country Study*. Washington, D. C.: Federal Research Division of the Library of Congress.

Kitagawa, Joseph. 1990. *The Quest for Human Unity: A Religious History*. Minneapolis, Minn.: Fortress Press.

Mahapatra, S. 1987. *Modernization and Ritual: Identity and Social Change in Santal Society*. Calcutta: Oxford University Press.

Mandelbaum, David. 1970. *Society in India: Continuity and Change*, vol. 1. Berkeley and Los Angeles: University of California Press.

Mazumdar, D. N. 1979. "Bongaism." In *The Santals: Readings in Tribal Life*, vol. 1, ed. J. Troisi, 324–38. New Delhi: Indian Social Institute.

Mittal, Kanailal. 1986. *Tribal Identity in Changing Industrial Environment*. Delhi: Metropolitan.

Mukherjea, Charulal. 1943. *The Santals*. Calcutta: np.

O'Flaherty, Wendy D. 1988. *Other Peoples' Myths: The Cave of Echoes*. New York: Macmillan Publishing Company.

Orans, Martin. 1965. *The Santal: A Tribe in Search of a Great Tradition*. Detroit: Wayne State University Press.

Panikkar, Raimundo. 1987. "The Jordan, the Tiber and the Ganges: Three Kairological Moments of Christic Self-Consciousness." In *The Myth of Christian Uniqueness: Toward a Pluralistic Theology of Religions*, eds. John Hick and Paul F. Knitter, 89–116. Maryknoll, NY: Orbis Books.

Raj, Selva. 1994. "Interactive Religious Systems in Indian Popular Catholicism: The Case of Tamil and Santal Catholics." Ph.D. Dissertation. University of Chicago.

Roy, S. C. 1979. "Primitive Religion." In *The Santals: Readings in Tribal Life*, vol. 1, ed. J. Troisi, 417–22. New Delhi: Indian Social Institute.

Sahay, K. N. 1986. *Christianity and Culture Change in India*. New Delhi: Inter India Publications.

Singer, Milton. 1980. *When a Great Tradition Modernizes.* Chicago: University of Chicago Press.

Thomas, L. V. 1987. "Funeral Rites." In *The Encyclopedia of Religion,* vol. 5, ed. M. Eliade, 450–58. New York: Macmillan Publishing Company.

Troisi, Joseph. 1978. *Tribal Religion: Religious Beliefs and Practices among the Santals.* Delhi: Manohar.

————. 1979. "Tribal Communion with the Supernatural: An Analysis of the Santal Flower Festival." In *The Santals: Readings in Tribal Life,* vol. 1, ed. J. Troisi, 458–70. New Delhi: Indian Social Institute.

————. ed. 1979. *The Santals: Readings in Tribal Life.* 10 volumes. New Delhi: Indian Social Institute.

Turner, Victor. 1985. *Ritual Process: Structure and Anti-Structure.* Fourth Edition. New York: Cornell University Press.

CHAPTER 4

Past Selves and Present Others: The Ritual Construction of Identity at a Catholic Festival in India*

Margaret Meibohm

In his treatment of the development of Hindu and Muslim religious identities in India and the formation of "religious nationalism," Peter van der Veer (1994) draws on Charles Taylor's (1985) notion that self-awareness emerges through interaction with others in order to emphasize the importance of ritual communication in the formation of identity. A sense of identity, van der Veer argues, answers the questions of "Who am I?" and "What do I do?" and is often found in community. While, in India, the community of Muslims forms what is by far the largest religious minority, there are also a small number of Christians who make up about two percent of the total population. The Indian Roman Catholics who are the primary subject of this essay face the problem of defining a self-image that is both Indian and Christian in a country where Christianity is largely perceived to be a product of the West. They must simultaneously construct a place for themselves in a nation diverse in languages and ways of living.

In this essay I would like to build on van der Veer's argument that identity can be produced through ritual but add a qualification to his secondary argument that ritual construction of identity involves the demonization and subjugation of an Other, whether conceived of as external, in another community, or internal, in the form of emotions or inclinations that need to be controlled. I use the example of the annual festival at the Catholic shrine of Velankanni in southern India to suggest that there are alternate means of creating identity through ritual. The questions of "Who am I?" and "What do I do?" can be partially addressed through the additional queries of "Where have I come from?" and "Who have I been?" Such questions about the past may find answers in images of, and interactions with, Others located in the present.[1] The festival at Velankanni, through enabling the blending of past

61

and present along several dimensions, provides a means of constructing and expressing a multifaceted sense of Indian Catholic identity for those who participate. My analysis will focus primarily on the importance of the festival for urban devotees from Mumbai.

The Velankanni shrine, dedicated to the Virgin Mary as Our Lady of Health, is located in the town of that name, approximately two hundred miles south of the city of Chennai and six miles south of the port town of Nagapattinam on the coast of the Bay of Bengal in the south Indian state of Tamil Nadu. It is a shrine that draws Hindus and Catholics from within the state of Tamil Nadu and Indian Catholics from all over the country and abroad. It is known as a place of syncretic or hybrid religious practice, where pilgrims offer coconuts, shave their heads, and don the saffron dress of Indian ascetics. It is the most well-known place of apparition of the Virgin Mary in India, and the origin stories of the shrine report three miraculous visits by her to the site.

The apparitions (*kāṭci*) are said to have taken place beginning in the sixteenth and seventeenth centuries when Velankanni was a small village. The first two manifestations were to local village boys and resulted in the building of a small thatched hut for a chapel. The third was to a group of Portuguese sailors who were rescued from a storm and brought safely to land at Velankanni on September eighth, the birthday of the Virgin Mary and the closing day of the annual festival. The sailors built a church of solid construction to replace the thatched hut and returned on subsequent visits bearing gifts to embellish the church. Historical records indicate the presence of a church in Velankanni dedicated to Our Lady of Health in the first half of the seventeenth century, presumably under the control of Portuguese Franciscans (Meersman 1962).

The original clients of the church are held to be members of a fishing community of Velankanni known as the Ariya Nattu Chettiyars (Āriya Nāṭṭu Ceṭṭiyar).[2] In recognition of their claim to the church, they retain certain key ceremonial roles in church celebrations. The Velankanni group includes caste members who, though staunchly Hindu, also take part in the festival and other events. The community is linked by marriage and caste to another group of Ariya Nattu Chettiyars in Nagapattinam, who also have traditional rights in the annual festival on the basis of the fact that the Velankanni church once belonged to the same parish.

The annual festival (*tiruvilā*) at Velankanni, which, as I have noted, celebrates the traditional birthday of the Virgin Mary on September eighth, is the longest, most elaborate, and most well-attended celebration of the church year. The festival draws a crowd of both Hindus and Catholics estimated at one million from throughout Tamil Nadu, making it one of the largest religious celebrations in the state (India 1968).

Since the mid-1950s, notable contingents of Catholics have been coming to the event from the city of Mumbai, formerly known as Bombay, over six hundred miles away on India's opposite coast, in the state of Maharashtra. The "Bombay people," as they are called by the residents of Velankanni, include "East Indians," that is, Catholics native to Mumbai who speak a dialect they refer to as East Indian Marathi, speakers of other varieties of Marathi, and Konkani speakers from the former Portuguese colony of Goa, two hundred miles south of Mumbai. They typically stay for the entire festival and take a prominent role in the daily processions.

Mumbai, India's financial and entertainment capital, is the largest city in the nation, with a population of almost ten million (Bose 1997) and one of the highest population densities in the world. The southern core of present-day Mumbai, Bombay Island, was developed from seven islands usually said to have been originally inhabited by a group of fisherpeople known as Kolis. It was ruled by a series of Indian kings until ceded to the Portuguese in 1534 by Sultan Bahudur Shah, the ruler of Gujarat, along with the islands of Salsette and Vasai, also known as Bassein, immediately to the north. The Portuguese converted a number of inhabitants of these areas to Catholicism. The Portuguese lost control of Bombay in 1661 and of Salsette and Vasai in 1739, but many Catholic churches in Vasai as well as some in Salsette and Bombay remained under Portuguese ecclesiastical administration until 1928, when they were joined with other area churches that had been under the direction of Rome, under the missionary organization known as Propaganda Fide (Baptista 1967; Gense 1960; Hull 1927–30).[3] Civically, most of Salsette was made part of Mumbai in 1950 (Kosambi 1986).[4] As the population of Mumbai continues to expand, residents from that city are moving into Vasai.[5]

The Velankanni Festival

My description of the festival is in the present tense, though I do not intend this usage to imply that the festival exists unchanging in a timeless realm of Otherness (Fabian 1983). The account will be based primarily on the events as I observed them in 1998, supplemented with information from church associates and key participants and from the festival as I observed it in 1992 and 1999. It concentrates on the two primary ritual events of flag hoistings and processions, both of which draw on similar practices at local Hindu temples and both of which are repeated daily. Throughout the festival, a crowd streams continuously into the main shrine to present candles, garlands, and other votive offerings to Our Lady. Masses and novena prayers are held in multiple [Indian] languages to accommodate the diverse crowd: Tamil, English, Malayalam, Marathi, Konkani, Hindi, and Telugu.

The Hoisting of the Flag

At Velankanni, the main shrine building, which holds the statue of Our Lady of Health, faces east toward the ocean, which is some one hundred to two hundred yards away along a wide, sandy path. In an inner courtyard on the north side of the shrine stands a flagpole, enclosed within a metal fence. Flags fly only during the primary festival and during the feast of Our Lady of Mount Carmel. Beyond the church building to the west is a path lined with the Stations of the Cross on the southern side and tableaus depicting the fifteen Mysteries of the Rosary on the northern side. The path leads to a pond known as Our Lady's Tank (*Māta kuḷam*), where Mary is said to have first appeared; a common group practice is to stage "Way of the Cross" prayers while going to the tank and recite the Rosary on the way back.

The festival begins on August twenty-ninth and officially concludes on September eighth. It opens with the hoisting of a flag (*koṭi*) bearing the image of Our Lady of Health, Velankanni and closes with the lowering of a flag on the evening of the eighth. On the intervening days are nightly processions (*tēr pavaṉi*, *ūrvalam*), which reach a climax on the night of September seventh, and daily hoistings of a flag, a different one each day. Before the initial hoisting on the twenty-ninth, the flag is taken through the streets of Velankanni along with a decorated palanquin carrying a statue of Our Lady. Conspicuously directing the manipulation of the flag as it is raised on a cart at the beginning of the procession and then lifted over the wall of the church courtyard is an elder from the Velankanni Ariya Nattu Chettiyar community. The flag raising on the twenty-ninth is conducted jointly by members of the Velankanni and Nagapattinam Ariya Nattu Chettiyar communities.

On a typical day the crowd begins to gather under the hot sun in the outer courtyard by 11:30 a.m. Those who have received passes from the parish priest are allowed in the inner courtyard. These include the families of the sponsors of that day's procession (*upayātār*), the flag donor and family, foreign scholars, and nuns. As noon approaches, the flag is brought out of the church into the courtyard, where it is spread open and held by male members of the designated family that has the right to make the donation (*upayam*) for that day, providing expenses for the flowers, lights, and fireworks for the evening procession. By tradition, each day is assigned to a different group, each of which was identified to me by family or caste name and town or village. Among the groups that sponsor the procession, the most important are the Ariya Nattu Chettiyar community of Velankanni and their sister community of Ariya Nattu Chettiyars in Nagapattinam. These two groups give the *upayams* for September sixth and September seventh, respectively, the days on which the processions are the most grand.

Despite announcements discouraging the practice for reasons of safety, people begin to throw coins at the flag. Coins that reach it are pocketed by the sponsors, while those falling on the ground are seized by onlookers, who often break through a police line to grab them. The sponsors shred garlands of roses onto the flag. At noon, church bells ring out. A priest standing at the flag blesses it with a prayer and holy water, then, over the loudspeakers, priests read prayers in English and Tamil. When the prayers conclude, church bells ring once more and a recorded song written especially for the event and played at every hoisting sounds over the loudspeakers as the flag is raised. The crowd throws more coins as the flag begins to rise but otherwise watches with rapt attention as it ascends. The gates to the inner courtyard are opened, and the crowd rushes in, scrambling for rose petals fallen from the flag and making their way to the flagpole, where they hang on to the surrounding fence in prayer and devotion.

The Procession of Our Lady

Every night from August thirtieth to September seventh, devotees carry palanquins in procession through the streets of Velankanni. Statues of St. Michael the Archangel, St. Sebastian, and Our Lady are taken on the thirtieth through the fifth. The palanquins of the two male saints, carried by women, are kept in the open on the southern side of the church and a larger palanquin for Our Lady, carried by men, is kept in a garage-like structure nearby. Devotees desiring to carry the palanquins arrive as early as ten hours before the procession to secure a place. A large majority of the palanquin bearers, in the judgment of Velankanni church workers and the bearers themselves, are Mumbai devotees. Our inquiries indicated that in addition to those from Mumbai, who included East Indians, Goans, and an occasional Tamil, there are individuals from elsewhere in Maharashtra, from Goa and Calcutta, and Indians, originally from Mumbai, working in the Persian Gulf region.

Prior to the procession, in view of the public, including those waiting to carry the palanquins, the statue of Our Lady carrying the child Jesus is wrapped in an ornate silk sari by the same elder from the Catholic Velankanni Ariya Nattu Chettiyar community who directs the flag raising on August twenty-ninth. In recent years, he has been joined by one of his sons, who is also a church sacristan. The statue is crowned and adorned with decorative garlands, and a rose garland is placed over Our Lady's hand.

As the James Band plays in front of the church, people stand in line to give flower garlands to the palanquins. The women waiting to carry the small palanquins decorate them with the donated flowers. Shortly before eight p.m.

the palanquin of Our Lady, preceded by the others, is brought in front of the church where it waits, while a short sermon in Tamil and prayers in Tamil and English are said over the loudspeakers.

Following the prayers, the procession goes forward, led by the James Band. The small palanquins follow, the way through the crowd held open by police and scouts. A priest, accompanied by altar boys carrying candles and a cross and by men carrying colorful royal umbrellas, precedes the palanquin of Our Lady. Following it are prayer groups in Tamil, English, Konkani, Marathi, and East Indian Marathi. Aside from the Tamil group, which is organized by the church, they are led by laity from the western part of India. Each group has its own sound system and uses the procession to recite decades of the rosary interspersed with prayers and songs. They are accompanied by a small brass band from Mumbai, not in uniform, but with a drum proclaiming them to be the "Velankanni Pilgrims Band, Bombay."

As the palanquins progress, the bearers chant "Ave Maria," and onlookers shower the statues with flowers and salt. As the palanquins reach the beach, they are met by fireworks. At the close of the procession, there is a mad rush to grab the garlands that have adorned the palanquins.

On the nights of September sixth and seventh, additional small palanquins are carried for St. Anthony of Padua, St. Joseph, and Our Lady. The large palanquin of the previous nights is again taken, but it is followed by an even larger one that carries a third statue of Our Lady.[6] On these two nights a greater number of Tamils join the Mumbai devotees in carrying the palanquins; the largest palanquin is divided, so that one side is taken by Tamil men and the other by men from Mumbai and other parts of India. The night of the seventh is the grandest celebration, featuring a Mass celebrated by the bishop. The James Band is joined by additional brass bands and dancing animal mascots.

Hindu and Catholic

I have proposed that the festival blends past and present along more than one dimension, making possible the construction of an integrated, multifaceted sense of Indian identity. Along the religious dimension, the Velankanni festival provides a hybridity of Hindu and Catholic that appeals to a wide range of people and helps to foster a sense of Indian Catholicism. In sharing elements with Hindu temple festivals, the Velankanni festival makes use of the recognized religious past and surrounding cultural present of Indian Catholics.[7] It also, however, combines these elements with Catholic ones or opens the door to new interpretations with a Christian theme.

As Younger (1992) has pointed out, in length and structure the Velankanni festival is similar to those of Tamil Hindu goddess temples, which have ten-day celebrations with a climactic event on the ninth day. The Velankanni festival time, though calculated on the basis of a recurring date in the Gregorian calendar rather than on a system involving the Tamil lunisolar calendar and the position of the moon relative to the stars, is scheduled, like temple festivals, by fixing the commemorative day as the final day of the festival and then counting the appropriate number of days backward to establish the start of the event (Clothey 1982; Merrey 1982).

In its allocation of social roles and sponsorships to particular groups or individuals, the Velankanni festival follows local Indian custom. However, there is some effort to foster a spirit of egalitarianism. Names of sponsors are not published as they are in some major Hindu festivals (Hudson 1982; Martin 1982) and receipt of transvalued substance made sacred or powerful by association with the holy figure, such as the garlands which decorate the palanquins and the coins which are thrown at the flag, is on a "first-come first served" basis rather than on the basis of perceived group rank (Hanchett 1982).[8]

The key rites of processions and flag raisings at Velankanni draw on similar events at Hindu temple festivals but lend themselves to adaptation and reinterpretation. Martin (1982) considers the procession to be the major public event of the Tamil temple festival. In major temple festivals described by Hudson (1982) and Smith (1982) there are minor processions of deities and/ or other holy figures nearly every day of the festival and a climactic procession near the end of the festival in which a massive wooden chariot is pulled through the streets by devotees.[9] As at Hindu temples, separate processional images are used in the Velankanni festival; the statue of Our Lady, like the Hindu statues, is dressed and adorned with garlands. Umbrellas, which are signs of royalty, and musical performers may accompany the holy figure, and fireworks greet its arrival (Hudson 1982).

At Velankanni simpler processions are followed by the more elaborate processions with the large palanquin of Our Lady processing on the sixth and seventh of September. Hudson (1982) and Younger (1982) have singled out certain processions or events as being most popular to the attendees at particular festivals. In the standardization of ritual events, repeating the popular processions each day, the Velankanni festival maximizes its appeal and caters to the pilgrim crowds, permitting them to come for a brief stay in the midst of the festival and still obtain a desired devotional experience. Processions with palanquins and music, sometimes singing, are also major events at Maharashtrian Hindu festivals described by Mate (1962), Stanley (1977), and Courtright (1988), and Mumbai devotees use the Marathi term *pālakhi* to refer to the palanquins.[10] Stanley (1977) describes the special power attributed to images of a god taken in procession at a Marathi festival and the consequent desire of people to touch the palanquin on which the image is carried. Devotees battle each other physically to gain an opportunity to carry the palanquin and to maintain contact with it for the longest period of time.

Processions in south Indian Hindu tradition are thought to bring blessings on the town, as the deity journeys into the mundane world (Martin 1982; Smith 1982). Tamils at Velankanni give this interpretation but in addition say the procession confers benefits also on anyone who watches, indeed, it gives everyone who can't go to the shrine a chance to see Our Lady.[11] Mumbai Christians cited a variety of reasons for the purpose of the procession: the alleviation of ills, the honoring of Our Lady, and the following of tradition. One pilgrim said that the function of the procession was for people to join together.

The Velankanni processions highlight not only the Hindu but also the Christian aspects of identity. They are overlaid with Christian elements: priests, crucifer and candles, crosses on the palanquins, the prayers at the start, and the prayers and songs throughout. Focusing on the Christian elements, two Mumbai Catholics said that the prayers were the reason for the procession. Another said that the procession builds up faith. A Tamil Catholic uttered a related sentiment, saying that the procession serves to provide a display of Mary's grace and power and thereby proclaim the might of Jesus.

The ceremony that has been most transformed and reinterpreted, however, is the flag hoisting. As at south Indian Hindu temple festivals and at other Catholic festivals in Tamil Nadu, it is an act that indicates the opening of the festival, the beginning of sacred time.[12] However, at Velankanni it has become as well a daily repeated rite evoking great emotion, often expressed in tears. The flag itself seems to confer great benefits when touched, judging by the attempts of pilgrims to grasp it and to obtain the coins and flower petals with which it has been in contact. Devotees report intense devotion and prayerful concentration during the flag raising, which causes them to "forget themselves" or "forget everything." One Tamil Catholic man said, "I do not know what I am praying, I am only crying." Many pray for favors during the hoisting, and there seems to be an idea that requests made during this time are especially likely to be granted. One Goan saw it very concretely: when the flag is raised, his wishes go up to God, when the flag comes down they are fulfilled. Devotees report that they become thrilled, enthralled, or elated while watching the flag. What may be the reasons for these beliefs and experiences? Some said the importance of the flag was that it contained Our Lady's form. Like the procession, then, the flag raising brings the image of Our Lady out of the church and nearer to the devotees' ordinary world. Some made this explicit. A Tamil Catholic woman from Mumbai said, "Eyes closed,

forgetting myself, I feel the nearness and love of Mother (*annai*)." Another
Catholic woman from Mumbai said, "I feel very happy . . . my heart jumps
with joy and my neck bows in adoration to Our Lady."[13] Perhaps the feeling
consciously expressed by one Tamil pilgrim, who remembered the apparitions that form the basis for the shrine's importance, is more widely shared:
"I feel that Mary appears again before us to bless us."

The hoisting of the flag refers to Indian Catholic history not just in
evoking the appearance of Our Lady on Indian soil, but also in marking the
transformation of Self from Hindu to Catholic. From both resident and pilgrim, but particularly from those from western India, I have heard that the
flag hoisting is in honor of the Portuguese sailors who were rescued by Our
Lady and built the first brick-and-mortar chapel, or that it is a custom started
by them. This interpretation was given wide circulation in the popular 1970s
Tamil film about Velankanni, in which the flag pole was described as the
mast of the Portuguese ship; a man from western India has also pointed out
to me its resemblance, in being marked by crossbars, to a ship's mast. Since
1996, a model of the Portuguese sailors aboard their vessel, formerly displayed at the chapel at Our Lady's tank, has been located within the fenced
flagpole enclosure. It was the Portuguese who brought Christianity to the Goa
and Mumbai areas and to parts of Tamil Nadu in the sixteenth century. Thus,
the flag hoisting is a reminder of Our Lady's appearance in India, and of the
conversion to the present religious faith, especially perhaps to the East Indian, Goan, and Vasai Catholics, who carry the evidence of Portuguese
influence in their surnames.[14]

Through its blending of Hindu and Catholic rites the Velankanni festival
creates an Indian Catholicism and allows performance of the Hindu past.
Though rites such as processions are also Catholic, and could be described as
"Indic" rather than "Hindu," the position of Hindus as a religious majority,
along with the many features the Velankanni events have in common with
Hindu practice, clearly calls to mind Hindu references. Hindu practices are
not only of the Other, and of the religious majority, but also of the past Self.[15]
As indicated in their dedication to carrying the palanquins, the shared Hindu
practices may be especially appealing to devotees from western India, whose
reports suggest that such practices as tonsuring, flag raising, and grand processions are rare at Catholic churches there. Tonsuring, for example, submitted to by significant numbers of the palanquin bearers, was said by them to
be done only at Velankanni or at Hindu temples, as was the practice of offering
coconuts. One man from western India suggested that where processions and
flag raisings do exist at churches in that region, they are new practices brought
back by pilgrims to Velankanni.[16] Another from that region, whom I spoke to
in 1992, when asked why he had come to the festival, replied that it was the
only Catholic festival in India. Thus the Hindu-Catholic hybridity experiences

at Velankanni create an Indian national festival for Catholics. The sharing of elements with Hindu temples, while enabling an encounter with the Other, can be simultaneously viewed as valid Catholicism, since the Roman Catholic Church now encourages "inculturation," the adapting of local practices. This was the view of a Tamil man from Mumbai, who proclaimed Velankanni a very "orthodox" church because it conforms to Vatican edicts in its use of Indian tradition. He felt this was especially attractive to Goans who, he said, have a very Westernized way of worship.[17]

From Village to Nation

In social as well as religious aspects, the festival integrates the past and the present and provides an image of a diverse India. I have noted that identity is often tied to community. My description of the festival has revealed the existence of multiple, overlapping social groupings that exist in connection with it. One social division is the one between pilgrims and residents, as the residents wait to carry the palanquins during additional processions that follow the flag lowering on September eighth. Though the bearing of palanquins is allocated on a "first-come-first-served" basis, other devotional services and privileges are held traditionally by different social groups. The right to perform certain devotional services has been listed among the "honors" distributed at south Indian temples (Appadurai and Breckenridge 1976). At Velankanni, the donation or *upayam* for a procession is a traditional service that brings along with it the duty and privilege of raising that day's flag. The procession sponsors closest to the geographical center are the Velankanni Ariya Nattu Chettiyars, accepted as the original clients of the church. In recognition of their historical claim, they hold the right (*urimai*) to raise the flag on August twenty-ninth, they have the right to give the *upayam* on the sixth of September, and members of their community prepare the statue of Our Lady before the processions. Next are the Nagapattinam Ariya Nattu Chettiyar, their close relatives, who have the right to the important *upayam* on the seventh of September in recognition of the fact that Velankanni and Nagapattinam were once part of the same parish. Then there are the family and caste groups, which give the *upayams* for the other days of the festival. With the exception of one group each from the cities of Tiruchirappalli and Pondicherry, eighty and one hundred miles distant, respectively, these groups are, or were traditionally, located within a few miles of Velankanni. It is not clear how long they have had the rights to give the *upayams*; it is at least prior to the 1950s, when Tamil priests took over the running of the shrine.

Finally, there are the processional groups from the western parts of India, which form along linguistic lines: the English language group from Mumbai, the Marathi group, the East Indian Marathi group, and the Konkani group. All except the East Indian Marathi group have formal associations; all have lay leaders who conduct the prayers in the nightly processions. Each group typically organizes priests and a choir for Masses said in their language, and at least once during the festival they hold a vernacular performance of the Way of the Cross followed by the Rosary. They also produce special booklets of prayers and hymns for festival use. The Marathi association, based in Vasai,[18] does social work in its own community as well.[19] Some of the groups make donations to the church in the names of their associations. One group recently attempted to purchase a property in Velankanni to be used as headquarters but was swindled out of its money. All of these groups have Mumbai connections; the Konkani group consists of Goans residing in both Mumbai and Goa.

The links between ceremonial roles and social groupings reflect the expansion of the shrine's popularity, from village to region to nation. The village past of Velankanni is enshrined in its origin stories in which Our Lady first appears to rural children in natural settings marked by ponds and trees. This aspect of Velankanni's heritage also plays a role in the appeal of the festival and the definition of Indian identity. Urban devotees may find in Velankanni and in the exposure to the countryside offered in walking pilgrimages to the festival the nostalgic pull of the rural (Meibohm 1995). In the imagining of Velankanni as an unspoiled rustic haven, the part played by the Ariya Nattu Chettiyar in the festival is not irrelevant. As Velankanni inhabitants and historical clients of the shrine, the Ariya Nattu Chettiyar are the closest link to the original recipients of Our Lady's apparitions, and a Nagapattinam Ariya Nattu Chettiyar family that has the privilege of decorating the palanquin of Our Lady on August twenty-ninth claims to be descended from a Nagapattinam man who features in the story of the second manifestation. But the link to Velankanni per se might not be as important as the perception of a rural atmosphere. A young Anglo-Indian from the city of Chennai once told me that the man in charge of the flagpole in the opening day's procession was not from Velankanni but from the undeveloped village across the river, whose landscape is frequently featured in a recent shrine promotional video. This village, I have argued elsewhere (1995), has come to symbolize Velankanni's own rustic past as Velankanni has become larger and more urban. But Velankanni itself can still evoke rural nostalgia for some. The organizers of the Marathi devotional group routinely stay during the festival at the house of the Ariya Nattu Chettiyar elder in charge of the flag procession and the palanquin of Our Lady and have told me they enjoy the social encounters that make Velankanni like a village.

This nostalgia for the village is linked to identity. Urban Indians often speak of ancestral homes in a village. For those native to urban areas, however, a substitute may have to be found. Saying, "We're from Bombay. We have no native place. Velankanni is our native place," a leader of one of the Mumbai groups linked rurality to identity and the bucolic atmosphere of Velankanni to his own ethnic past, as he said that Velankanni served as a place of origin for East Indians, since the fields and trees that once marked their own homelands had been erased by the development of the city.[20] A young woman taking part in carrying the palanquins noted that there could be no such processions in Mumbai, since there was no open space. Thus the history of the Ariya Nattu Chettiyars caste links to the church, the continued survival of a small-scale community, and physical setting all contribute to the rural appeal of Velankanni and enable an experience of a village past for urban devotees.

But it is not only an experience of the past. The continuing urbanization and "development" of Velankanni, which the Mumbai devotees have witnessed and helped foster over the past forty years, recapitulate the transformation of Mumbai from a collection of villages to a major metropolitan center.[21] The festival provides for both village nostalgia and a sense of modern cosmopolitanism. Until recently, traditional musicians playing a flat drum (*tappaṭṭai*) used to announce and lead the procession, providing a counterpoint to the more modern music of the James Band, who play Western airs and recent Christian devotional hits. The mix of ethnic groups draws sightseers like the man I met in 1992 from the Tamil city of Madurai, who came solely to meet different types of people. In 1992 I spotted a man wearing a T-shirt advertising a "run" to the festival from Chennai, and a group of ham radio operators from the city of Bangalore, a Silicon Valley of India, volunteered their services for security and crowd control and also coordinated a special broadcast from the Vatican. Some pilgrims who came from Chennai on foot wear matching polo shirts with Velankanni insignias; male members of English-speaking groups may wear shorts instead of the traditional lower garment (*vēṭṭi*), usually *de rigueur* for south Indian male walking pilgrims.

Social roles and groupings also exhibit the contrast between now and then. The traditional *upayams* of the festival and the roles of the Ariya Nattu Chettiyar emphasize caste distinction. Indeed, the Velankanni Ariya Nattu Chettiyars state that on the day of the initial flag raising, there is no Catholic and no Hindu, only Chettiyar. For the urban devotees, however, caste may no longer be as relevant as religious and ethnic identity. The East Indians and the Catholics from Vasai claim to recognize no caste distinctions among themselves; Baptista (1967), in her study of East Indians conducted in the 1950s, found this to be true at that time for the urbanites and for the group known as Salsette Christians. Perhaps more relevant are the linguistic divisions that mark a different place of origin for various Catholics now residing in Mumbai. Indeed, the East Indians mobilized as a group and adopted their name in the late nineteenth century in order to distinguish themselves to the British colonizers from Goan and Mangalorean Catholics, who had begun immigrating to Mumbai and, as "Portuguese Christians," were capitalizing on the reputation of East Indians as educated people fit for service in the British administration (Albuquerque 1984; Baptista 1967). Consequently, at that time, as Albuquerque (1984: 31–32) describes it, "the Roman Catholic community of Bombay was terribly split up from within. Europeans, Anglo-Indians, East Indians, Goans and Mangaloreans—all formed separate compartments, each vieing [sic] to outdo the other and looking with suspicion at one another."

Groupings based on linguistic or ethnic identity have obviously not dissolved nor, I would argue, has the competition between them. One means of acquiring relative prestige is gift-giving. I was once told by a Velankanni man with long history of festival patronage that the Marathi and English groups had each donated an organ to the shrine, in seeming rivalry. I was able to verify the donation of an organ by only one group, but the perception of competition between the groups is notable. At least one group leader has said that there are no disputes about the order of the groups in the procession; expressing pride in their peaceful accommodation and equality, he thus implicitly acknowledged the potential for conflict. I was also invited to attend Masses or performances of the Way of the Cross by more than one group and then asked to evaluate the expression of devotion, presumably in comparison with the other associations; one leader spoke proudly of his group's performance of the Rosary, which is sung, rather than spoken.

There is some evidence hinting that flag donations may be becoming an additional means of ethnic expression. Although the names of flag donors are not announced or published, there is evidently some information spread by word-of-mouth since, in 1998, a Goan nun temporarily resident in Velankanni was able to inform us of the donation of a flag by a Goan family. There was also in 1998 a flag that bore the name of Nagpur, a city in the northeastern portion of Maharashtra. At the least, these two flag donations indicate the interest among non-Tamils in donating a flag and in making known their regional affiliations. Along with the claimed participation of a Mumbai leader in the flag selection process in 1998, they may also indicate that one of the criteria of flag selection may now be the ethnic or geographic background of the donors, with an attempt being made to spread the honor among different heritage groups and locales.[22]

What is at stake in these competitions? In south Indian festivals for which the clienteles are more localized, the results of contests for honors may directly influence caste rankings and interactions in the year to follow (Hanchett

1982). While I do not know the particular ramifications of participation in the Velankanni festival for the individuals, formal associations, and larger ethnic groups in Mumbai, we can assume that the competitions for rights and honors at Velankanni are implicated in more complex and large scale social arrangements. Within the relatively small world of the pilgrimage center, privileges such as the right to choose and arrange the saris on Our Lady's statue may carry rewards of respect and influence. But for the pilgrims, the social rewards may be more diffuse, tied to a generalized sense of ethnic identity rather than to specific interactions or status rankings within the city of Mumbai. Palanquin bearers report for instance that they do not associate with the friends they make at the festival when back in Mumbai, except perhaps to exchange greetings if they happen to meet. The Velankanni organizations, with the exception of the group from Vasai, do not engage in many activities at home. Though Baptista's (1967) report on 1950s Mumbai indicates that Goans, East Indians, Mangaloreans, and "Malabar" Catholics (from the state of Kerala, west of Tamil Nadu) continued to have separate organizations and publications. Albuquerque (1984) also writes that the ethnic rivalries of the last century have been eased by educational and social institutions, which have brought together Catholics of different backgrounds. The East Indian prayer group organizers said that the general East Indian Association of Mumbai (i.e. not associated with Velankanni) was largely a social club, requiring entrance fees prohibitively expensive for most people. Since the material rewards of jobs in the British Administration are no longer at issue, what are the reasons for the continuing division among the Mumbai Catholics?

One factor in the existence of different prayer groups at Velankanni, at least, is the desire to participate in prayers and Masses in the language one can best understand. Differences in "home language" and geographical location are agreed by the East Indians and Vasai Catholics to be what separates them from each other.[23] Languages of education are also a factor in the division. The Vasai Catholics use the standard Marathi taught in schools for their prayers and hymns. If not too complex, this is understood by middle-aged and younger educated East Indians—the East Indian Marathi prayer group leader mentioned above attends the Marathi Mass, among others—but East Indians generally pursue English rather than Marathi as the language of education, and the East Indian processional prayers are printed in Roman script rather than the Indian script normally used for Marathi. Vasai Catholics, on the other hand, are more likely to be educated in Marathi-medium schools. Lack of comfort with English led them to fight for decades to have their own diocese, separate from Mumbai, in which Marathi could be the primary language, a goal that was reached in 1998.[24]

The presence of the English language prayer group may also indicate the influence of education. While it obviously can accommodate those whose vernaculars are not provided for, it also caters to East Indians and Goans. One person estimated that the English Mass is attended primarily by East Indians, and the Bombay Velankanni Pilgrims' Band, which plays outside the church after the English Mass, has been described to me as an East Indian band. The existence of English-language activities organized by devotees from Mumbai presumably reflects class and generational differences, as it sometimes does in India, but it does not directly correspond to linguistic competency. The leader of the East Indian Marathi prayer group is also the director of the choir that sings in the English Mass, a fact which indicates the bilingual proficiency of some of the participants and the desire to encourage expression of the vernacular language even by those who are fluent in English.

The prayer groups are thus a way of preserving ethnic language and identity, but not only that. An Indian resident in the U.S. once told me, explaining his active participation in a group oriented around a particular language and region, that though he had for himself tried to cultivate a pan-Indian identity, when it came time to pass along Indian traditions, especially language, to his children, he found that he had to teach them something specific. In this way, participation in a linguistically oriented group is a way of asserting not only an ethnic identity but also, through it, a national one. At Velankanni, the festival, with its display of various languages in Masses and processions, constructs and expresses the totality of the nation as an amalgamation of diversities, in a show of what in India is termed "national integration." The focus on the nation is made explicit in the only prayer repeated at both processions and flag raisings, "Our Lady of Health, Velankanni, pray for us. Our Lady of Health, Velankanni, pray for India. Our Lady of Health, Velankanni, pray for the peace of the world." Processional prayers for the English group on the night that I heard them in 1998 included appeals on behalf of the leaders of the nation; on one night in 1999, the devotion of the group's entire processional walk was dedicated to Indian soldiers defending the "Line of Control," which separates the area of Kashmir occupied by India from that occupied by Pakistan.

Hudson (1982), analyzing a popular myth that links two Hindu festivals in Madurai, has described the coexistence of the ideal of familial unity with the recognition of ongoing tensions. At the Velankanni festival, the ideals of unity and harmony were expressed by the linguistic associations when participants said that they had no struggle over processional order; indeed a number of respondents to a survey in 1992 said that the very significance of the festival was that it brought people of different types together as one.[25] That these ideals are imperfectly realized is seen, on the one hand, in the feelings of a Hindu man from the city of Pune, the husband of a Catholic, who joyfully reported that the palanquin bearers join as one family and, on the other, in the division between Tamil men and those from western India who carry the palanquin, on September sixth and seventh, respectively. Bell (1997, 235) sees this encompassment of contradiction as part of the process of ritual construction of community: " . . . rituals do not build community by simply expressing sentiments of collective harmony; they do it by channeling conflict, focusing grievances, socializing participants into more embracing codes of symbolic behavior, negotiating power relations, and ultimately, forging images by which the participants can think of themselves as an embracing unity."

The division of roles in the festival is a palimpsest on which the expansion of the shrine's popularity to evermore distant communities and the consequent evolution of the event are written. The festival's social structure is revealed as both stable and flexible, with each enactment making and remaking community. It has maintained key roles for the Ariya Nattu Chettiyar of the original village, while allowing new groups to participate. It changed to accommodate Tamil groupings in various *upayams* when, according to a Velankanni Ariya Nattu Chettiyar man, the expenses grew too much for the Nagapattinam and Velankanni groups to handle, and has since further expanded to include nontraditional residents of Velankanni in postfestival processions. Flag and sari donations have allowed individual donors from different areas to participate. The processions have allowed Mumbai and Goa devotees to take an active role in the proceedings; while the palanquin carrying unites participants from outside Tamil Nadu, the Masses and prayers in the processions construct and express language-based ethnic divisions within the larger unit of the nation. For the Mumbai devotees, participation in the festival thus allows the past village self to be seen and experienced while simultaneously evoking a present ethnic identity within an encompassing India.

Conclusion

Both socially and culturally the Velankanni festival has shown a mix of stability and flexibility. The stable side of the festival allows a sense of continuity with the past. A Hindu man from Nagapattinam involved in some of the practical affairs of the festival told me in 1992 that he had been associated with it for eighty years, and that in that time it had remained the same. The Velankanni man who was in charge of the procession for about forty years, until illness caused him to stop in 1991, highlighted as changes in the festival the use of electric lights, the improvement of the roads to Velankanni, and what he perceived as a Christianization of the music. A priest has acknowledged the beginnings of women carrying the palanquins as an innovation brought by the Mumbai devotees, and recalls the introduction of prayers at the beginning of the processions in the 1950s. Overall, however, the maintenance of the key rites of flag hoisting and processions allows "the feast" to be talked of as unchanging.

History is part of the fabric of meaning of the festival, from the recurring celebration of the birthday of Our Lady, to the remembrance of the Portuguese being brought to shore on that very day. The visible role of the Ariya Nattu Chettiyar elder who supervises the flag hoisting on the twenty-ninth and often rides with the palanquin of Our Lady after dressing her statue reinforces this history. But flexibility of cultural forms and interpretations, of social roles, and of accommodation to individual devotion has allowed the festival to adapt to expanding circles of devotees. Though we cannot travel back in time to recover past meanings of the festival celebrated by a smaller group of devotees, we can posit a new layering of significance for those coming from Mumbai, who typically stay for the entire proceedings. For them the festival provides an extended retreat away from the cares and pressures of ordinary life, from the urban density and intensity of Mumbai, to a location with open space and a rural character, materially and socially simplified, where uninterrupted devotion is possible. Here, Catholicism allows them to feel their Indianness. Younger (1982) has noted the flexibility of a Hindu festival at Srirankam in Tamil Nadu, which, he argues, allowed the introduction of sectarian interests at a particular historical conjuncture, while the popular devotional meaning, a movement between the poles of transcendence and intimacy with the god, was maintained. Similarly, the Velankanni festival has evolved by maintaining, with adjustments, a core set of rituals that allow it to fit into the local landscape and be perceived as traditional. The adjustments bring it into the present of Catholicism, urbanness, and ethnic interaction, all aspects of an Indian selfhood for Mumbai devotees.

In van der Veer's formulation with which I began, ritual production of identity requires the demonization and domination of the Other. The Velankanni festival, however, illustrates that juxtaposition to, and partial merging with, the Other, especially when the Other can be defined as past Self, are also potent ways of constructing self representations. Presenting a multiplex image of an India diverse in religions, languages, and degrees of urbanization, the festival reveals itself as a ritual that is, to adapt a phrase from Kelly and Kaplan (1990, 135), both "rooted . . . and transformed," in which the past is used as a resource for the present (Appadurai 1981) to create a vibrant and popular expression of contemporary Indian identity.

Notes

*I would like to thank Jerome Bauer, Anne Meibohm, Mark Whitaker, and the editors for commenting on earlier versions of this essay. Research in Velankanni in 1991–93 was supported by a grant from the American Institute of Indian Studies and a Fulbright-Hays Doctoral Dissertation Research Abroad award. My use of "we" in this essay reflects the hard work of "V. Prema," M. Elongo, and K. Srinivas, who helped gather information. I am grateful to the priests and staff members of the Shrine Basilica of Our Lady of Health, Velankanni, who facilitated the research in many ways. Special thanks are due to Fr. R. K. Samy and the Arokia Niketan Institute of Mariology and to A. Arulanandam, A. Aruldass, A. Arumai Raj, A. John, and Sebastian. My biggest debt is, of course, to the devotees of the shrine for tolerating my intrusions and sharing their experiences. In this regard, the aid of the leaders of the language-based associations was invaluable. As always, any errors remain my responsibility.

1. The use of the Self/Other distinction is not meant to imply that binary classifications are always predominant. For instance the sphere of religious identity in India is not limited to Hindu and Catholic. However, in the context of the Velankanni festival, it is these two identities that are given prominence. My discussion of ethnic identity, below, presumes that a Self can be constituted in relation to multiple Others.

2. There are a number of caste groups in Tamil Nadu known as Chettiyars. Their traditional occupation is usually said to be trading. "Ariya Nattu" translates as "Aryan Country."

3. Propaganda Fide (Congregation for the Propagation of the Faith), now known as the Congregation for the Evangelization of Peoples, is a department of the Catholic Church, based in Rome, with responsibility for overseeing missionary efforts. It was formally begun in 1622. In India, it competed for control of churches with the Padroado, or system of patronage of the Portuguese, which was based on rights granted to the Portuguese king by Rome in the fifteenth century. Disputes between the Propaganda and the Padroado were common in India, with successive attempts to divide territory by means of various concordats, until the Padroado was put to an end in 1953 (Silva Rego 1967).

4. The term "Mumbai" here now refers to the civic entity known as Greater Bombay, which consists of Bombay City (Bombay Island) and adjacent territory. The population figure of ten million given above is for Greater Bombay. David (1995) puts the extension of Greater Bombay into Salsette into two stages, the first completed in 1950 and the second in 1957.

5. In 1991 Christians made up 2.34 percent of the population of India, 5.69 percent of the population of Tamil Nadu, 4.45 percent of that in Greater Bombay (see note 4) and 29.85 percent of that of Goa (Bose 1997). In 1981, they were 20.44 percent of Vasai *tahsīl* and 26.09 percent of Vasai municipality (India 1984).

6. Approximately fifty women carry each of the small palanquins. A male palanquin carrier told us there were 250 men to carry the medium-sized palanquin and 350 men to carry the large palanquin on the sixth and seventh of September. My own calculation is that there are only 150 and 200 men, respectively, who carry the medium-sized and large palanquins.

7. In opposing Hindu and Catholic in this way, I do not mean to suggest that in the realm of spiritual or intellectual contact the spheres of Hinduism and Catholicism in India are necessarily mutually exclusive. When speaking of socially relevant identities, however, Hindu and Catholic are discrete categories.

8. In practice, of course, those who wrap the saris and ride on the palanquin and those who carry the palanquins have privileged access. Male sponsors have extended contact with the flag and are best able to pick up the coins and flower petals at the flag raising.

9. At Velankanni some carry the palanquins to fulfill a vow or gain a particular favor. Others may do it out of affection or respect for Our Lady. Some consider it a sacrifice—a Goan woman once told me that if I carried one I would "feel the pain"—but others say it is not an onerous task.

10. Eck (1998) treats the festival procession as a general feature of Hinduism. Palanquins carrying silver replicas of the feet of saints are also central in the most important pilgrimage in Maharashtra, in which groups of devotees travel as far as 150 miles to the temple of Pandharpur (Eleanor Zelliot, personal communication).

11. The act of seeing and being seen by the holy image and thereby attaining blessings is known in Sanskrit as *darśan* and is, according to Eck (1998, 1), "the single most common and significant element of Hindu worship."

12. Informal sources indicate that in Maharashtra saffron flags without insignia fly on a permanent basis at temples, not just during festival periods. The 1961 census report's descriptions of numerous festivals (India 1969) indicate that the hoisting of a flag to open a festival is not a general feature of Maharashtrian festivals.

13. Clothey (1968–69) writes that the flagpole in a Tamil Hindu temple represents a pillar connecting heaven and earth. The flags at Tamil Hindu temples do not carry the image of the god, but of his or her vehicle, usually an animal (Beck 1969; Clothey 1968–69).

14. Baptista (1967, 27–28) presents evidence suggesting that Christians in the Mumbai area may have a history dating back to the supposed visit of the Apostle Bartholomew, but she acknowledges that this possibility is foreign to the East Indians since the Portuguese had "liquidated every trace" of the previous Church and imposed Portuguese customs upon them.

15. When answering questions about syncretic practices at Velankanni, devotees from Mumbai and Goa sometimes stated that these were very old customs or that Velankanni was a very old church.

16. Robinson (1998) finds processions to be a part of village Catholic practice in Goa but also states that the Mass and elaborate meals are the most important aspects of feast days. Baptista (1967), in a brief description of East Indian village feasts, does not mention processions. Nor is a procession mentioned in the census description of the popular Catholic festival at the church of Our Lady of the Mount in Mumbai, the dates of which overlap those of the Velankanni festival (India 1969).

17. Stirrat (1982) argues that the syncretism of Catholicism in Sri Lanka increased during the seventeenth and eighteenth centuries after the Portuguese had been displaced by the Dutch, due to the cessation of enforcement of orthodoxy and the need to adapt to the local culture in order to survive. The current situation in India is more

complex, since neocolonial power relations and improved transnational communication promote stronger ties to the Vatican. But the loss of direct colonial control and the rise of Hindu nationalism, which tries to define "Indian" as "Hindu," may result in Indian Catholics feeling a greater need to connect to their Hindu roots.

Robinson (1998) states that historically in Goa, in contrast to south India, Catholics were socially and often geographically separate from Hindus. She adds, "Further, the missionaries made particular efforts to ensure that 'Hindu' practices were eradicated among the converts" (18).

18. In the 1981 Indian census report, Vasai *tahsīl* is considered a separate entity from Mumbai, one reason being that it is in a separate district. The town of Vasai is part of an "urban agglomeration" that includes two other towns (India 1984).

19. Baptista (1967) includes Vasai Catholics in her category of East Indians, but this is not the current understanding of either the East Indians from Mumbai or the group from Vasai, whose leaders belong to specific Vasai-based caste groups, which she includes in her definition.

20. David (1995) writes that East Indians, along with the Catholic religious orders, owned most of the land in Bombay Island until the seventeenth century, when they began gradually to lose most of it. Baptista (1967, 84), writing of the 1950s, speaks of "rural Salsette villages" and even of Christian villages in Bombay Island "no longer surrounded by fields."

21. Statistics from Kosambi (1986), which cannot be given here for lack of space, document the rapid rate of population growth in outer areas of Bombay in recent decades.

22. Or, more cynically, the presence of flags from different groups may simply reflect the success of these groups in gaining influence in the festival.

23. An early twentieth-century national linguistic survey isolated dialects related to the Vasai castes, supporting the contentions of the Vasai group and the East Indians that the basic differences between them are linguistic and geographic (Grierson 1968 [1908]).

24. Language statistics of the early 1990s for the Bombay Archdiocese presented by Rajan (1993) confirm the reports of the Velankanni devotees and suggest that many East Indians consider their primary language to be English.

25. Most of the people expressing this sentiment were Tamils, but there were far fewer people from Mumbai represented in our survey.

References

Albuquerque, Teresa. 1984. "The Coming Together of Christians in Bombay." *Indian Church History Review* 18, no. 1 (June):30–57.

Appadurai, Arjun. 1981. "The Past as a Scarce Resource." *Man (n.s.)*16:201–19.

Appadurai, Arjun, and Carol Appadurai Breckenridge. 1976. "The South Indian Temple: Authority, Honour and Redistribution." *Contributions to Indian Sociology (n.s.)* 10, no. 2:187–211.

Baptista, Elsie W. 1967. *The East Indians: Catholic Community of Bombay, Salsette and Bassein.* Bandra, Bombay: The Bombay East Indian Association.

Beck, Brenda E. F. 1969. "Colour and Heat in South Indian Ritual." *Man (n.s.)* 4, no. 4 (December):553–72.

Bell, Catherine. 1997. *Ritual: Perspectives and Dimensions.* New York: Oxford University Press.

Bose, Ashish. 1997. *Population Profile of Religion in India: Districtwise Data from 1991 Census.* Delhi: B. R. Publishing.

Clothey, Fred W. 1968–69. "Skanda-Ṣaṣṭi: A Festival in Tamil India." *History of Religions* 8, no. 3 (August 1968–May 1969):236–59.

Clothey, Fred W. 1982. "Chronometry, Cosmology, and the Festival Calendar in the Murukan Cult." In *Religious Festivals in South India and Sri Lanka*, eds. Guy R. Welbon and Glenn E. Yocum, 157–88. New Delhi: Manohar.

Courtright, Paul B. 1988. "The Ganesh Festival in Maharashtra: Some Observations." In *The Experience of Hinduism: Essays on Religion in Maharashtra*, eds. Eleanor Zelliot and Maxine Berntsen, 76–94. Albany: State University of New York Press.

David, M. D. 1995. *Bombay: The City of Dreams.* Bombay: Himalaya Publishing House.

Eck, Diana L. 1998. *Darśan: Seeing the Divine Image in India.* Third ed. New York: Columbia University Press.

Fabian, Johannes. 1983. *Time and the Other: How Anthropology Makes its Objects.* New York: Columbia University Press.

Gense, J. H. 1960. *The Church at the Gateway of India, 1720–1960.* Bombay: St. Xavier's College.

Grierson, G. A., compiler and editor. 1968 [1908]. *Linguistic Survey of India, Volume VII, Indo-Aryan Family, Southern Group: Specimens of the Marathi Language.* Delhi: Motilal Banarsidass.

Hanchett, Suzanne. 1982. "The Festival Interlude: Some Anthropological Observations." In *Religious Festivals in South India and Sri Lanka*, eds. Guy R. Welbon and Glenn E. Yocum, 219–41. New Delhi: Manohar.

Hudson, D. Dennis. 1982. "Two Citrā Festivals in Madurai." In *Religious Festivals in South India and Sri Lanka*, eds. Guy R. Welbon and Glenn E. Yocum, 101–56. New Delhi: Manohar.

Hull, Ernest R. 1927–30. *Bombay Mission History: With a Special Study of the Padroado Question.* Two vols. Bombay: Examiner Press.

India. Superintendent of Census Operations, Madras. 1968. *Census of India 1961, Volume IX, Madras. Part VII-B. Fairs and Festivals.* Madras: Superintendent of Census Operations.

India. Maharashtra Census Office, Bombay. 1969. *Census of India 1961, Volume X, Maharashtra. Part VII-B. Fairs and Festivals in Maharashtra.* Delhi: Manager of Publications.

India. Director of Census Operations, Maharashtra. 1984. *Census of India 1981, Series 12, Maharashtra. Paper 1 of 1984: Household Population by Religion.* Nagpur: Government Press.

Kelly, John D., and Martha Kaplan. 1990. "History, Structure and Ritual." *Annual Review of Anthropology* 19:119–50.

Kosambi, Meera. 1986. *Bombay in Transition: The Growth and Social Ecology of a Colonial City, 1880–1980.* Stockholm: Almqvist and Wiksell International.

Martin, James L. 1982. "The Cycle of Festivals at Pārthasārathī Temple." In *Religious Festivals in South India and Sri Lanka,* eds. Guy R. Welbon and Glenn E. Yocum, 51–76. New Delhi: Manohar.

Mate, M. S. 1962. *Temples and Legends of Maharashtra.* Bombay: Bharatiya Vidya Bhavan.

Meersman, Achilles. 1962. *The Franciscans in Tamilnad.* Schöneck-Beckenried, Switzerland: Nouvelle Revue de Science Missionaire.

Meibohm, Margaret. 1995. "Romance of the Rural: 'Development' and Difference in South Indian Pilgrimage." Presented at the 47th Annual Meeting of the Association for Asian Studies, Washington, D.C., April 6–9.

Merrey, Karen L. 1982. "The Hindu Festival Calendar." In *Religious Festivals in South India and Sri Lanka,* eds. Guy R. Welbon and Glenn E. Yocum, 1–25. New Delhi: Manohar.

Rajan, S. Irudaya. 1993. *Catholics in Bombay: A Historical-Demographic Study of the Roman Catholic Population in the Archdiocese of Bombay.* Shillong: Vendrame Institute; Calcutta: Firma KLM.

Robinson, Rowena. 1998. *Conversion, Continuity and Change: Lived Christianity in Southern Goa.* Walnut Creek, Calif.: AltaMira Press.

Silva, Rego, A. da. 1967. "Patronato Real." *New Catholic Encyclopedia* 10:1113–15. New York: McGraw-Hill.

Smith, H. Daniel. 1982. "Festivals in Pāñcarātra Literature." In *Religious Festivals in South India and Sri Lanka,* eds. Guy R. Welbon and Glenn E. Yocum, 27–49. New Delhi: Manohar.

Stanley, John M. 1977. "Special Time, Special Power: The Fluidity of Power in a Popular Hindu Festival." *Journal of Asian Studies* 37, no. 1 (November):27–43.

Stirrat, R. L. 1982. "Shrines, Pilgrimage and Miraculous Powers in Roman Catholic Sri Lanka." In *The Church and Healing*, ed. W. J. Shiels, 385–413. Oxford: Blackwell.

Taylor, Charles. 1985. "The Person." In *The Category of the Person: Anthropology, Philosophy, History*, eds. Michael Carrithers, Steven Collins, and Steven Lukes, 257–81. Cambridge: Cambridge University Press.

van der Veer, Peter. 1994. *Religious Nationalism: Hindus and Muslims in India.* Berkeley and Los Angeles: University of California Press.

Younger, Paul. 1982. "Singing the Tamil Hymnbook in the Tradition of Rāmānuja: The *Adyayanōtsava* Festival in Śrīraṅkam." *History of Religions* 21, no. 3 (February): 272–93.

―――. 1992. "Velankanni Calling: Hindu Patterns of Pilgrimage at a Christian Shrine." In *Sacred Journeys: The Anthropology of Pilgrimage*, ed. Alan Morinis, 89–99. Westport, Conn.: Greenwood Press.

CHAPTER 5

Transgressing Boundaries, Transcending Turner:
The Pilgrimage Tradition at the Shrine of St. John de Britto[1]

Selva J. Raj

Introduction

In *Contesting the Sacred: The Anthropology of Christian Pilgrimage*, Eade and Sallnow stress that, given the essential heterogeneity of the pilgrimage process, pilgrimage discourse should be "less concerned to match empirical instances with a preconceived ideal . . . than to deconstruct the very category of 'pilgrimage' into historically and culturally specific behaviours and meanings" (1991:2–3). The pilgrimage tradition at the shrine of St. John de Britto in south India provides a poignant illustration of the problems in matching empirical data with a preconceived interpretive paradigm. Drawing on the pilgrimage practices and performances in this shrine, this essay will examine the merits and limitations in applying Victor Turner's paradigm—particularly his twin concepts of liminality and communitas—to the religio-cultural context of Tamil Catholics.

The Shrine, the Saint, and the Festival

Situated at the extreme northeast end of the district of Ramnad—now known as Pacumpon Muthuramalinga Thevar district—the shrine of John de Britto at Oriyur is a popular pilgrim center for Tamil Catholics of the region. The history and popularity of the shrine are related to the events surrounding the martyrdom in 1696 of John de Britto, a Portuguese Jesuit missionary, who spearheaded a mass conversion movement in a portion of southeast Tamil Nadu, known as the Marava country. Tradition holds that, soon after arriving in India, Britto earned a reputation as a holy man of great power. He

85

became such a threat to Setupathi, the Raja of Ramnad, that the king had the missionary's head impaled on a stake after decapitation (Bayly 1989, 403). Oral tradition maintains that the king later repented his action and carried stones for the construction of the shrine. It is also reported that shortly after the martyrdom of Britto, the king and his entire household converted to Catholicism and were buried near the site of martyrdom.

The beheading of Britto had its own political dimensions, which historians like Susan Bayly have painstakingly emphasized. Through his campaign of mass conversion, Britto came to be perceived as a source of awesome sacral and political powers, which the local ruler feared were being deployed against him. Consequently, Christianity was unlike other south Indian religious traditions of the time in that it was a source of both sacral and political powers. According to Bayly, the local rulers perceived Christianity as a basis on which to build new political alliances. A variant of the martyrdom legend, on which Bayly bases her view, alludes to this political dimension. The executioners beheaded the saint, so goes the legend, then cut off his hands and feet, and tied them to the execution post because they feared his power. His limbs had to be tied down to immobilize his power and spirit. "What is implied here," observes Bayly, "is that . . . de Britto became a focus, a source of power and dynamism . . . This is why it was not enough to kill the missionary . . . de Britto's limbs had to be nailed down so as to immobilise his vengeful spirit. . . . de Britto could not be neutralized as a source of danger to the Ramnad realm unless his body was 'immobilized'; only this could de-activate his power as a rival dominion-builder" (403).

Thus the development of the Britto cult in the Marava country and the popularity of the Oriyur shrine are closely linked to his martyrdom and his assumed sacral powers, especially his fertility powers.[2] A rich collection of legends and folk songs celebrate these life-giving powers. According to one legend, a rooster sacrificed to Britto crowed even after it was beheaded. A folk song celebrates this theme: "The place of the Oriyur saint is a highly exalted space. It can be reached in a day and a half walking. Even the beheaded rooster crows in the sacred shrine of Britto."[3] The fertility motif is also evident in the legends concerning the coloration of the soil surrounding the shrine. Whereas the soil in the immediate vicinity of the site of beheading is red (an area of one square km), all other areas in the vicinity have black soil. Oriyur residents and devotees attribute this unique phenomenon to the martyrdom of Britto, whose blood is believed to have transformed the site into a sacred center of extraordinary fertility. "The saint's blood," writes Mosse, "was taken into the earth and turned it red. The earth representing his blood then became a source of healing and fertility" (cited in Bayly 402).

The three dominant caste groups of the region—namely, Pallar, Kallar, and Udayar, collectively known as Marava castes—and their diasporic population distributed in the adjacent districts of Tanjore, Pudukottai, Madurai, and Trichy constitute the principal cultic constituency of Britto and his shrine. A notable feature of the Britto cult is that it is centered around caste identities rather than religious affiliation. Thus, regardless of their individual religious affiliation, all members of these caste groups—Catholics and Hindus alike—regard him as their favorite clan/family deity (*kula teyvam*). Special marks of honor and affection are accorded to the saint during the festival season. Members of these communities who have moved to urban centers return to the shrine during the festival season to perform passage rites and a wide array of vow rituals. So extensive is Britto's patronage among the Marava caste groups that he is affectionately called the "Marava saint." In addition to these caste groups, Britto also commands the devotion of some Vellala Catholics of the area.

As for the demographics of Oriyur, when I conducted field research in 1990, the total population of the village was comprised of 120 Catholic families. Pallars, who constitute the largest caste group (75 percent), and Vellalas (25 percent) are the two caste groups in the village. Occupationally, Pallars are farmers and unskilled laborers, whereas the Vellalas, who have had more formal education than the Pallars, serve as parish catechists and teachers in the parochial elementary and high schools. The Vellala Catholics were brought by European missionaries from distant Vellala villages to help with catechetical instruction. Though Udayar and Kallar Catholics do not reside in Oriyur, there is a heavy concentration of them in the neighboring villages. As for caste status, Pallars, Udayars, and Kallars are considered lower than Vellalas.

The extraordinary sacral powers of St. John de Britto and his martyrdom site have transformed the remote village of Oriyur into a famed regional pilgrimage center. Tens of thousands of pilgrims and devotees of diverse religious affiliations from all over Tamil Nadu go on annual pilgrimage to this sacred site, where animal sacrifice is a regular feature. Though animal sacrifice is performed in many local Catholic shrines, the shrine of Britto is one of the few reputed regional sites in Tamil Nadu where this practice has survived.[4] Wednesdays are considered particularly auspicious for animal sacrifices, since the martyr was beheaded on a Wednesday. Thus it would not be unusual to find, on any Wednesday, a group of pilgrims offering animal sacrifices at the shrine. However, large-scale goat or chicken sacrifices occur during the three annual shrine festivals: the feast of St. John de Britto (January 26–February 4), the anniversary of the canonization of Britto (June 20–22), and the feast of the Nativity of Mary (August 30–September 8).[5]

Of these three festivals, the nine-day September festival[6] is considered the most auspicious and popular moment for pilgrimage, as evidenced by the sheer volume of pilgrims and animal sacrifices. The annual festival begins with an elaborate flag-hoisting ceremony modeled after Hindu flag-ceremonies.[7] Church authorities estimate that over 50,000 pilgrims visit the shrine during this festival, when the volume of goat sacrifices reaches its peak. According to a conservative estimate, the number of animals sacrificed would be in excess of 800 goats and countless chickens.[8] However, this number fluctuates greatly from year to year. For example, during the September festival in 1990 nearly 600 goats were slaughtered at the shrine.

The Journey to the Center

Pilgrims adopt one of the three modes of travel to the center: walking, bullock-cart, or bus. These three modes of travel in turn suggest the three types of Oriyur pilgrims: ascetic, traditional, and modern pilgrims. The particular mode of travel chosen by a group of pilgrims not only serves as a vehicle for affirming their social status, religious fervor, and caste identities, but profoundly affects, if not defines, their ritual performance.

In rural Tamil Nadu, *pata yattirai* (pilgrimage on foot) is valued by both Hindus and Catholics as a salutary, self-purificatory ascetic exercise. Like their Hindu brethren, many Catholic pilgrims who choose this particular mode of journey also wear saffron clothes. Dressed in saffron, these *pata yatris* (foot-pilgrims) start their journey several days before the festival and stop at villages en route to rest and enjoy hospitality from strangers. Apart from physical relief, such stopovers also afford an opportunity for the pilgrims to talk about their particular personal or familial needs, gain moral support, and strengthen their resolve. The *patayatri* group usually comprises persons who share common ties such as caste, village, faith, and family ties that enhance and strengthen intragroup fellowship.

However, the bullock-cart journey remains the preferred mode of travel among the rural Catholics of the region because of the hardship and austerity it requires. With sacrificial animals, pilgrim families of a particular village travel in small groups. Several practical considerations justify this preference. It is inexpensive and appropriately tedious. It provides an opportunity for strengthening family and village ties. It also gives pilgrims a certain flexibility and freedom to return home as and when they wish. Upon arrival at the shrine, clusters of families make their temporary residence in the church premises, under trees, in the school verandas, and in classrooms. In selecting their "shrine space," pilgrims are guided especially by caste, family, and village considerations. Invariably, members of a particular village or caste mark out a separate space that becomes their temporary residence. Such arrangements, however, are made amiably without any quarrels or unpleasant incidents. More importantly, these groups often have a communal or collective religious intent and hence their rituals have a communal character. The coconut sapling procession, cattle procession, and communal meal are three concrete examples. Depending on the makeup of the group, these collective performances create and reinforce a feeling of family unity, caste communitas, and village solidarity among the members. While some bullock-cart pilgrims stay for three days, many remain at the shrine for the duration of the festival. This extended stay enables them to appropriate the sacred atmosphere of the shrine, share their religious experiences with other pilgrims, and listen to their stories.

Given the easy availability of public transportation today, bus journey has become an attractive third option. A growing number of rural and urban pilgrims prefer this modern means of travel to the slower and more arduous bullock-cart journeys. Whereas rural pilgrims tend to spend several days at the shrine, the urban diaspora visit the shrine for a day, usually on the last day of the festival. Most arrive in the morning, perform the required rituals, often in a perfunctionary manner, and depart in the evening. Inadequate lodging and the lack of modern amenities in this rural shrine often shorten their stay. Their presence is commonly brief, their participation in communal activities (like the *tēr* procession) minimal, and their ritual performance economical and abridged. Nor do they typically mingle or commiserate with other pilgrims. A certain individualism is characteristic of their religious behavior and ritual performance. One might classify them as "jet-set pilgrims." These differences notwithstanding, seemingly all pilgrims prefer, whenever possible, to travel in groups.

Pilgrimage Rituals at Oriyur

The Oriyur pilgrimage tradition encompasses a wide array of ritual performances including hair-shaving, ear-piercing, coconut sapling processions, cattle processions, participation in the Mass, chariot *(tēr)* processions, and the ceremonial recording of the promissory note. However, the centerpiece of the pilgrimage is the animal sacrifice—usually goats and chickens— offered to Britto. Taken together, these various ritual actions constitute the complex *nerccai* (vow) ritual system so prominent in Tamil popular Catholicism in general and the Oriyur pilgrimage tradition in particular.[9] In this essay I shall examine only the sacrifice of animals, the hair-shaving rite, and two fertility/healing rites.

Goat/Chicken Sacrifice

Preparations for the goat sacrifice begin several months prior to the September festival. Depending on the terms of the contractual agreement documented in a promissory note (*muri*), pilgrim families set aside one or more goats or chickens to be sacrificed to Britto at his shrine.[10] From this moment on, these goats are known as Britto's goats. Set apart from other animals through common signs of consecration, these sacrificial animals obtain a sacred character and identity as evidenced by the particular affection and deferential treatment extended to them by the pilgrim families and their neighbors. Mistreatment of the sacrificial animals is believed to be not only improper, but fraught with dangerous consequences. Oral tradition and legends reinforce the efficacy of this taboo.

A popular miracle story recounted by many Oriyur pilgrims well illustrates the privileged status and special treatment accorded to animals set aside for ritual purposes. Arul Samy, headmaster of the parochial elementary school in Oriyur, recounted this story to me. Once a poor Dalit Christian had set aside a goat to be offered to Britto in fulfilment of a vow. With great care, he fed the animal and fattened it. One day, a Hindu landlord of his village demanded this goat for a wedding feast. The poor man replied: "Sir, ordinarily I would be happy to sell any goat of your choice. But I cannot sell this particular goat because I have dedicated it to St. Britto. This is *his* goat and must be offered to him." But the landlord insisted on purchasing this particular goat as it was well fattened. When all efforts to persuade the poor Christian failed, in a fit of anger the wealthy Hindu said: "What is so special about Britto's goat? Does it have three horns?" Miraculously, a third horn sprouted on the goat the next day. When the Hindu landlord saw the third horn, he apologized to the poor Christian and agreed that the goat should be offered to Britto.[11]

The rubrics and contents of the sacrificial rite are quite straightforward. As for auspicious time, most pilgrims prefer to slaughter the animal around 7 a.m., as it gives sufficient time to prepare the communal meal that generally takes place at noon. Adorned with garlands, vermilion powder, and other ornaments, the sacrificial animal is led by the pilgrim family to the martyr's shrine, where the priest blesses it with holy water, often reluctantly (figure 5.1). Pilgrims solicit this blessing not to insure the efficacy of the rite but primarily for psychological satisfaction, as it gives some semblance of official validation for *their* ritual. The animal is then led to the slaughter area—located behind the shrine of Britto's martyrdom—where family elders bless it by tracing the sign of the cross on its forehead (figure 5.2). As a rule, women are not permitted to enter the slaughter area.[12] A senior member of the family then pours holy water on the animal, blesses and venerates it, followed by the actual slaughter witnessed only by men and children (figure 5.3). A notable feature of the slaughter rites is the prominence of the laity in the performance of ritual functions and the exclusion of ordained priests.[13] The carefully collected blood is an important item in the communal meal that follows. I was told that in the past it was customary for pilgrims to offer a portion of the sacrificial meat—usually the best portion of the animal—some

Figure 5.1: Pilgrims gather with sacrificial goats in front of Britto's shrine for an official blessing by shrine priests prior to goat sacrifice.

measure of rice, vegetables, and other cereal offerings to the shrine's priest. This practice was discontinued due to a Church prohibition. Today, however, pilgrims leave a portion of the meat and the animal's skin at the "priest's booth," where they are auctioned off quickly and the proceeds given to the shrine priest.

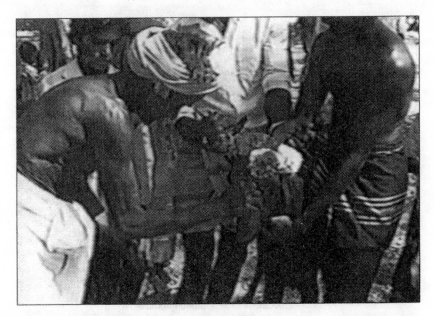

Figure 5.2: A family elder blesses the sacrificial goat by tracing the sign of the cross on its forehead before it is ritually slaughtered.

Figure 5.3: The scene of a goat slaughter.

Meanwhile, a communal meal is prepared with the sacrificial meat. Before partaking in the meal, family members take a ritual bath, circumambulate the shrine with coconut saplings in their hands, and approach the martyr's altar to offer candles and other token offerings either as petitionary prayer for specific favors sought or as thanksgiving for favors received. After the distribution of the sacred meal to the poor, family members and relatives partake of the communal meal, which has dual significance. Religiously, it expresses the pilgrims' desire for communion and fellowship with the saint. Socially, it helps strengthen family ties and the kinship bond.

A series of taboos and prescriptions govern the proper ritual etiquette concerning the consumption of sacrificial meat. An important prescription concerns the treatment of leftover meat as sacred food (*piracatam*). Pilgrims insist that the sacrificial meat should be consumed by family members at the shrine or distributed to the poor before returning home. Under no circumstances may leftover meat be carried beyond its premises. Any violation of this taboo would have disastrous consequences. Hence, pilgrims exhibit great care in disposing the leftover food. Several shrine stories recount the fate of those who dared to defy this taboo.

According to one such legend, a particular family who had plenty of sacrificial meat left over decided to take the leftovers home. As soon as the bullock-cart in which the family was traveling crossed the shrine premises, so goes the legend, the bullocks went wild and caused the cart to tumble and break. A member of the family was seriously injured. The pilgrim family was forced to stay on in the shrine for another day and consume the leftover meat. Devotees attribute this mishap to the family's attempt at appropriating what rightfully belonged to St. John de Britto.

Another popular *piracatam* myth reinforces this taboo regarding sacred leftovers. Long ago a group of pilgrims had lots of sacrificial meat and cooked rice left over after the communal meal, as there were not too many poor people to feed. Not knowing what to do with the large amount of leftovers, the pilgrims prayed to Britto and sought his guidance. He reportedly instructed them to bury the food on the shrine grounds. After consulting the shrine priest, the pilgrims buried the food in the shrine premises and returned home. When the pilgrims returned to the shrine a year later, they dug up the place where they had buried the leftovers and were amazed to find the food just as they had buried it a year ago—steaming rice and unspoiled meat! Devotees ate this rice and meat without suffering any physical ailment.[14]

Pilgrims may dedicate animal sacrifices to Britto for a variety of human and/or spiritual needs.[15] Marital stability, domestic well-being, health and healing, fertility of land and cattle, and agricultural success are some of the more common motives. For some of Britto's most ardent devotees, for whom the saint is a family patron, annual animal sacrifices are also expressions of loyalty and devotion. The following testimonial from Arul of Ilaiyangudi well illustrates this dimension.

> For over a hundred years, our ancestors have been offering goats to Britto. He is our family patron, our *kula teyvam* (family deity). During family rituals and celebrations, we show special devotion and affection for the saint. For example, every firstborn child in our family is named after Britto. Annual pilgrimage to Oriyur is another cherished family tradition. As long as I can remember, I have been coming to this shrine to offer goats to Britto. Economic depression, famines, droughts and agricultural failure have not deterred or eroded our faith in Britto. We don't come to Oriyur only when we need something from the saint. He is our guardian and protector, in good times and bad times. Also, we begin our agricultural season by dedicating special prayers to Britto. At the beginning of the sowing season, we pray to Britto and promise to offer goats and feed the poor if he would ensure good crops. And in my experience, Britto has never failed to answer our prayers.[16]

Hair-Shaving Rites

Hair-shaving is the simplest and most popular devotional activity at Oriyur. Though hair-shaving may be done at the shrine throughout the year, the festival season is considered especially auspicious. Oriyur pilgrims may perform this rite for any one or more of the following five different reasons thus the hair functions as a multivalent symbol: 1) The rite may be performed as a petitionary or promissory rite in which the devotee offers his/her hair as a token offering for favors sought (figure 5.4). In this case, the hair serves as a form of "down payment" to the saint. 2) As a thanksgiving or fulfillment rite for favors already received. Hair can serve as the full payment of debt (figure 5.5 and figure 5.6). 3) As a dedication rite the newborn child's first crop of hair is offered to Britto as a token of loyalty and devotion to the martyr as well as insurance of his protection and assistance for the child (figure 5.7). Here the hair takes the form of an insurance premium. 4) As a pilgrimage devotion through which pilgrims affirm their faith in and loyalty to the patron saint, a shaved head serves as a devotional emblem to the pilgrims and their neighbors. 5) Even if they do not pray for any specific favors, some devotees have their head shaved just because it is a family tradition.[17] In the two last instances, hair functions as an annual tax or tribute owed to the patron saint for his continued protection for the devotee and his/her extended family.

Figure 5.4: Female hair-shaving rite as a token offering for favors sought.

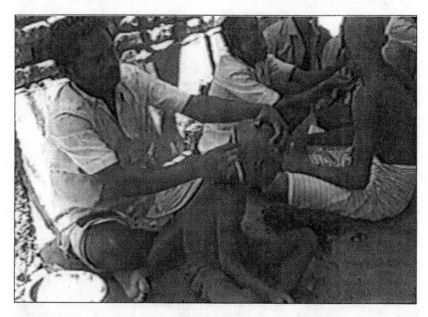

Figure 5.5: Male hair-shaving rite undertaken either as thanksgiving for favors received or as a promissary rite for favors sought.

Figure 5.6: A pilgrim mother stands in front of the shrine after fulfilling her promise to offer her child's first crop of hair to St. Britto in thanksgiving for the gift of the child.

Figure 5.7: After ritual shaving of the hair, a young child has his ear pierced.

During the September festival, a continuous stream of devotees flows to the church-sponsored tonsure houses for the hair-shaving ceremony, where several professional barbers—many of them Hindu—are pressed into service.[18] On the last day of the festival, an average of 600-700 devotees have their heads shaved. The rite itself is simple and straightforward, devoid of any religious or liturgical components. Conspicuous by his absence is the shrine priest who has no part or function in this rite. However, according to an elderly catechist of the shrine, in the past the priest used to cut off a few plaits of hair prior to the actual hair-shaving.[19] Today the shrine priests have no such symbolic roles. In fact, many shrine priests deliberately distance themselves from these popular practices, even though the vast majority of devotees who take tonsure at Oriyur are Catholics. Besides Catholics, many Hindu pilgrims also observe this rite.[20] Following the hair-removal, pilgrims bathe, apply sandal paste on their head, circumambulate the shrine, and offer prayers, candles, flowers, fruits, grains, and other offerings at the altar of Britto. Depending on the context, the promissory note (*muri*), which contains the terms and conditions of the pilgrim's promise, is submitted along with other votive offerings when the contract between Britto and the pilgrim is either initiated or fulfilled. If the contract has not been fulfilled, either by the saint or the devotee, then the *muri* is burned privately or torn to pieces, indicating that the transaction has been nullified.

Raymond Firth's detailed discussion of the complex symbolism of hair and its social, cultural, personal, and sacrificial significance serves as a useful theoretical framework for interpreting hair-shaving rituals at the shrine of St. John de Britto. He writes:

> . . . [I]n most general terms shaving the head is a sign of *tristitia* . . . of diminution of the self, whether in terms of status or of relation to the world and human affairs. The hair of the head is an intimate element of the personality, and to remove it by intention is to effect a reduction or at least a change in the personality. Yet there is a kind of dialectical relationship here. For reduction of the personality in one direction may allow of its growth in another. (290)

Firth furthermore asserts that the "lowering of status may be only temporary, a reduction of the individual to order in the name of a collectivity or an extra-human being with which association gives the individual a special new status" (291). He concludes his cross-cultural analysis by noting that hair cutting not only implies an abasement of the personality but sacrifice as well (298).

The Oriyur pilgrimage tradition serves as an illustration for Firth's analysis. As noted above, Oriyur pilgrims have their hair shaved during rites of passage for children and as a devotional/sacrificial exercise. In the case of the adult pilgrim, hair-shaving represents a sacrificial act involving self-abasement through which the pilgrim affirms or negotiates a reciprocal relationship between a consenting adult and the saint. Though the hair-shaving ritual functions as a rite of passage for children, it also operates as a form of sacrifice sponsored by their parents. The spiritual and mundane benefits of this sacrificial act accrue to the child as well as to the child's parents. While the child whose head is treated is inducted into a privileged patron-client relationship with Britto, bringing a special new status for the child, this ritual also assures parents of the saint's continued protection for the child and its family. While Firth's theory of abasement applies more directly to adult pilgrims, the themes of sacrifice and status-elevation pertain to all pilgrims. The elevation of the pilgrim's status is acknowledged by the pilgrim community and the larger society, for whom a shaved head functions as a public emblem and statement of the devotee's newfound or renewed spiritual status and identity.

Fertility and Healing Rites

No human need attracts pilgrims to the shrine of Britto as much as the need for fertility. So prominent is the fertility motif that we may consider it the ritual nerve center of the Oriyur pilgrimage system. Indeed, the bloody rites of sacrifice are inspired by fertility concerns as well. Miracle stories and legends celebrate the extraordinary fertility and healing powers of the saint and his shrine. According to local tradition, for example, "a drop of his [Britto's] blood fell into the blind eye of his Pallar executioner and restored it. The saint's blood was taken into the earth and turned it red. The earth representing his blood then became a source of healing and fertility" (cited in Bayly: 402). Shrine priests assert that over 50 percent of the pilgrims attend the September festival to pray for fertility—fertility of land, cattle, crops, and humans. Of the numerous fertility rites that gain prominence during the pilgrimage, the coconut sapling rite and the cattle procession are the most colorful. Unique to Oriyur, the cattle procession is especially relevant for our purposes, as it demonstrates that social boundaries and caste distinctions are neither renounced nor forgotten during pilgrimage but are in fact displayed, preserved, and reinforced.

THE COCONUT SAPLING RITE

Offering coconut saplings to Britto is a popular ritual activity especially among women. Women praying for children write a promissory note (*muri*) documenting the specific favors sought and the type of offering promised to the saint in return for favors. Then they have their head shaved in the church tonsure house, take a ritual bath, apply sandal paste on their head, and circumambulate Britto's shrine three times with a coconut sapling in hand. After circumambulating the shrine in this manner, pilgrims place the sapling and the promissory note at the altar of Britto. Occasionally, some pilgrims circumambulate the shrine on their knees to demonstrate to the saint the extent of their devotion and the urgency of the petition. The use of a coconut sapling has much symbolic significance. In Tamil folk tradition, the coconut sapling is a common fertility symbol. The Tamil word for it (*tennam pillai*) is similar in tone and meaning to the Tamil word for a child (*pillai*). Pilgrims purchase the coconut saplings at the church-administered stall and have them blessed by the priest (figure 5.8). Shrine officials deal with the high demand for coconut saplings by retrieving them from Britto's shrine and reselling them to devotees, thereby generating additional revenue. As with hair-shaving, devotees may perform the coconut sapling rite either as a promissory or fulfilment rite.

The following testimonials by two Catholic devotees capture the essential spirit of the rite. With a coconut sapling in hand and sandal paste generously dabbed on her newly shaved head, Flora Rani of Murugatharampatti said to me: "I have been married for several years but did not have a male child. Last year I submitted a *muri* (promissory note) to Britto in which I promised I would shave my hair and carry a coconut sapling around the shrine if he would give me a male child. Through Britto's blessing, this year I gave birth to a son." Pointing to the child in her arms, she continued, "This child is Britto's gift to my family. As promised, I shaved off my hair and

Figure 5.8: With coconut saplings in hand, pilgrims gather in front of the rectory for an official priestly blessing.

carried a coconut sapling as thanksgiving for his favor."[21] Saverimuthu of the village of Pillamari, who is a regular pilgrim to Oriyur, stated:

> I got married in 1967 and had two daughters. But we did not have a male child. My neighbors suggested that I go on a pilgrimage to Oriyur and offer a vow to Britto. So I came to Oriyur on pilgrimage in 1971, wrote a *muri*, prayed for a male child and promised Britto that, if my prayer would be answered, our entire family would shave our heads and sacrifice a he-goat to Britto. The saint gave us a male child the following year. We fulfilled our promise and offered a he-goat during the festival season and shaved our heads. Presently I have acute pain in my right hand and I have come to pray for healing. I just wrote a *muri* for seven rupees and will carry a coconut sapling around the shrine. I have full confidence and faith that my hand will get better through Britto's blessing.[22]

Though formerly the coconut sapling rite was observed only when praying for children, today the coconut sapling functions as a generic symbol for various fertility and healing needs. A variation of the coconut sapling rite is the "cradle ceremony." Pilgrim families who have received a child through Britto's favor carry the child in a makeshift cradle made of cloth and sugarcane stalks and circumambulate the shrine three times after which candles, money, fruits, flowers, and other cereal items are presented as thanksgiving offerings. Whereas the coconut sapling rite may be performed either as a promissory or thanksgiving rite, the cradle ceremony is exclusively a thanksgiving rite.

THE CATTLE PROCESSION RITE

On the last day of the September festival, the men wash their cattle in a nearby tank and decorate them with ornaments, garlands, and vermilion powder, after which the entire extended family, including children, women, and cattle, assemble in front of Britto's martyrdom shrine to offer homage and thanks for favors received and/or to solicit his continued protection for themselves, their land, and cattle. The shrine priest then prays over and blesses the congregation with holy water, again reluctantly. With coconut saplings in their hands, family members lead the cattle in a colorful procession around the shrine three times and place the coconut saplings inside the shrine as votive offerings (figure 5.9 and figure 5.10). According to a conservative estimate, over 100 such processions take place during the September festival.

Of particular relevance for us in this essay is the makeup and caste identities of devotees who observe this rite and the social themes embedded

Figure 5.9: With coconut saplings in hand, pilgrims lead the cattle in ceremonial procession around the shrine.

Figure 5.10: The main Gothic Church at the shrine of St. John de Britto.

in it. Observed by both Hindu and Catholic devotees, participation in the cattle procession is based on family, village, and caste identities. Only members of a particular family, village, or caste are allowed to process together. Although there is no explicit prohibitive code, there is an understanding among pilgrims that outsiders do not join the procession. Furthermore, while other shrine rituals are performed by devotees of diverse socioeconomic status, the cattle procession is specific to devotees from the farming community, since their livelihood and well-being understandably depend on the health and fertility of their cattle. The general congregation of pilgrims witnesses this colorful ceremony with mixed feelings of piety and curiosity. Thus in addition to its religious value, the cattle procession serves an important social function in that it provides a sacred context and occasion for the pilgrims to display, affirm, and strengthen their caste identities, family ties, and social status.

Transgressing Boundaries

The description furnished above confirms the fact that boundary crossing is a striking feature of the Oriyur pilgrimage process. There is little difference between Oriyur and Hindu pilgrimage patterns. While the locus, sacrificers, and recipients of rituals may be Catholic, their contents, rubrics, and idiom are essentially Hindu in character and origin. As for pilgrims themselves, it is difficult to know whether they are Catholic or Hindu. Their dress, ritual performance, and shrine behavior are not markedly different. These facts suggest that Oriyur Catholic pilgrims both transgress and transcend the normative boundaries of official religion. As to the specific form of boundary crossing noticeable at Oriyur, however, the following may be considered the general pattern.[23] Catholic pilgrims import a series of Hindu rites and ritual idioms into their pilgrimage practices and direct them to the European martyr-saint, investing in him certain indigenous religious ideas, powers, and meanings—largely derived from village Hinduism—so that the European saint resembles, in personality, power, and function, the tutelary deities of their Hindu counterparts. One specific example of this localization process is the geographical extent of Britto's power. As with Hindu village deities, Britto's sacral powers are believed to be contained and grounded in a specific locale, i.e., his shrine.

Boundary crossing also results in the temporary suspension of a particular religious identity, evident in the temporary relegation of official rituals such as the Mass to secondary status. In fact, many pilgrims explicitly stated that one's religious identity is not crucial for the efficacy of rituals. Commenting on this phenomenon, Rev. Nedungatt, pastor of Oriyur shrine, said:

"We [clergy] preach about faith, the cross, and the kingdom of God but for them [rural Catholics] religion is pilgrimage, festivals, and rituals. Official Catholic rituals like the Mass and sacraments have only secondary importance."[24] It is instructive that while many Catholic pilgrims skip the Mass and other devotional exercises when at the shrine, many Hindus attend Mass and scrupulously observe these exercises. Some Hindu pilgrims also receive communion as *piracatam* (food offered to and blessed by the deity). There are therefore ways in which Catholic pilgrims behave like Hindus, and Hindu pilgrims behave like Catholics.

While the Catholic hierarchy would be likely to view such violations of sacred boundaries with dismay and disdain, and as signs of dysfunctional Catholicism, the practitioners themselves regard them as necessary and efficacious instruments to provide relief from specific human and/or spiritual crises. Thus communal faith in the efficacy of popular rituals acts as a powerful motivation for such transgressions.[25] Consequently, the efforts of the hierarchy to map and reinforce the sanctity of religious boundaries are met with disregard and protest. One layman echoes the practitioners' general complaint: "Our priests do not understand or respect our feelings; when that happens, we do not care whether they approve or disapprove of our practices." So pronounced is this sentiment that the pilgrimage tradition at Oriyur has the appearance and marks of a "protestant Catholicism." Let me turn now to a brief analysis of the cultural conditions and factors that drive Tamil Catholic pilgrims to adopt a protestant stance.

The Liminality of Oriyur Catholic Pilgrims

In *The Rites of Passage*, Van Gennep (1960) has shown that all rites of passage possess a tripartite structure—separation, margin or limen, and re-aggregation. Building on Van Gennep's classic three stages, Turner delineates a similar structure in pilgrimage that includes the start of the journey, the journey itself and the encounter with the sacred (liminality), and homecoming. Turner identifies liminality as the crucial middle stage.[26] So central is this category that in *Image and Pilgrimage in the Christian Culture* (1978), Turner describes pilgrimage itself as a "liminoid phenomenon," characterized by a sense of transcendence, an awareness of temporary release from established social structure, the freedom to step out of normalcy and experiment with other invisible possibilities, and a strong sense of bonding and classlessness which he calls communitas (1–39).

The Oriyur pilgrimage process displays some, if not all, of the classic symptoms and features that Turner associates with liminality—a sense of transcendence from established structure, freedom from normative structures and boundaries, some sense of bonding, and an excursion into antistructure and chaos. Nevertheless, a notable liminal feature absent in the Oriyur process is the type of communal bonding that Turner attributes to liminal situations and entities. Although there is a sense of intragroup bonding among the three types of Catholic pilgrims as well as a bonding between Hindu and Catholic pilgrims, class, caste, and religious distinctions are not entirely absent, an issue that will be explored in the final section of this essay. This limitation notwithstanding, Turner's expanded notion of liminality is a useful interpretive tool in understanding Oriyur pilgrimage tradition and the phenomenon of boundary crossing.

What is distinctive about the Oriyur pilgrimage tradition is that its rituals reveal not only the liminal phase through which Tamil Catholic pilgrims pass during pilgrimage, but the pilgrim community's cultural and religious liminality. In other words, for these pilgrims, liminality is not merely a temporary stage but an enduring state of mind and being, a way of life. Given their dual identity as Tamils and Catholics, these pilgrims exist in a state of permanent liminality, a certain transcendence and freedom from official structures and normative boundaries as well as a certain bonding and communitas with Hindu neighbors. It is this consciousness of permanent liminality as neither Hindu nor Catholic, I believe, which allows Tamil Catholic pilgrims to move in and out of structure. It also gives them the freedom to defy, in a guilt-free manner, the doctrinal and ritual boundaries of normative Catholicism, to indulge in what appears as chaotic ritual behavior, and to experiment with other redemptive possibilities and solutions to their human and/or spiritual crises unavailable within official Catholicism.[27] This excursion into antistructural experiments, which gains prominence during pilgrimage, also occurs beyond the pilgrimage context.

While this sense of liminality is most visible among pilgrims, it is interesting to note that similar patterns are also reflected in the imaging of the saint and the actions of the clergy. Though Britto is represented in iconography as a European saint wearing a European cape, the powers and qualities attributed to him make him an indigenous figure who resembles the local Hindu tutelary deities. Furthermore, like his Catholic pilgrims, Britto both supports and confounds the status quo. As the Marava saint, he supports caste identity; he is a Catholic saint who also "acts" like a Hindu tutelary deity. Located at the juncture between European and Tamil, Catholic and Hindu, high caste and low caste, he is a preeminent liminal figure reflected in his personality and powers. As such, he functions as a sacred metaphor reflecting the religious and cultural liminality of his Catholic pilgrims.[28]

A different sort of liminality is characteristic of ecclesiastical authorities—most of them natives—who find themselves between regulations and directives from the Vatican, on the one hand, and pastoral exigencies or realities predicated by their flock's own cultural and religious liminality, on the other. Though many priests disapprove of the religious practices of their flock on theological grounds and are disdainful toward these practices, pastoral considerations compel them to look the other way. The recurring demand for pastoral compromises produces in the clergy a certain personal and theological liminality. This sense of liminality is not unique to Oriyur shrine priests but is widespread among many Catholic priests in Tamil Nadu. The following incident well illustrates this fact. A Catholic bishop in Tamil Nadu issued a decree in December 1974 banning all *tēr* (chariot) processions during Catholic festivals. A few days later, the bishop presided over festival celebrations in one of his parishes and reiterated the ban he had issued earlier. As the bishop came out of the church after the service, a group of local parishioners asked him to bless the *tēr* that was kept ready to be taken out in procession. Despite his condemnatory sermon against such practices minutes before, the bishop blessed the *tēr*. When one of his priests sought an explanation for his quick turnaround, the bishop said: 'We have no choice but to respect the traditions and sentiments of our people.'[29] Thus all the principal actors in the Oriyur ritual drama are liminal entities, each reflecting and reinforcing the other's liminality.

Transcending Turner

The concept of communitas is another crucial category in Turner's pilgrimage theory. He defines communitas as "an essential and generic human bond" which is "undifferentiated, and egalitarian"(1978, 250). "What is sought in communitas," writes Turner, "is unity, not the unity which represents a sum of fractions . . . but an indivisible unity" (254–55). According to him, the pilgrims "are impregnated by unity, as it were, and purified from divisiveness and plurality," so that social distinctions and boundaries are dissolved in the pilgrimage context (255). He argues that communitas occurs both during the journey and at the shrine. Thus, for Turner communitas is an integral aspect of religious pilgrimage inasmuch as pilgrims realize their common humanity and human kindness at the sacred center despite social distinctions. Over the past decade, however, his pilgrimage theory has been tested in different social and religious settings—Morocco (Eickelman 1976), Nepal (Messerschmidt and Sharma 1981), Sri Lanka (Stirrat 1992), and Peru (Sallnow 1981). These case studies demonstrate that rather than dissolving distinctions, pilgrimage centers and practices in fact reinforce social distinctions and boundaries, even if pilgrims exhibit some of the conditions and features underscored in Turner's concept of communitas.[30]

Oriyur data also suggest limitations in Turner's concept of communitas as a universal feature in religious pilgrimage. Even if we acknowledge the value of his communitas thesis in some cultural and religious contexts, its universal validity, particularly the theme of "indivisible unity" in communitas, remains problematic. Admittedly, Oriyur pilgrims do exhibit some of the typical features that Turner associates with communitas. However, further investigation of Oriyur pilgrims' behavioral, performative, and relational patterns—particularly their modes of travel, goat sacrificial rites and related practices, and their social interactions with one another—suggests that families, villages, and caste-groups maintain their distinctive identities both during the journey and at the shrine. While there is ample intracaste and intravillage communitas, particularly during the journey, intercaste communitas is not only absent but consciously avoided and discouraged. For example, Vellala Catholics do not stay with Pallar Catholics. Nor do they commiserate or partake in communal meals with them. Also, urban pilgrims neither mingle nor share fellowship with rural pilgrims of their own caste, much less with pilgrims from other caste groups. Although as Catholics these pilgrims are expected to transcend caste and social boundaries and demonstrate their catholicity in faith, Catholic pilgrims at Oriyur are deeply conscious of and committed to caste identities and distinctions. The cattle procession offers a good example of this recurring pattern. Curiously, while caste identities and class distinctions are carefully preserved and consciously displayed, pilgrims' religious identities and delineations remain quite fluid, both during and beyond the pilgrimage experience. These facts suggest that caste identities and class distinctions are not entirely repressed nor obliterated but in fact reinforced in pilgrimage contexts, which compels us to distinguish between a superficial feeling of solidarity, a kind of "cocktail communitas," and the actual breakdown of social groups. It is this "cocktail communitas" that is most visible among the pilgrims at the shrine of John de Britto.

Conclusion

Recent cross-cultural studies on pilgrimage have shown that "pilgrimage is above all an arena for competing religious and secular discourses, for both the official co-optation and the non-official recovery of religious meanings, for conflict between orthodoxies, sects, and confessional groups, for drives towards consensus and communitas *and* for counter-movements towards separateness and division" (Eade and Sallnow, 2–3). Our case study lends support to this thesis. At the shrine of John de Britto, the identity and powers of the saint and his shrine are construed differently by different constituencies. For example, the identity and status assigned to the saint by the Church hierarchy significantly differ from those invested by the Catholic laity. This clash of conflicting perceptions between the hierarchy and the laity played out in the pilgrim center is further compounded by the saint's multireligious clientele and their differing perceptions of the saint and his shrine, whereby Hindu and Catholic devotees invest in the saint their respective perceptions, meanings, and ideas, some of which are drawn from their shared cultural data-bank, while others are drawn from their own religious tradition.

In this sense, the Oriyur pilgrimage tradition serves both as a mirror and as a window—a three-way mirror to insiders and a window to outsiders. To insiders, pilgrimage provides a ritual context in which the liminality of pilgrims (Catholics and Hindus), the saint, and Church leaders gains public ritual expression. To outsiders, it serves as a window to the multiple characters, the fluid identities, the complicated relations, the complex negotiations, and the enduring tensions that define Tamil popular Catholicism. To that extent, Turner is right in arguing that pilgrimage is a "metasocial commentary."

Notes

1. I am grateful to my colleagues Corinne Dempsey, William Harman, and Frank Frick for their careful comments and suggestions on an earlier draft. This essay is primarily based on data collected during a four-month (June–September, 1990) dissertation field research at the shrine of St. John de Britto.

2. David Mosse has traced the themes of asceticism, death, and blood sacrifice that characterize the Britto cult. Mosse argues that the blood-stained martyr is a source of new life and regeneration who fits the south Indian model of the slain renouncer-king. Cited in Bayly, 428–33.

3. This is my translation of the folk song that Arul Samy of Oriyur recited to me on September 7, 1990.

4. During field research I learned that in the past, animal sacrifice used to be practiced at the shrine of Our Lady of Good Health in Velankanni. However, this practice has been discontinued due to church prohibition. But animal sacrifices are quite common in many rural shrines. The shrines of Augustinus Capelli, a saintly Jesuit who died at Kalugermadai near Madurai, St. Sebastian at Manganur near Trichy, and St. Antony at Uavari near Tuticorin are three such rural shrines in Tamil Nadu. Goat sacrifices are a regular feature at the shrine of Capelli especially during the annual festival. While the shrine of Britto attracts a large number of Marava Catholics, the vast majority of Capelli's devotees are Vellala Catholics from the region. For basic information on Capelli and his shrine, see Ponnad's (1990) *Tiruttala Varalaru* (History of the Shrine), the shrine brochure. On Kalugermadai rituals, see my dissertation (1994, 157–60).

Animal sacrifices are also common at the shrine of St. Sebastian at Manganur when devotees—Catholics and Hindus—seek Sebastian's favors to gain relief from such frightful diseases as chicken pox or smallpox. He is the Catholic version of

Mariamman, the Hindu goddess of disease and healing. Devotees praying for healing from chicken pox wear a yellow wristband and offer salt to the saint. Devotees attach much symbolic significance to the use of salt. That the disease, like salt, might melt away is their fervent prayer. Besides, salt is also said to be a favorite item of St. Sebastian. Tamil Catholics of the Vannia caste form the principal caste-group at this shrine. This information was gathered during an interview with Nevis of Manganur on August 2, 1990.

The shrine of St. Antony at Uvari is another popular pilgrim center for the Parava Catholics of the fishery coast where goat sacrifices are a regular feature. While on average twenty to forty goats may be sacrificed on any Tuesday, the number of goats sacrificed increases during the shrine festival in February (17–19). I am told that animal sacrifices are also popular at the shrine of St. Antony in Puliampatti and numerous other rural Catholic shrines in Tamil Nadu. These facts suggest that caste considerations and identities play an important role in the establishment of sacred sites.

5. The annual clergy pilgrimage in the archdiocese of Madurai coincides with the anniversary of Britto's canonization that attracts many pilgrims to the shrine. The physical presence and known opposition of Church authorities do not deter Catholic pilgrims from performing their traditional shrine rituals, including animal sacrifices. Ironically, while the archbishop celebrates Mass inside the church, animal slaughters occur outside the church.

6. The length of the September festival corresponds to the annual festival at the shrine of Our Lady of Good Health in Velankanni that lies about sixty miles north of Oriyur. Younger (1992, 89–99) has argued that the length and structure of Catholic festivals in India are similar to those of Hindu goddess festivals in Tamil Nadu.

7. In her study of Catholic festival practices at the shrine of Our Lady of Good Heath in Velankanni in Tamil Nadu, M. Meibohm suggests identity symbolism in the flag-hoisting ceremony. She argues that "the hoisting of the flag refers to Indian Catholic history not just in evoking the appearance of Our Lady on Indian soil, but also in making the transformation of Self from Hindu to Catholic" (69). (See her essay in this volume.)

8. A number of devotees stated that in the past over 2,000 goats used to be offered to Britto during the September festival. In 1990 I met a family of forty that sacrificed nine goats, one for each day of the festival. Changed patterns of travel and the steady migration of Marava Catholics to urban settings are the two main reasons for the fluctuation and decline in the number of goats sacrificed.

9. In Tamil, the term *nerccai* or *nerrikatan* is a generic term for a wide array of vow rituals like hair-shaving and animal sacrifice that may be performed as thanksgiving or promissory or propitiatory rites. For a detailed discussion of Tamil Catholic *nerccai* rituals, see my dissertation, 115–95.

10. Although devotees consider Britto's shrine as the ideal locus for goat sacrifices, human exigencies such as illness have given rise to at least three types of substitution regarding the site and victim of the sacrifice. The first type of substitution occurs when transportation of the animal poses practical difficulties. In such situa-

tions, devotees may sell the designated goat or chicken and offer cash to Britto. Here money functions as a substitute for the animal. We may call it victim substitution. In the second type, pilgrims slaughter the animal in their homes and partake of a festive meal. When they visit the shrine during the festival, devotees would complete the rite by offering money and rice in lieu of the customary skin and meat due to Britto and/ or his earthly representative. Though money is again a substitute for the animal, what differentiates the first and second types of substitution is that in the second form, the profane space of devotees' home serves as a substitute for the shrine. We may call it spatial substitution. In the third type of substitution, the sacrificer may have the sacrifice performed by a relative or neighbor, which might entail either sending the animal to the shrine or cash offerings. We may classify this type of substitution as proxy-substitution. A notable feature of these various forms of substitution is that devotees neither seek nor receive dispensation from church officials but themselves act as the dispensing authority. During my field-research I did not come across anyone who expressed regret or guilt for making these substitutions.

11. Based on an interview with Arul Samy at Oriyur, September 7, 1990.

12. Most male devotees said that women are not allowed in the slaughter area because animal slaughter and skinning are gruesome for women to watch. Another explanation was that this rule would free women for other preparations for the communal meal. I could not find out how women themselves view this custom. I am inclined to think that the Hindu idea of female pollution has inspired this exclusionary rule.

13. While some priests are willing to bless the animals before the slaughter, many refuse to witness or participate in the actual killing of the animal.

14. These stories were gathered during an interview with Jebamalai Muthu at Oriyur, September 6, 1990.

15. Devotees use the terms 'offering' and 'sacrifice' interchangeably, and in this essay I have retained their usage.

16. Based on an interview on September 6, 1990.

17. Based on recent field research in a south Indian Muslim shrine, Vasudha Narayanan (1998) has proposed a typology of vows similar to my typology.

18. The Oriyur tonsure house is relatively small when compared to the large concrete building at the shrine of Our Lady in Velankanni.

19. Information furnished by Rev. K. S. Arulanandam, S.J., in a personal communication.

20. A Tamil proverb captures the symbolic and religious significance attached to the offering of hair in Tamil popular religious culture: "Uyirai kotutha aandavanakku, mayirai kotu," meaning, "to the god who has given you life, give your hair."

21. Interview at Oriyur on September 6, 1990.

22. Interview at Oriyur on September 7, 1990.

23. For a discussion of the various forms of boundary crossing in Tamil popular Catholicism, see my dissertation, 251–57.

24. Interview on September 5, 1990, at Oriyur.

25. The following narrative by Rev. K. S. Arulanandam, S.J. (1989) reinforces the efficacy argument. "Arumainathan was one of my students at St. Mary's Higher Secondary School in Madurai. At school and later as a government official he was a devout Catholic. In 1972 he married Jeyamary. For twelve years, they had an unhappy marital life because they had no issue. Depressed by this, Arumainathan gave up all religious practices. Around this time, I met him one day and advised him to go on a pilgrimage to the shrine of John de Britto in Oriyur. He and his wife took a pilgrimage to Oriyur that year and prayed to Britto. A year later I saw Arumainathan. He was totally excited that he had now become a father of a boy child and asked me to perform the child's baptism in Oriyur. As a token of gratitude to the saint, the parents named the child 'arul' which is the Tamil Catholic conventional name for Britto." (Personal communication to the author on November 1, 1989.)

26. Turner (1969) expands Van Gennep's notion of limen into an autonomous category present in all ritual processes. This is well documented in his *Ritual Process: Structure and Anti-Structure.*

27. European pilgrims also defy doctrinal Catholicism in their popular practice. What distinguishes the Oriyur tradition is the extreme ways and limits to which Oriyur pilgrims seem to go in order to express their defiance of normative rules as well as the remarkable ease and guiltlessness they exhibit.

28. Special thanks to Corinne Dempsey who prompted me to reflect on Britto's own liminality.

29. Based on an interview with a priest who witnessed this incident. In deference to his wishes, I have withheld his identity.

30. For example D. Eickelman's study (1976) shows that Islamic pilgrimage in Morocco preserves and legitimizes secular inequalities in the wider society.

References

Arulanandam, K. S. 1989. Letter to the author, November 1.

Bayly, Susan. 1989. *Saints, Goddesses, and Kings: Muslims and Christians in South Indian Society 1700–1900.* Cambridge: Cambridge University Press.

Eade, John, and Michael J. Sallnow. 1991. *Contesting the Sacred: The Anthropology of Christian Pilgrimage.* London: Routledge.

Eickelman, D. 1976. *Moroccan Islam.* Austin: Texas University Press.

Firth, Raymond. 1973. *Symbols: Private and Public.* Ithaca, N.Y.: Cornell University Press.

Meibohm, Margaret. 2002. "Past Selves and Present Others: The Ritual Construction of Identity at a Catholic Festival in India." In *Popular Christianity in India: Riting Between the Lines,* eds. Selva Raj and Corinne Dempsey, 61–83. Albany: State University of New York Press.

Messerschmidt, D. A. and J. Sharma, 1981. "Hindu Pilgrimage in the Nepal Himalayas." *Current Anthropology* 22, no. 5:571–52.

Narayanan, Vasudha. 1998. *Religious Vows at the Shrine of Shahul Hamid.* Paper read at the American Academy of Religion, Ritual Studies Group & Religions in South Asia Section, Orlando, Florida (November 23).

Ponnad, G. 1990. *Tiruttal Vavalaru* (History of the Shrine) brochure. n.p.

Raj, Selva. 1994. "Interactive Religious Systems in Indian Popular Catholicism: The Case of Tamil and Santal Catholics." Ph.D. Dissertation. University of Chicago.

Sallnow, Michael J. 1981. "Communitas Reconsidered: The Sociology of Andean Pilgrimage." *Man* 16:163–82.

Stirrat, R. L. 1992. *Power and Religiosity in a Post-Colonial Setting (Sinhala Catholics In Contemporary Sri Lanka).* Cambridge: Cambridge University Press.

Turner, Victor. 1969. *Ritual Process: Structure and Anti-Structure.* Ithaca, N.Y.: Cornell University Press.

Turner, Victor, and E. Turner. 1978. *Image and Pilgrimage in the Christian Culture: Anthropological Perspectives.* New York: Columbia University Press.

Van Gennep, Arnold. 1960. *The Rites of Passage.* Chicago: University of Chicago Press.

Younger, Paul. 1992. "Velankanni Calling: Hindu Patterns of Pilgrimage at a Christian Shrine." In *Sacred Journeys: The Anthropology of Pilgrimage*, ed. Alan Morinis, 89–99. Westport, Conn.: Greenwood.

PART II

Saints and Wonderworkers:
Healing Disease and Division

CHAPTER 6

Lessons in Miracles from Kerala, South India: Stories of Three "Christian" Saints[1]

Corinne G. Dempsey

Highlighted in the following pages are stories of three well-established Kerala Christian saints, champions of healing and miracles. They are also champions who seemingly defy the "laws" of religious distinction. One miracle-worker and patroness of an Orthodox Christian church, a pious Jewish woman, is conspicuously non-Christian. Another saint, although Jacobite Christian, gleans a portion of his powers from questionable—seemingly de-monic—magical sources.[2] The third figure, recently beatified by the Vatican, elicits much of her fame and institutional recognition from the miraculous healing of a Muslim boy. Besides their miraculous bestowal of health and well-being upon their devotees, these saints bestow (miraculous?) lessons upon us as well.

The most important lesson has to do with the healing shrine's (de)construction of religious boundaries. In spite of the various affiliations and cross-affiliations embodied by these saints, stories about them tend to underscore a single, unifying feature: their capacity for miraculous power. Their seemingly bold mixing of traditions thus becomes inconsequential, particularly for those on the receiving end of saintly boons. This is not to say that saints and devotees consciously defy "orthodox" delineations between religions. Rather, in the face of real life matters such abstractions simply matter less.[3]

Speaking of delineations, Malayali Christians are often quick to distin-guish for Christian foreigners their unique lineage, one that stems from the peaceful conversion of Brahmins by St. Thomas the Apostle himself. As one Syrian Catholic man told me, his people were Christian and/or Brahmin, while most Europeans were "still running around like barbarians." Although Indian, Kerala Christians consider themselves no less Christian than their

European counterparts and, although Christian, no less Indian than their Hindu neighbors. Moreover, for some Kerala Christians, their Indian tradition is the hegemonic center that situates western European Christianity as peripheral Other.[4] Methodologically, for those of us influenced by modern European Christianity—which Talal Asad argues is most of us in the academic community—this position as peripheral Other in relation to south India presents a crucial challenge. It is something to keep in mind while digesting the following "unorthodox" stories and a subject to which I will return at the end of this chapter.[5]

Marttaśmūni of Peroor: The Jewish-Christian Saint

I first learned of Marttaśmūni from two middle-aged men, one Hindu and the other Christian, in Ettamanur town near Kottayam. During our discussion over tea in the Hindu gentleman's photo shop, the two men compared Marttaśmūni of Peroor to the more famous Mary at Manarcad.[6] Both saints and their shrines, they agreed, were equally popular among Hindus and Christians. Before I was able to learn more about Marttaśmūni, however, our conversation drifted irretrievably onto other subjects. Perhaps this explains my initial confusion several days later when I arrived at an Orthodox Syrian church in Peroor and found the customary oil lamps and Christian paraphernalia alongside tables filled with Jewish menorahs (figure 6.1). After searching the deserted church grounds for someone who could explain, I noticed three men setting up a tea stall near the rear entrance to the church. After some small talk and introductions, I asked if they could tell me the story of Marttaśmūni and their church. While the youngest of the three brought a bench out of the stall so I could sit down, the sixtyish elder of the group obligingly narrated the following.

> Marttaśmūni Mother had seven children. Mosil of Karakosil was their village [in present day Iraq], 157 years before Christ. She had deep faith in God, that saintly woman. She was compelled to venerate idols and eat pork by a king called Antiochus but she was not willing to do it. She was a woman with her seven children who lived according to the Jewish tradition's beliefs in Yahweh. Her husband died, so she had a guru named Eliyāsar.
>
> When she was fifty-five she was invited to the king Antiochus's palace. The king promised her one-half of the kingdom if she would give up Yahweh, worship idols, and obey them. So the Mother said, "I don't care for powers and positions of this world. I will only worship Yahweh the true God."

Figure 6.1: Display of menorahs and hanging oil lamps inside the Marttasmuni Church, Peroor.

The enraged king condemned her to an immediate death, thus she was handed over to be tortured. The children were bound to a stake and whipped, while her skin was peeled off, and her limbs were cut off. Then, each one of them was thrown into boiling oil and fried. Finally, they did the same to the Mother also. Thus they went over to God. Then, they appeared as saints. Since then, even to date, they go on making apparitions as saints.

The man then explained to those of us listening (whose ranks were gradually increasing) that Marttaśmūni, her guru, and her seven children appeared once a year as shadows cast on the walls of a church in Musil. Someone apparently decided to drape a silk cloth on the wall before one apparition and the figures stayed on the cloth for five minutes. Luckily for the community in Peroor and all of Kerala, the archbishop of Iraq brought this cloth to Peroor and enshrined it in the local church. Extolling the potency and popularity of Marttaśmūni's local apparitions, the teller's account concluded: "They appear even now on this holy cloth before the people who have real faith. Many miracles occur. Many people from India and from abroad come here. Many patients and people who suffer from dire poverty are saved from their troubles. Many tourists also come here."

During this narration I kept waiting for the "missing" link between the Jewish Marttaśmūni and the Christian churches visited by her shadows. I also was hoping for an explanation of the church's menorahs that so took me off guard. After the man finished speaking, thinking perhaps I had lost something in the translation, I stated for purposes of clarification, "Then, she is Jewish." The people around the tea stall, apparently also familiar with the story, simply nodded as though nothing more needed to be said. On asking if anyone could tell me the significance of the menorahs in the church, people seemed to think it best to go to the parish priest living nearby for further information. After a short tour of the church, a young woman led me along a path that edged along a rice field and into the back of Father Mani Kallapurathu's house. There we learned that Father Mani was on his way home from the hospital, where his wife had just given birth to a baby boy.

On returning, the priest kindly agreed to answer some of my questions, the most pressing of which still had to do with the menorahs. These he understood to be Syrian, the candles representing each of Marttaśmūni's seven children. Without further ado or provocation, he went on to explain that the cloth in the glass case was of central importance. Originally kept in a church in Iraq, it was brought to Peroor in 1993 by the Musil bishop, Isaac Zacha Zevarius, after the shadow appeared and fixed itself. The relationship between Peroor and Mosil apparently stems back around 100 years, when Malayali bishops Joseph Mar Dionysius and Kochuparambil Mar Kurilos visited Iraq and, in the Musil church, saw the holy shadows. The former of the two bishops returned to Peroor and built a church in Marttaśmūni's honor. I learned later that the Peroor church is not the only one dedicated to Marttaśmūni in Kerala but is currently the most famous.

Because Father Mani had many things to attend to and because I did not want to monopolize his time, we cut our conversation short. He performed a quick blessing over me, and I was on my way. As with my earlier exchange with village members outside the tea stall, I left with questions unanswered about the Jewishness of Marttaśmūni. I thought that an explanation of the church's menorahs would perhaps get to the heart of her religious affiliation, but it did not; instead it seemed the menorahs had been stripped of Jewish association altogether.

Nevertheless, the Jewishness of Marttaśmūni as portrayed in her story, related similarly in other oral and written accounts, seems far from erased or even incidental. It is precisely her staunch Jewishness, expressed by her choosing death rather than eating pork or worshipping idols, for which these pork-eating Christians give her honor. The story in the Hebrew Bible of the mother and her seven sons gruesomely martyred at the hands of Antiochus (in 2 Maccabees 7), although slightly different in detail, relates a similar central message of courage and faithfulness to Jewish tradition (figure 6.2).[7]

Figure 6.2: Paintings of St. George and of Marttasmuni, her guru, and her seven children before the boiling pot of oil. Marttasmuni Church, Peroor.

The fact that this martyred woman's story varies little—whether told outside tea stalls or related in 2 Maccabees or, as I would later read, in Malayalam publications—comes to me as no surprise. From my experience researching Kerala saint traditions I have found that hagiographies of saintly men and women often differ little between official pilgrimage pamphlets, church hymns, or local tellings regardless of the region, religion, or caste. Highly literate as a group, it seems that Keralites are more likely to have access to "official" versions of saints' lives and are therefore less likely to embellish hagiographical details. Nonetheless, this does not mean that the understandings or interpretations of saintly lives and miracles are by any means uniform.

In the case of Marttaśmūni, a clear exegetical difference appears in the introductory chapter to Father Mani's edited book of prayers, dedicated to her (Kallapurathu 1993, 147–50). Here, he links Marttaśmūni's Jewishness to her Christian devotion by framing the story in a way that encourages readers to view her in a Christian light. He introduces her story by writing, "163 years before the birth of Jesus, Marttaśmūni, her seven children, and their guru Eliyāsar, born in the tribe of the Maccabees (of Jesus) waited upon the coming of our Lord and led a holy life" (147). Father Mani then continues with the familiar story. Once finished, he again links this pre-Christian woman and her life to the Christian era.

> Later, when our Lord Jesus was born through St. Mary, the world remembered the woes of Mother Marttaśmūni and knew the power of her prophecy. Her prophecy that king Antiochus would die after three years and that his corpse be eaten by an eagle and fox was also fulfilled. Then a church was built in her name at Karakosh near Mosil. In that church, the mother and children appear every year (149).

Father Mani's portrayal of Marttaśmūni's story reflects a minority view that something is needed to weave her into the Christian fold—however loosely. It represents an element I thought to be "missing" from the narration outside the tea stall. The fact that I perceived this element to be missing, and therefore somehow necessary, testifies to the ways my understanding of religious distinctions is far more rigid—much more like Father Mani's—than that of the majority of Marttaśmūni's devotees.

Of greater importance to devotees, although not unimportant to Father Mani,[8] are the miraculous appearances and blessings bestowed by the martyred nine. To illustrate this, let me return to Father Mani's house. While I waited for him to come home from the hospital, the priest's father held forth in a discussion of Marttaśmūni's apparitions with a group of approximately fifteen of us who sat together as we waited. As the following fragment makes clear, in cases when apparitions and miracles are of focal interest, issues of religious delineation and institutional sanction tend to take a back seat.

FATHER MANI'S FATHER: The Mother appeared on the holy cloth installed there—the Mother and children. So all the people who went there saw it several times. From the face down we saw the whole figure, but the face and hands were the most visible parts. There was a cloak. The face and hands of Mother and the youngest child were very clear. The vest looked somewhat like a shadow. The youngest child was about two years old. They appeared on the cloth, and they walked up and down several times. This takes place within the case. The best vision is on Saturdays. All those who came to church saw that.

WOMAN: Before we installed the cloth, didn't we see an apparition?

FATHER: No, we didn't. The first sighting was three days after it was installed [by the Iraqi bishop]. The first appearance was to an Izhava woman [member of a Hindu community].

WOMAN: Yes, there *was* an apparition.

FATHER: Oh, that was only occasionally to individuals. The apparition to the Izhava woman did happen a few days before the installation. She was an old lady who came for prayer in the evening. This happened during examination time when many children came to pray. The woman was frightened to see the vision. She came out of the church and was looking inside when the children came. The woman then said, "Come over here, I'll show you something." When all the children entered, they saw the apparition walking on the walls, up and down, up and down above the sanctuary. So all of them screamed and shouted.

WOMAN: Out of fear?

Out of joy. So the children came here to report the matter, but by the time we got there it disappeared.

In the above dialogue, Father Mani's father wants to draw attention to the power of the Iraqi cloth (also important to Father Mani during our conversation). His emphasis runs counter to the woman who firmly insists that, in regard to apparitions, the church can hold its own. Similar to Father Mani's Christian frame around the Jewish Marttaśmūni story, the holy cloth, for some, helps to validate the church and devotion in Peroor through its connection to a larger tradition. For others, these kinds of connections do not seem worthy of mention or elaboration and, as expressed by the woman's response to the story told by Father Mani's father, they can even obstruct the force of the "real" story about a miracle. What seems important to many is the efficacy and immediacy of Marttaśmūni and her entourage: their ability to appear and perform miracles in Peroor itself for those who are devoted, without foreign mediation, and regardless of caste or creed.

Kaṭamaṭṭattachan and the "Problem" of Magic

Kaṭamaṭṭattachan's pilgrimage site is the St. George Jacobite Church in Katamattam near Ernakulam (figure 6.3). He draws, as does Marttaśmūni, devotees from a variety of religious backgrounds. Also like Marttaśmūni, Achan's status in relation to Christianity is variously interpreted—not because he was professedly non-Christian, but because his miraculous powers were decidedly unorthodox and, therefore, for some, suspect. During conversations in Kerala about famous or powerful saints, people often make refer-

Figure 6.3: Old style entrance to St. George Kadamattam Church.

ence to Achan as ranking among such saints. Yet opinions about his good standing as a Jacobite Christian seem polarized. The fantastic exploits of Kaṭamaṭṭattachan have such an appeal that they have been published in numerous forms, staged by acting troupes, and featured in two movie productions. Yet, in spite of Achan's fame, some people (predominantly Christians) told me that he was, in fact, excommunicated for his methods because they relied on magic. As a result, the Jacobite church apparently has nothing to do, officially, with his current devotion. For his devotees, however, Christian and otherwise—particularly pilgrims with whom I spoke in Katamattam—Achan is truly revered as a saint. So great is his popularity that his place of pilgrimage receives a steady stream of visitors. To accommodate the unusually large flow of offerings, a large receptacle stands on the roadside outside the church into which passengers on vehicles—from bicycles to buses—toss their coins as they ride past.[9]

In spite of the widely held perception that Achan is a kind of flawed saint, nothing in the many stories I heard and read—even those told by dissenters themselves—directly suggests anything of his questionable standing. Similar to Father Mani's frame around Marttaśmūni's tale, directing the reader to consider her in a Christian light, the message of Kaṭamaṭṭattachan's detractors usually stands as an exegetical prologue to his story and does little to alter the thrust of the account itself. Tales of Achan's miraculous exploits, rather than calling into question his means, describe him as serving a variety of noble ends such as managing evil, settling feuds, humbling the haughty, and winning wars.

A subtle exception to this, a story genre that seems to leave, for some, Kaṭamaṭṭattachan's techniques open for critique, are the tales depicting the saint as a youth and explaining the origins of his extraordinary powers. While these stories often contain great detail and variation, I offer here a summarized version of what was recited to me by a number of people. It also represents a rendition quite similar to the one told in a well-circulated pilgrimage pamphlet (Samuvan 1992).

Living approximately four-hundred years ago, Kaṭamaṭṭattachan (Paulos) was an orphan boy reared by the local church vicar. This vicar also acted as the boy's guru, training him for ordination and eventual succession. One day the guru's cow ran away into a nearby forest, and young Paulos was chosen to lead the search. Venturing deep into the forest after nightfall, the youth came upon a group of "hill people" (*malayarayan*) who brought him to their cave. Cannibalistic by nature, these *malayarayan* decided to make a meal out of Paulos and brought him to their leader. Recognizing Paulos to be an unusually good and talented young man, the leader spared him under the condition that he remain in the cave and not attempt to escape. Paulos agreed and lived with the hill people for a number of years, learning their magic.

Eventually he became restless and sad, longing for the outside world and for the company of his guru. The head magician "guru" took pity on his favorite pupil and, with hopes that Paulos would someday return, he begrudgingly granted the young man permission to leave. The other *malayarayan* (also referred to, particularly at this point, as *piśācu* [devils] or *rakṣāsan* [demons]), lacking such sentimental ties, chased after him, threatening to kill him. Paulos sought refuge in the village church where the doors miraculously locked behind him. His pursuers (in some versions) furiously beat the outside walls with chains, but Paulos, using his magical powers, made the church spin, frustrating their efforts and causing them to flee into the wilderness. United once again with his Christian guru, Paulos was ordained and, after the elder vicar's death, succeeded him as vicar (or "Achan," meaning "priest") of the Kadamattam church.

Other renditions of this story, although maintaining a similar sequence of events, differ most significantly in their portrayal of the cave-dwelling magicians. Some versions place the *malayarayan* in a more benign light: they are not cannibalistic, are not referred to as *piśācu* or *rakṣāsan,* and they allow Achan to leave their cave without further provocation. Painting the most benign picture of the cave-dwelling magicians is the story told to me by K. P. Isaac, the ninety-four-year-old vicar of the Katamattam Jacobite church (figure 6.4). (Although in good health when I met him in 1994, Father Isaac died two years later.) Highly esteemed by Kaṭamaṭṭattachan's devotees, this vicar was described by pilgrims as possessing some of the same powers as the saint himself, passed on in succession from vicar to vicar "like electricity." In spite of his locally exalted position, it seemed Father Isaac, as an ordained priest, had to negotiate the complex interests and skepticism of the institutional Church. The embellishments to Achan's story that he narrated (dramatically, in soft-spoken English) from his upstairs church office expressed this rather tenuous position.

Father Isaac began his tale by casting Kaṭamaṭṭattachan not as an orphan but as an only son to a poor widow. The boy and his mother, as Father Isaac put it, were discovered by a miracle-working bishop from Persia who later became the boy's guru.

> Once a bishop came from Persia to the house of Achan. He [Kaṭamaṭṭattachan] was then a small boy. They could not understand the teacher, but by gesturing with their hands, they could understand one another. Achan was very angry, and the mother was quite helpless. Nothing was there, nothing was there. This priest who had just arrived came to the house and asked for some raw rice, some three or four kernels in number. They handed over the rice and wondered, 'What could he be wanting with this?' He asked the lady to put on

Figure 6.4: 94-year-old vicar of St. George Kadamattam Church, K.P. Isaac.

a fire and boil the rice. When the rice was boiled it filled up the vessel, and the three ate and were fully satisfied.

Father Isaac went on to give details of other miraculous feats performed by the Persian bishop before describing the more familiar pursuit of the (bishop's) cow into the forest. The elderly vicar's elaboration and emphasis upon the foreign miracle-working bishop, replacing the local vicar-guru of other renditions, seems to give a boost to the institutional validity of the story and the saint on two accounts. First, the bishop's Persian origins, once the ecclesial center of Kerala's Syrian Christianity, gives official validation to the guru and, by association, to his magical powers. Second, because the bishop-guru performs holy feats of his own, Achan's magical capabilities, by association, become less suspect. We cannot attribute them solely to lessons learned from cave-dwellers; a high church official who transmits this "holy" knowledge to the boy is also responsible.

Father Isaac's rendition of the young Achan story further disassociates the saint from questionable forces by portraying the cave-dwelling "wild people" (his English term) as benign and shrouded in mystery. It seems the reason these people kept Achan captive was not due to nefarious intent but, rather, for the sake of their own protection: for the preservation of their sacred secrets. Unwittingly discovered by a young man searching at night for his bishop's cow, these wild people had no choice but to keep him captive.

> One day the [bishop's] cow ran away into the forest and it was feared that she would be eaten by the wild beasts. To search for the cow they sent this widow's son as a leader—he was a leader there. So he rounded up many people and they started out at night to search for the cow. To light their way, they burned coconut leaves, something which was done in those days. This light was necessary because of the wild beasts. In such a way they searched for the cow but nobody could find her. When the party returned, Achan was missing and no one knew where he was.

> In the forest there were wild people who lived in the caves in the rocks. Their work was as magicians. They went all over the place during the day gathering food for their meals and at night they brought whatever they had found and ate it. No one was allowed to find out the place where they were living. This deacon [Kaṭamaṭṭattachan], by chance, approached this cave. Finding him there at the entrance of the cave, they picked him up and entered the cave. He could not be let out at any rate. What is there, we do not know, but whatever they have is theirs. Their prayers they learned

by heart—by hearing alone. No books, no church. In such a way, Achan also, who was a deacon learned something. Perhaps. It is not so sure. That is a holy matter.

Noncannibalistic and prayerful yet ultimately cloaked in mystery, the wild people and their ways may have been—or maybe not—instrumental in Kaṭamaṭṭattachan's training as a powerful holy man. This, Father Isaac leaves up to our own imaginations.

For those who do not leave so much to the imagination—storytellers who seem less interested in disassociating Achan from questionable influences—descriptions of the cave-dwellers are rarely neutral. Nor are they always split between a good leader and his sinister cohorts. Rather, many oral accounts refer to these cave dwellers uniformly as *piśācu* and *rakṣāsan,* whose magic is clearly pernicious. These demonic characters cruelly take Achan hostage in their cave, flatly deny the homesick young man his freedom, and, when he eventually attempts an escape, they use their magical powers to keep him from leaving. But, since Kaṭamaṭṭattachan has observed and learned so well over the years, the young hero ultimately overcomes their evil efforts by using their powers against them. One might assume that devotees trying to spare Achan criticism might also spare him from associations with demonic powers as well, and that, as a consequence, the stories they tell would be less likely to expound on the magicians' evil ways and on Achan's acquisition of their powers. Yet I found that supporters and detractors alike often told tales of demonic cave magicians and lessons the saint learned from them.

For scholars of Hindu traditions, the theme in which "evil" gets converted for good ends is likely a familiar one. In Kerala, there are small shrines outside many Hindu temples—consisting of a *sarpa* stone and a *yakṣi* stone—which are meant to be sites for offering devotion to the snake and the *yakṣi*, respectively, thus transforming their potentially malignant powers. The Keralite *yakṣi* most commonly gets portrayed as a kind of vampire-like female—a deceptively beautiful woman who dwells in the night-blooming *pala* tree.[10] Lurking mainly in uninhabited areas, the *yakṣi*'s prey are commonly unsuspecting men whom she entices and later kills by sucking their blood. One of Achan's most widely told tales is his domestication of a fierce *yakṣi* (she works temporarily as a servant in his elderly aunt's home) by driving a nail into the top of her head. In this instance, Kaṭamaṭṭattachan not only channels potentially demonic magical powers for good ends but, on top of this, these powers work to tame and make good use of a potentially murderous woman.

The theme of transforming dangerous events and properties into benign forces—complicating normative distinctions between evil and good, calamity and cure—emerges not only within Hindu traditions but in Christian ones as well, and not only in India but also in Europe (far from Hindu influences). Among the many Christian examples is the tradition of Saint Agatha, a martyr from Sicily, who was tortured by rods, racks, and fire, culminating in the torment of having her breasts sliced (or twisted) off. Consequently she is invoked for protection against diseases of the breasts as well as against fire, especially eruptions of Mt. Etna—seemingly combining breast and fire motifs into one. The notion that "evil" is transformed into posthumous power strikingly emerges in Agatha's iconographical emblem: two bloody breasts on a plate (Farmer 1992, 6). According to tradition, Saint Apollonia was seized by pagan enemies who broke her teeth with blows to her jaws. Religious art most commonly depicts her as holding a tooth in a pair of pincers or else having her teeth extracted by an elaborate machine. As to be expected, Apollonia has traditionally been invoked by people with tooth pain (Farmer, 28).[11]

These examples of saintly transformations of and subtle complicity with evil suggest that Achan's use of nefarious encounters is not as unconventional as it first may seem. As is the case with Apollonia and Agatha, Achan's powers are not proven through his ability to banish or negate adversity (in the form of yakṣis or cave demons) but, rather, through his consistent association with and manipulation of the same. In fact, as reflected in the popularity of the demon cave dweller theme in Achan's story, the strength of his powers seems to rely on their relationship with and transformation of evil forces—forces over which their saint wields special control. As one Christian man who worked on the church grounds put it, "everything was under him, and, therefore, no one could control him." Lessons learned from both the church guru and the guru of the wilds are what make Kaṭamaṭṭattachan invincible. For those who come to his shrine, it is his invincibility, not his good standing within the Jacobite tradition, that enables him to bestow blessings and therefore be worthy of devotion. Similar to Marttaśmūni, it is the wonder-working capacity of the saint—not his official status—that draws devotees into the human-saint relationship.

Sister Alphonsa and the Story of the Muslim Boy

Although the final "saint" invoked to make my argument is not yet canonized, she is, in contrast to the two discussed above, beyond reproach or apology in the eyes of her Roman Catholic community. Sister Alphonsa (1910–1946), a nun from the Bharananganam Clarist convent, Kottayam district, was beatified in 1987 (one step short of full-fledged sainthood) by John Paul II. She epitomizes not only officially sanctioned female holiness but also, for some, Indian Christian identity.

Alphonsa's story, as told not only by her pilgrimage pamphlets but also by devotees, is primarily one of suffering. Official hagiography depicts her agony as life-long and multidimensional: she was raised by a stern foster mother, teased by school children, and endured serious illness throughout her twelve years as a Clarist Sister. Emphasized in songs, stories, and anecdotes are Alphonsa's later years of suffering, beginning with her courageous leap into a smoldering ash pit, causing severe burns to her legs. Alphonsa reportedly underwent this self-immolation in order to make herself an unsuitable match, securing her future as a nun.[12] This focus upon courageous self-sacrifice and bed-ridden agony in Sister Alphonsa's later life fits her squarely into the most common category for female Christian sainthood, "fortitude in illness" (Weinstein and Bell 1982, 234).

Commentaries on and interpretations of Alphonsa's life often portray her as an emblematic Indian Christian in that her life articulates reverse-Orientalist values privileging the "East" (i.e., spiritual, traditional, nonmaterialistic) over the "West" (i.e., hedonistic, modern, technological). Typical of sentiments related mostly by clergy and nuns but also by lay people at Sister Alphonsa's shrine, Salomi P. L.'s master's thesis argues that Alphonsa "reminds the materialistic world and inspires it to embrace suffering when it is not possible to avoid them [sic]" (1992, 82). She goes on to write that Alphonsa "understood the meaning and value of suffering. The modern man who seeks worldly pleasures and luxuries of life could not see anything special in Alphonsa's life of suffering" (89). Although the author does not explicitly link the "materialistic world" and those who seek "worldly pleasures and luxuries" with the West, such associations are often taken for granted by Malayalis, especially Christian clergy or nuns. Keralite Christians often perpetuate such Orientalist stereotypes to assert their Catholicism as not only genuine but in some ways superior, due to their position as Indian (read Eastern) rather than Western.

Perhaps because her cult is a fairly recent one, details of Sister Alphonsa's life tend to vary only subtly between official and local tellings and between those who knew her and those devoted to her. Somewhat like Marttaśmūni's narrative tradition, Alphonsa's life account is variously framed so as to offer storytellers' interpretations. Because clergy and nuns often (though not exclusively or consistently) think of Sister Alphonsa as emblematic for Kerala Christian living, they often describe her life of pain and suffering as a model of asceticism to follow. Many devotees understand Alphonsa's pain not as something to emulate but as a powerful source for her healing. Like Marttaśmūni's gruesome martyrdom and Achan's trials with demons, Alphonsa's life-long tribulations act to both validate and fuel her capacity as miracle worker in her devotees' lives.

As with Marttaśmūni and Achan, Alphonsa's reputation as healer draws people in large numbers and from various backgrounds to her shrine. It is the strength of her healing powers, not details of her life, that generates the greatest enthusiasm for storytelling. Within this narrative genre, devotees often put little emphasis upon their own or Alphonsa's religious affiliation—a statement in itself—while others applaud her apparent disregard for religious distinction as reflecting a generous power that transcends affiliation. A minority perspective, held primarily but not exclusively by priests and nuns, views such interreligious generosity differently. In such cases, Alphonsa's seemingly indiscriminate performance of miracles is perceived, in part, as spreading the Christian faith.

This brings me to the story of the Muslim boy, one of Alphonsa's most famous posthumous miracle accounts. This cure, involving the correction of a boy's clubbed feet, took place in the northern Kerala district of Thalassery about twenty years ago and is one of three official miracles investigated by the Vatican for Alphonsa's beatification process. The fact that storytellers—primarily nuns from the Clarist convent—consistently refer to the account as the story about "the Muslim boy" and not "the boy from Thalassery" or even "the boy with clubbed feet" attests to the fact that his religious affiliation is, for them, significant. If he were Catholic or even a non-Catholic Christian, it is doubtful that people would refer to his story as the one about "the Christian boy." Several nuns at the Clarist convent told me abbreviated versions of the story, some of which highlighted the fact that the healing of Muslims is a means by which Alphonsa helps to spread Christianity.

At one point during my stay in Kerala, I made a trip to Thalassery and arranged to meet with Bishop Sebastian Valopilly, an ardent devotee of Alphonsa. It was he who suggested to the Muslim boy with the clubbed feet that he pray to the saint for a miracle. Before meeting the now-retired bishop, I learned of his rather valiant reputation for championing the cause of needy people, regardless of religious affiliation. Particularly indebted to the bishop are the people who settled the thick forests of Thalassery during World War II and soon afterward. At that time, general shortages and hardships caused large numbers of Malayali Christians and some Hindus to move northward to take advantage of available cheap land. Combating serious obstacles such as wild animals and rampant malaria, these impoverished immigrants were particularly vulnerable during their early years of settlement. Before their arrival, large communities of Muslims were already established in the area but primarily in coastal trade centers. Valopilly, referred to as "our bishop" by people of all religious backgrounds, became famous for his ability to appeal to the government and other sources to assist the newly arrived agriculturists and poor Muslim locals. In 1957 when the Marxist Party came to power, a Brahmin politician leaving Thalassery for Thiruvananthapuram, Kerala's capital, "gave" (for a nominal price) Bishop Valopilly his oceanside estate as a token of his gratitude. This

Figure 6.5: Retired Bishop Valopilly in front of his favorite statue of Sr. Alphonsa. Bishop's House, Thalassery.

expansive property is the current bishop's headquarters and home to Valopilly, a number of seminarians, nuns, and priests.[13]

Prominently displayed in front of the main entrance to the bishop's house, raised up in the center of a large, lotus-filled pond, is an imposing statue of Sister Alphonsa (figure 6.5). During my visit with the bishop, he asked me to take a good look at the statue, to make sure I noted that it is more beautiful than the ones in Bharananganam, much more like the real person. The bishop's great devotion to Alphonsa is due, in part, to the fact that he spent some time with her during the last year of her life. Valopilly's first placement after his ordination was in Bharananganam, where he lived from December 1945 through March 1946. Here, he was commissioned to regularly administer Communion to Alphonsa "with these very hands," as he put it. He explained to me that it was God's will that he meet her, so that he could spread the news about her. This was the theme of his homily that morning at a Mass celebrating the first day of his jubilee year, marking fifty years of priesthood.

It was in the context of his reminiscing about Alphonsa and his own part in spreading her devotion that the bishop asked if he had told me the story about the Muslim boy. After telling him that I had heard it from others but not yet from him, he enthusiastically proceeded to relate his own account, filling in the missing details of the nuns' more abbreviated versions:

> About ten years ago, when I was in a small village in Wayanad outside Manatavady, I saw a boy walking with some difficulty, using a stick. As he approached me I noted that both of his feet were turned upside down. I had a stack of holy cards in my pocket with Alphonsa's picture on them, so I pulled one of them out and gave it to the boy. When I told the boy that he should pray to this woman for the cure of his feet, the boy—he was quite smart for a ten-year-old boy—replied, "But I'm a Muslim and, besides, I was born this way." I replied that God is very powerful, so let's pray. A few months later, a boy and a gentleman appeared at the house here. I didn't recognize them at first but soon learned that it was the Muslim boy with his father, here to tell me that his feet had been cured through their prayers to Sister Alphonsa. They showed me the calluses on the tops of his feet, and you could see the marks which had been made from the years of his walking with his feet turned under. Before they left, the three of us had our pictures taken.

The two visitors explained to the bishop that the boy had taken the holy card in his hands and "simply asked Alphonsa that, if she could help him, could she please fix his feet." Several days later, one of the boy's feet turned around. He and some members of his family then took up praying in earnest for the healing of his other foot. It eventually turned around as well.

Conditioned by the frame some of the nuns at the Clarist convent give to Alphonsa's miracle stories and anticipating a similar perspective from this high Church official, I felt compelled to ask the bishop, once he finished his story, whether "the Muslim boy" had become a Christian as a result of his cure. Responding as though I had not heard him during his recital, the bishop insisted rather sternly, "No, he's *Muslim*." Conversion, for the bishop, was not a foreseeable or even a desirable result of the boy's healing. Consistent with the views of a man known for his efforts to improve the material well-being of those within his jurisdiction—regardless of religious affiliation—the bishop concerned himself with the healing of a physical disability, not a denominational one. Bishop Valopilly does tell this story to demonstrate his part in spreading good news throughout the region—but it is not The Good News of Christianity. It is that of Alphonsa's healing power.

This is not to say that the bishop does not, in other contexts, strongly identify with and celebrate his own Catholic Christian tradition. In spite of his concern for the community's health and well-being in a way that transcends religious division, the bishop still refers to this story as the one about "the Muslim boy," and he takes care to note that this "smart boy" initially resisted a cure from a Christian saint. Likewise, non-Christian devotion to Achan and Marttaśmūni, although involving a departure from normative religious delineation, does not necessarily mitigate the devotee's sense of affiliation. Moreover, portrayals of Marttaśmūni as unapologetically Jewish and Kaṭamaṭṭattachan as learning from demons does not compromise, for most people, these saints' connection with their Christian places of devotion. Ultimately, it appears that involvement with and perceptions of religious healing offer instances in which normative categorizations of religious traditions—that is, institutional and scholarly—are breached but not obliterated.

It is also important to emphasize that the bishop's tale breaks the dichotomy between local and official sentiments set up in this article's first two saint cult examples, in which priests and nuns appear to be more concerned with traditional parameters than do the devotee "folk." Father Mani distinguishes himself from the devotional norm by framing Jewish Marttaśmūni's story so that she becomes a spokeswoman for the coming of Jesus. Likewise, Father Isaac describes Achan's powers in ways that are somewhat institutionally palatable. To be fair, it only makes sense that those closely tied to institutional structures will more likely be interested in clearly distinguishing their parameters. Yet there are important exceptions to this trend, the Thalassery bishop being one of them.

Some Final Stories: Scholars, Colonizers, and Politicians

To conclude, I wish to point out that this tension or continuum between religion as a means for delineating belief and religion as conduit of miraculous power—typically between institutional or scholarly representations and localized expressions—is by no means limited to Indian Christianity. Arguing along these lines, Talal Asad notes that the category and function of religion as currently and broadly construed by religion scholars—by theologians and anthropologists alike—invariably reflect post-Enlightenment Christian understandings. Because, as Asad argues, the particular lens through which we view religion tends to see it as offering and reflecting internally held beliefs, religious symbols are thus meant to be understood, and rituals are meant to reflect meaning. Asad identifies this narrow and disembodied construction of religion as part of a dehistoricization that allows religion "to be abstracted and universalized" (Asad, 42). It is ultimately problematic that religion as a dehistoricized cognitive construct "invites us to separate it conceptually from the domain of power" (29). While Asad's critique is aimed primarily at analyses of religion that underestimate its connection to political and institutional power, I am saying that to overlook the importance of miraculous power in our understanding of religion likewise runs the risk of dehistoricizing and universalizing.

As the preceding stories demonstrate, perceptions and delineations of religion are often tied to efficacy rather than creed. To overlook the importance of a saint's miraculous power would largely be, from the perspective of his or her devotees, to miss the point. Yet the institutional and scholarly focus, if we are to buy Asad's argument, often does miss the point. Speaking of missing the point, it seems my initial confusion about the healed Muslim boy who remained Muslim as well as "Christian" Marttaśmūni's Jewishness reflects, in a basic and perhaps typical way, my narrow expectation that religion is tied to belief rather than to healing power. Demonstrating approaches similar to mine, Father Mani and Father Isaac's versions of the Marttaśmūni and Achan stories seemingly shift the emphasis away from miraculous efficacy. At the very least, the priestly versions complicate the "point" of the stories by introducing issues of belief and institutional delineation into the equation—concerns that many devotees find, in this context, somewhat expendable.

Pushing this critique of dehistoricized, decontextualized constructs a bit further and on slightly different terrain is Nicholas Dirks's analysis of the caste system in India. Dirks argues that "caste itself as we now know it is not a residual survival of ancient India but a specifically colonial form of civil society." In contrast to what many people today understand to be the eternal order of things in India, "Kings were not inferior to Brahmins; the political domain was not encompassed by the religious domain" (1992, 59). According to Dirks, current rigid notions of caste identity have emerged through imperialist reductions of what was in fact a complex weave of societal forces existent in precolonial India. This process that reduced Indian society to a "religious" category reflects "a striking disregard for ethnographic specificity, as well as a systematic denial of the political mechanisms that selected different kinds of social units as most significant at different times" (Dirks, 60).

Although I do not claim that religion scholars or even religious institutions can unilaterally shape local perceptions in the same way that colonizers shaped Indian society (which I think can also be overestimated),[14] it seems Dirks describes a dynamic not totally unrelated to Asad's view of the construction of religion. In the same way that British colonizers imposed abstracted Orientalist formulas reducing India to religion and caste, religion scholars' privileging of familiar forms and interpretations logically lead to similar reductions and misunderstandings. Decontextualized understandings of religion that focus solely upon established or projected belief systems and creeds at the expense of seemingly less-than-tidy practices forfeit vital complexities and differences and, as much of this volume demonstrates, notions of boundaries and identities that are more permeable than rigid.

In line with Dirks's argument, the problem with abstracted imperialist or scholarly views is not merely one of inaccuracy or insufficiency. Ahistorical constructions of overly tidy categories—for example, "Hinduism" (or "Christianity" for that matter) in its most narrow sense—have created situations where religious tension and violence erupt.[15] It thus seems we have a responsibility to pay attention to and document contextualized religious expressions and practices. This is particularly the case when such lived expressions reflect religious affiliations and identities that defy politically contrived rigidities.

As I understand it, redefining or at least broadening our constructions and interpretations of religion through greater contextualization should be about decentering ourselves epistemologically or, put another way, paying heed to other epistemological centers. The fact that Christians from Peroor house a Jewish patron saint in their church or that Muslims from northern Kerala garner blessings from a Christian figure or that Hindus flock in large numbers to all three of the shrines described above make these people no less rooted in Christianity, Islam, or Hinduism, respectively. As I have argued, the context of real life in which material suffering and hope are a part of religious expression often causes the center of gravity to shift. Or, more accurately put, such contexts reveal entirely different centers, ones that complicate scholarly and institutional delineations yet do not entirely negate them. As Akeel Bilgrami puts it in his argument against Islam as a dehistoricized monolith, "'(c)ontext is only the beginning of wisdom.' It does not sweep conceptual problems away nor does it herald the end of theory; it merely removes the rigidities of a long standing theoretical tradition" (Bilgrami 1993, 274). Ultimately, while theological and institutional parameters are of great importance to many, to scholars and devotees alike, they do not—and must not—tell the whole story.

Notes

1. My thanks to Craig Burgdoff, Ann Gold, Mary Keller, Bill Preston, and Selva Raj, for helpful conversations and suggestions incorporated into the following. Also thanks to Anitha Chrisanthus for assistance in translation and to the American Institute of Indian Studies for supporting fieldwork in Kerala in 1994. Interviews and stories emerged from this eleven-month research period.

2. The Orthodox Syrians and Jacobites are branches of the ancient Syrian Christian tradition in Kerala. Their split occurred in 1911 when about half their members switched their allegiance from the Patriarch in Antioch to the Katholicos based in Kerala. Those who maintain their allegiance to the Patriarch are today referred to as the Jacobites (Yakoba), and those who follow the Katholicos are Orthodox Syrian. The following stories' references to Syrian Christian seats of power—contemporary Iraq and ancient Persia—demonstrate how Kerala's Syrian Christian ties to the Middle East continue to play themselves out on a number of levels. For an extensive discussion of contemporary Jacobite-Orthodox Syrian relations, see Vishvanathan (1993).

3. The richly pluralistic context that sustains Kerala Christianity allows ample opportunity for issues of religious delineation to arise. Approximately one-quarter each Muslim and Christian and one-half Hindu, Kerala also hosts a remnant of the thriving Jewish community that emigrated to Israel in the late 1940s.

4. My discussion of Alphonsa, below, briefly picks up this subject of Kerala Christian hegemony. For a fuller discussion of the ways in which Kerala Christian saint cults articulate distance from and superiority over European culture and religion, see Dempsey 2001.

5. While I distinguish between understandings of religion as belief versus religion as power, as witnessed in Kerala, this is not to say that current European or North American Christianity does not also concern itself with power and healing. For U.S. examples see Orsi (1985, 1996) and MacDannell (1995). For European examples, see Badone (1990).

6. For a description of Manarcad's annual festival honoring Mary, see Younger (2001).

7. The most significant difference between the Keralite and biblical stories is in their cast of characters. In 2 Maccabees all seven children are sons, whereas Marttaśmūni's children seem to include girls (see fig. 2). Also, the Maccabees story makes no mention of a male companion for the Mother. The tortures involving severing limbs and frying in oil are included in both accounts. My thanks to Selva Raj for bringing Maccabees to my attention.

8. In his book Father Mani makes an exhaustive list of Marttaśmūni's many blessings.

9. I discovered the function of this unusual receptacle the hard way. I was standing in front of it waiting for the bus, directly in the line of fire, when a bus stopped on the other side of the road and let loose a shower of coins in my direction.

10, For more on Kerala *yakṣis,* see Dempsey (2000) and Caldwell (2000).

11. For further discussions of ambivalent Christian powers that complicate institutional prescriptions for benign sanctity, see Caroll (1992), Christian (1981), and Dempsey (2001).

12. A woman who burns herself as a form of resistance is a common motif in Indian folklore (Narayana Rao 1986, 140–41). For a discussion of this and other ways in which Alphonsa's story resonates with Indian motifs of female sanctity, see Dempsey (2001).

13. Although Bishop Valopilly is best known for his politicking on a grand scale, he is also famous for having qualities of personal integrity and humility unusual in a bishop. For instance, Sr. Josephina, my research collaborator in Bharananganam, described her first encounter with the bishop over thirty years ago, when she and another Sister were in Thalassery for a teachers' evaluation. When they arrived at the bishop's house he went into the kitchen and served them himself – unthinkable behavior for a bishop. Reflecting on the incident, Sr. Josephina remarked that "he acted just like a father to us." On second thought, she said, "No, better than a father. He was like a mother to us."

14. For elaborations upon the hybrid nature of colonial power and native responses, see Nandy (1983); Bhabha (1985); and Suleri (1990). For a fuller discussion of the tenacity and resilience of indigenous agendas in the face of colonizing forces in Kerala—in spite of outward appearances—see Dempsey (2001).

15. In an argument similar to Dirks's, Pandey convincingly proposes that an overly tidy understanding of "Hinduism" that has led to communalism and religious violence has been created by those who choose to ignore history. More broadly speaking, Pandey states that "(n)ationalisms are fundamentally ahistorical" (1993, 267).

References

Asad, Talal. 1993. *Genealogies of Religion: Discipline and Power in Christianity and Islam.* Baltimore, Md.: Johns Hopkins University Press.

Badone, Ellen, ed. 1990. *Religious Orthodoxy and Popular Faith in European Society.* Princeton, N.J.: Princeton University Press.

Bayly, Susan. 1989. *Saints, Goddesses, and Kings: Muslims and Christians in South Indian Society, 1700–1900.* Cambridge: Cambridge University Press.

Bhabha, Homi. 1985. "Signs Taken for Wonders: Questions of Ambivalence and Authority under a Tree Outside Delhi." *Critical Inquiry* 12:145–65.

Bilgrami, Akeel. 1993. "What is a Muslim? Fundamental Commitment and Cultural Identity." In *Hindus and Others: The Question of Identity in India Today*, ed. G. Pandey, 273–99. New Delhi: Viking Press.

Caldwell, Sarah. 2000. *Oh Terrifying Mother: Sexuality, Violence, and the Worship of the Goddess Kali*. Delhi: Oxford University Press.

Caroll, Michael. 1992. *Madonnas That Maim: Popular Catholicism in Italy since the Fifteenth Century*. Baltimore, Md.: Johns Hopkins University Press.

Christian, William. 1981. *Local Religion in Sixteenth-Century Spain*. Princeton, N.J.: Princeton University Press.

Dempsey, Corinne. 2001. *Kerala Christian Sainthood: Collisions of Culture and Worldview in South India*. New York: Oxford University Press.

———. (2000). "Nailing Heads and Splitting Hairs: Conflict, Conversion and the Bloodthirsty Yakṣi in South India." Presented at the Annual Meeting of the American Academy of Religion, Nashville, Tennessee.

Dirks, Nicholas. 1992. "Castes of Mind." *Representations* 37:59.

Farmer, David Hugh. 1992. *The Oxford Dictionary of Saints*. Oxford: Oxford University Press.

Kallapurathu, Rev. Father Mani. 1993. "Marttaśmūni Ammayum Eḻumakkaḷum Guruvāya Eliyāsaṟum." In *Prārtthana Manjari*, ed. M. Kallapurathu, 147–50. Peroor, Kottayam, n.p.

MacDannell, Colleen. 1995. *Material Christianity: Religion and Popular Culture in America*. New Haven, Conn.: Yale University Press.

Nandy, Ashis. 1983. *The Intimate Enemy: Loss and Recovery of Self under Colonialism*. Delhi: Oxford University Press.

Narayana Rao, Velchuru. 1986. "Epics and Ideologies: Six Telegu Folk Epics." In *Another Harmony: New Essays on the Folklore of India*, ed. A. K. Ramanujan and S. Blackburn, 131–64. Berkeley and Los Angeles: University of California Press.

Orsi, Robert Anthony. 1985. *Madonna of 115th Street: Faith and Community in Italian Harlem, 1880–1950*. New Haven, Conn.: Yale University Press.

———. 1996. *Thank You, St. Jude: Women's Devotion to the Patron Saint of Hopeless Causes*. New Haven, Conn.: Yale University Press.

P. L. Salomi. 1992. "Sister Alphonsa of Bharananganam." Masters Thesis. University of Madras.

Pandey, Gyanendra. 1993. "Which of Us Are Hindus?" In *Hindus and Others: The Question of Identity in India Today*, ed. G. Pandey, 238–72. New Delhi: Viking Press.

Samuvan, C. T. 1992. *Kaṭamattattacharande Māntrika Vidyakaḷ*. Allepey: Vidyārmbam Publishers.

Suleri, Sara. 1990. *The Rhetoric of English India*. Chicago: University of Chicago Press.

Vishvanathan, Susan. 1993. *The Christians of Kerala: History, Belief, and Ritual Among the Yakoba*. New York: Oxford University Press.

Weinstein, Donald, and Rudolph Bell. 1982. *Saints and Society: The Two Worlds of Western Christendom, 1000–1700*. Chicago: University of Chicago Press.

Younger, Paul. 2001. *Playing Host to Deity: Festival Religion in the South Indian Tradition*. New York: Oxford University Press.

CHAPTER 7

Finding a Path in Others' Worlds:
The Challenge of Exorcism

Richard D. MacPhail

Mātā cōlletāṅka (*Mātā* has said), so we went for prayers.
Dr. Kumar pressed his point vigorously:
Nobody—I can challenge—can do this . . . no priest.
A service like this can be done by no priest. It's tremendous. . . .

The cult of the Virgin Mary in south India is a dynamic tradition capable of broad creative variation. Active followers of the Tamil Marian cult, whose numbers rival those of the largest Catholic pilgrimages in the world, are developing a range of culturally distinctive responses to the problem of evil as manifested in human experience. Even casual inquiries will produce recommendations to visit healers and wonder-workers, tied to the powers of the Virgin, patronized by Christians and Hindus alike. Much of the work of these specialists involves the interplay of curse and blessing and, in the transit between them, reputations stand to be made and broken.

This essay examines the functions of possession and exorcism in the construction of sacred and human identity in a popular religious discourse on *Ārōkkiya Mātā*, the Blessed Virgin Mary as Our Lady of Good Health, in Tamil Nadu.[1] It illustrates how Tamil symbolic resources are used to imagine and represent sacred power, to connect ritually with that power, and to symbolically construct social and personal identities in the face of supernatural evil. It also shows how the truth-claims, history, and effects on human lives of the events described here have, for adherents and participants, a coherence all their own—despite the cultural and theological tensions they manifest.

The People of the Cepakulam

The *Kōvai Tūya Mariyannai Cepakulam* (pronounced "jepakulam")[2] is an urban prayer-assembly or community devoted to the Blessed Virgin Mary located in Coimbatore (*Kōvai*), Tamil Nadu. Three sisters, Mrs. S. P. Lourdu Mary, Mrs. K. Sagaya Mary, and Mrs. P. Philomena Mary are at the heart of the *cepakulam,* locally renowned for exorcism and healing. Their Roman Catholic family belongs to a commercial caste, the *vellam ceṭṭiyār*, and is comprised of their parents, Kulandaisami Chettiyar and Savariammal, a fourth sister, Mrs. S. Fatima Mary who resides in the Andaman Islands, and the sisters' husbands and children. They have no brothers. The aged parents are poor, depend on the income of their sons-in-law, and reside with Lourdu Mary, the eldest of the sisters.[3]

Philomena Mary, the youngest sister, is a visionary medium and the central charismatic figure in the *cepakulam*. She was married in 1971. Her husband works in sales, travels regularly, and is away from home for up to four months at a time. Their only child, a daughter, had just completed her high school education at the time of my first visit in June of 1993.

At the heart of the *cepakulam* is the presence of the Blessed Virgin Mary, communicating through Philomena on most Fridays and Saturdays. The fifteen or so homes where *cepakulam* members meet and pray together are invariably packed with devotees—predominantly Roman Catholics with a large minority of Hindus—on these two days. When I first encountered the *cepakulam*, the meetings were being held in Lourdu Mary's three-room thatched and mud-walled house. Lourdu's home was unquestionably the most modest in her neighborhood. The crowd filled its veranda and spilled out into the narrow street.

Dr. S. Kumar, a professor of organic chemistry in a Salem college, Tamil Nadu, became my most useful informant about the workings of the *cepakulam*. He had been summoned from Salem as a semiofficial English-fluent spokesperson when I turned up unexpectedly in June 1993 enquiring about these devotions. What follows is an account of his version of events, a perspective that carries a certain "institutional" authority that interviews with casual visitors might not.

History

According to Dr. Kumar, the origins of the *cepakulam* can be traced to the first Saturday of February 1990, when Sagaya Mary's second daughter, Bernadette, was praying the Rosary after Mass in the Seven Dolours Church near her home. As she prayed, Bernadette heard a voice from Mother Mary's

statue saying, "Come, come." Dr. Kumar related that Bernadette was reluc-
tant to respond because, "such things as feeling like we are being called can
be imagined," so she ignored it. After hearing the same call from the statue
again and again, Bernadette summoned her courage, went to the statue, and
touched it. "Today, at three o'clock I'm coming to your house," said the
voice from the statue, "go and tell your Mommy." Bernadette immediately
went home and related her experience to her mother.

Sagaya responded to her daughter's story with disbelief. "What a fool
you are! How is it possible that Mother Mary will speak? Don't tell this to
anybody else. Definitely they will misunderstand you. You'll be branded as
mad. Go." In spite of her mother's dismissal, Bernadette held her ground.
"Although you speak like this, one day She's definitely going to come. That
day, you'll understand that what I am saying now is true."

After lunch, while Lourdu Mary and Sagaya Mary were sitting and
talking in the veranda, the matter apparently having been dismissed, Bernadette
was in the kitchen, praying the Rosary before Mother Mary's picture.
Bernadette suddenly began to shout, "*Mariyē vālka! Mariyē vālka!* Hail Mary!
Hail Mary!" Lourdu and Sagaya protested this disturbance from the veranda:
"There must be some time spared for prayer, but not prayer at any time you
like. Why do you do all these things? Don't be mad after prayer." Bernadette
would not stop, however, and continued chanting, "*Mariyē vālka! Mariyē vālka!*
Hail Mary . . . !" Alarmed, the two women rushed into the kitchen.

Bernadette ceased her chanting and addressed her mother with authority,
"*Cākāya, en makalē* (Sagaya, my daughter), don't you know who I am?"
Holding her own mother's chin, she commanded, "Just look at my eyes.
Don't you know who I am? I told Bernie that I would be coming to your
house at 3 o'clock today, but you did not believe it. I have come. You may
not believe that I am Mother Mary, but do not suspect that I am an evil spirit
or something like that."

After narrating the above series of events, Dr. Kumar informed me that
Sagaya had married a police constable posted in the remote Andaman Islands. Although both wife and husband were originally from Coimbatore, all
four of their children were born in the Andamans. When Sagaya's husband
found that it was too costly to keep a family there, he decided to leave her
and the children in Coimbatore with her relatives and visits them only on his
annual leave. According to Dr. Kumar, Bernadette went on to narrate to her
aunt and mother events known to them concerning her father in the Andamans,
details of which she could not have been aware.

Sagaya's nature, said Dr. Kumar, is to be thoroughly suspicious and
sceptical, and to never take anything for granted. In spite of this, Sagaya
began to suspect that, although evil spirits can take possession of people, this
might well be Mother Mary. After narrating many confidential events in

Sagaya's life, Bernadette said, "I am Mother Mary, *Vēḷāṅkaṉṉi Ārōkkiya Mātā.*" She then prescribed certain devotions for the family to observe strictly—to perform novenas to the Infant Jesus on Thursdays, to pray to Jesus on Fridays, and to perform novenas to herself on Saturdays. Sagaya agreed, despite her reservations about what had just happened to her daughter. Sagaya's rationale for accepting *Mātā'*s instructions, as she later told Dr. Kumar, was that the family had already been in the habit of conducting novenas, so there was nothing new in that, nor was there anything improper about praying on Thursday, Friday, and Saturday, as *Mātā* had asked.

From the second week of February 1990, the prescribed prayers were conducted by all members of the extended family. On each occasion, after the Rosary, Mother Mary would speak to them through Bernadette. After two months, however, Sagaya became concerned that if Mary continued to come to Bernadette, the relatives might avoid arranging her marriage and thus asked Mother Mary to choose some other woman through whom to speak. While *Mātā*'s presence was indeed a grace, and the family did not want to seem ungrateful, it was an inconvenient and uncomfortable favor.

Another woman, a relative who had miscarried three children consecutively, spent much time praying in the Seven Dolours Church where *Mātā* had first come to Bernadette. One evening in April 1990, during the Rosary in the *cepakulam,* before *Mātā* came to Bernadette, this woman began to call, "*Makaḷē cakāya,*" just as Bernadette had done the first time. This meant, said Dr. Kumar, that Mother Mary had selected her. *Mātā* spoke through this second medium for nearly six months. It was during this time that Dr. Kumar, who is also a relative, became active in the prayer group.

After some months, a sister of the second medium became distressed, like Sagaya, about the potential consequences for her family. Dr. Kumar explained that when *Mātā* gives a revelation, she directs people to take the medium and conduct prayers in the clients' own house. The medium is obliged to go, often to distant places in the company of strangers and to stay away for several days, leaving the children at home alone. The second medium's husband, a commercial traveler who is often away from home himself, also objected. Thus it was that *Mātā* finally chose to speak through Mrs. Philomena. Dr. Kumar had spoken with Mother Mary through both the second medium and Philomena and attested that the pattern of *Mātā*'s speech through both women was the same, without any detectable change.

Philomena likens her visions to a video cassette being played; she can see the house where she is to go. When she prays in the *cepakulam,* she sees people's names written in golden letters and calls them to her. Although Philomena covers her head when *Mātā* comes to her and cannot see who is entering and leaving, unknown newcomers are often summoned by name or

by some distinctive characteristic. Dr. Kumar became convinced, after check-
ing with many such people, that neither their presence in the *cepakulam* nor
their problem could have been known to Philomena when *Mātā* called them.

"We can put any questions to Mother Mary," Dr. Kumar told me. "She'll
give answers, but we cannot ask Philomena. Philomena does not know anything." This observation is consistent with many accounts of possession states,
but not with Philomena's own curious assertion that it is she who sees the
houses of the afflicted and the written names of clients to be called. Clearly
there is some ambivalence in Philomena's process of passing bodily control
over to *Mātā* as she moves into the trance state in which *Mātā* knows as
Philomena does not, and speaks as Philomena cannot.

Regarding Sagaya's role in the *cepakulam,* Kumar asserted, "While I am
God's servant (*ūḻiyaṉ*), coming for these three years, and I have spoken with
Mātā over a hundred times, whenever she speaks it is always Sagaya who is
by her side." Indeed, as I observed, Sagaya is central to *cepakulam* functioning. It was her daughter, Bernadette, who first heard the voice of *Mātā* and
it is she who always sits next to the second medium during her trances and
accompanies her on visits to clients' homes. Sagaya is also the main actor in
the Saturday *maraṇapāṭu* (death-wounds)[4] exorcism rite as well as the leader
of the *ūḻiyar*, the *cepakulam* "servants."

The *Āvi Kaṭṭu,* a Para-liturgy

The *āvi kaṭṭu,* or "spirit-binding," is the central ritual process within the
cepakulam and a primary technique used for dealing with the forces of evil,
understood principally as *māntirikam* or sorcery. For participants in the
cepakulam, the *āvi kaṭṭu* appears to be a highly successful, "wide spectrum"
antidote to *māntirikam* of all sorts.

Friday activities at the *cepakulam* begin at 3:00 p.m. Participants in the
āvi kaṭṭu bring with them twenty candles, which they turn over to the *ūḻiyan*.
The liturgy itself is preceded by a series of testimonies, lasting about ninety
minutes. Participants recount how *Mātā*, speaking through Philomena, had
resolved their problems, how this had changed their lives, and the importance
of following, for long periods if necessary, the rituals prescribed for correct-
ing their supernatural afflictions. Clients' testimonials always concern serious
emotional, physical, or social problems and extol the treatment provided by
the *cepakulam*. One mother reported how, when her son was ill, dying in the
hospital, *Mātā* had saved him. "Anyone who even *steps* into this home," the
mother insisted, "will be blessed." Counseling patience to those who might
have come many times without any result, she assured them: *"Mātā will
definitely bless you when you need it."*

Such testimonials appear to be critical to the construction of Philomena's and the *cepakulam*'s efficacy, truth-value, and power. Without such verbal evidence, constantly reiterated, an initial failure of the *āvi kaṭṭu* to yield the desired effect might send the clients away with nothing good to say for it. Instead, persistence in following the prescribed regimen becomes a recipe for eventual success. Initial failure is only an early indication of the serious and refractory nature of the affliction.

During testimonials, one man speaks of his conversion through the *cepakulam* and his eventual selection as *ūḻiyaṉ*. Involved with alcohol and knife-fights, always in trouble with the police, he was impatient and rude and condemned by his whole family. After his parents had experienced healing in the *cepakulam,* they invited Philomena and Sagaya home to pray over him. *Mātā* asked him for a written commitment that he would not drink. He kept his commitment for a few days, but drank again. "Very little," he confessed, "yet my limbs began to ache and become stiff, and I returned home." Realizing the magnitude of his transgression, he repented and lit the five candles. "*Mātā* spoke to me and asked me to serve her," he declared. "Now I accompany the sisters wherever they go. I have changed now because of their patience."

There are also testimonies to unresolved affliction. A widow reports that her only son has fallen ill. With three unmarried daughters, she is beset with worries, and the crops have failed. She asks the congregation for prayer. The para-liturgy begins with a prayer by Philomena, followed by an intercession from Sagaya: "They have come seeking your help. Bless their families. Grant their wishes. The problems in each of their families, Father, look at them and bless them. . . ." The congregation recites the Rosary, then sings a hymn, "*Ārōkkiya Tāy* (Health-Mother), grant us health." There are announcements about the *āvi kaṭṭu* to take place the following day, Saturday, and about payment for the candles to be used in it.

As these announcements are concluding, Philomena begins to sing quietly and mournfully in the background. All direct their attention to her. "Your body is covered with wounds. Oh, *Anpin Rācā* (Love-King),[5] why did you do this divine sacrifice?" Expressing her agony, Philomena describes in the first person how a sword is piercing her heart, "How I quiver and flail about in agony!! Is this why you came as my son?" Philomena wails, "*Ammā, Mātāvē, Yēcuvē* (Mommy, O Mother, O Jesus), I'm feeling giddy." This appears to be a transition stage when Mother Mary's and Philomena's persons are in contention for—or comingled within—Philomena's mind and organs of speech. The process seems to be cooperative rather than a struggle.

In trance, Philomena speaks as *Mātā*, identifying members of the congregation who are suffering and in need of treatment by name, by what they are wearing, or by those with whom they have come. She often specifies the nature and cause of the affliction. Those identified as having some problem— all but a few in attendance—are given five candles lit from a *kuttuviḷakku* (brass oil lamp) to hold in their hands. They hold them until they have almost entirely melted and are forbidden to extinguish them until instructed. The odor of melted wax, dripping to the floor over cupped hands, is pervasive. When Philomena comes out of the trance, she collapses, exhausted, and eventually revives after resting for some time. As Sagaya explains afterward, "It is *Viyākula Mātā*, the Mother of Sorrows, who is singing through her. When Philomena prays like this, and so many of God's children are set free from the bondage of sin, the Evil One is unhappy and tries to hurt her. She bears all that pain for the good of others. Those who work for the Lord will share in his wounds or death-marks (*maraṇapāṭu*)."

After *Mātā* has identified all the afflicted for this iteration of the *āvi kaṭṭu,* and they have burned their candles as prescribed, Sagaya calls one family or client at a time to sit close to her on the floor. All others observe intently. She is given five candles from those handed over by the client to the *ūḷiyar*. She places them at the corners of an eight-inch (20-cm.) square, with one at its center, representing the *maraṇapāṭu,* the five wounds in Christ's hands, feet, and side. As the candles burn, Sagaya holds her Bible and prays, at least two minutes by each candle, asking Jesus to "wipe out" the client's problems. Tapping the flames with the Bible one by one, Sagaya then snuffs out each candle. The whole process takes about fifteen minutes.

The client for whom this prayer is performed must relight these same five *maraṇapāṭu* candles, usually in some other part of the house and must remain with the candles, or at least within the house, until all five have burned down and extinguished themselves. No effort may be made to extinguish them prematurely. I observed several parties carefully tending the flames to ensure the maximum consumption of wax.

Clients are given a third, fourth, and fifth set of five candles by an *ūḷiyaṇ* and instructed to do the same thing, with prayer, at home. They are to do it as the last act of the day, just before going to bed. The doors and windows must be shut, and they should kneel in front of the candles, arranged in the "five wounds" configuration, and pray. They may read the Bible or say the Rosary. Under no circumstances should they get up from the place until the candles have completely melted, and all five have burned out by themselves.

This process completes one iteration of the *āvi kaṭṭu,* "spirit tying or binding." It is repeated weekly on Fridays, according to the instructions of Mother Mary, without variation. Clients are instructed to return for prayer the following day and for three successive Saturdays. They receive three more sets of candles and repeat the ritual at least three more times, depending on the perceived intransigence of the problem. "If," as Dr. Kumar put it, "we come for three weeks, definitely the problem will be wiped off. Even then, if it is not wiped off. . . . It's similar to taking injections; some diseases are not cured with a few injections and we have to undergo a surgery."

Dr. Kumar also related *āvi kaṭṭu*'s efficacy in the process of exorcism. The brother of his academic colleague, an economics lecturer, was involved with *cēviṉai* (black magic). [6] When the man was reformed his wife began to do *cēviṉai*. Brought to the *cepakulam* under duress, her gold bangles turned black the moment she held the *maraṇapāṭu* candles. This visible sign could not have been merely a psychological effect, insisted Kumar. "If possession is only psychological," continued Kumar, "why should such physical signs occur and why should all the possessed give the same answers?" Elaborating on this point, he described meeting a *mantiravāti* (sorcerer) who could remove gold from a locked and sealed box without opening it through the power of a *pēy*, or dead person's spirit. By the same power, he explained, *mantiravāti*s put *tāyittu* (amulets) and other objects inside places such as walls, and even within persons, without any visible mark of insertion.

Dr. Kumar is confident that it is not by such evil powers that healing takes place in the *cepakulam*, because Jesus' five wounds are honored with five candles by the *āvi kaṭṭiṉār* (spirit binders). He proved to be a fine spokesperson for the truth-value and power manifested in the *cepakulam*, for the authority Philomena derives from *Mātā*, and for the imperative to drain supernatural evil of its resources. He had once been a victim of *cēviṉai;* so severe was his condition that Philomena and her party performed the *āvi kaṭṭu* at his home in Salem. *Mātā* spoke of the presence of a folded copper sheet tied with yellow thread inside which she saw a rusted nail and a tooth along with a *tāyiṭṭu* (charm) hidden somewhere in his house. As *mātā* revealed this, Philomena sank to the floor, speechless, a sign of resistance to an evil spirit. Unable to speak, *Mātā* gestured for a pen and paper and wrote that the objects had been secretly stowed in the loft of Kumar's kitchen. Searching the loft with a candle and much trepidation, Kumar retrieved the items. Grasping them with tongs to prevent any evil force from entering her, Philomena cut the thread with scissors and opened the sheet to find exactly what *Mātā* had described: a tooth and a rusted nail.

Dr. Kumar contended that such powers cannot be attributed to evil spirits acting alone. A *mantiravāti*, one who works with evil spirits, generally for remuneration by malicious clientele, captures *pēy* by performing a *pūcai* (Sanskrit *pūjā*, an offering rite). The *pēy* then becomes subject to the will of the *mantiravāti* and will do anything he commands.

> But here in the *cepakulam* we don't do any such thing. Suppose there is an evil spirit and we want to chase it off. Anybody else, however powerful, will have to give coconuts and other *pūjā* materials. But here, the sisters command it to leave in the name of Jesus

Christ and the spirits have to go. They will undertake anything—
cēvinai, piḷḷicūṇiyam—however toughly it has been done. I once
thought that all this is only psychological, but after coming here, I
have seen with my own eyes. These people are not just acting.

When I returned to the *cepakulam,* four years later, on a Friday in
September 1997, the *āvi kaṭṭu* was being held in Philomena's new three-
story, neatly plastered, reinforced concrete and brick house called *Cepa Iḷḷam*
(Prayer House), a short walk from Lourdu's hut. The ritual was performed in
an upstairs room especially designed as a prayer hall and was packed with
over one hundred clients. Because of the size of the group the entire process
lasted from midafternoon until well into the night. Several *ūḷiyar* replicated
Sagaya's *maraṇapāṭu* work elsewhere in the enhanced facilities, indicating a
devolution of functions and increased social complexity in the *cepakulam.*
The new house is unmistakable evidence of the prosperity the patrons of the
cepakulam have brought to the sisters in a very short time.

Shades of Possession and Spiritual Hierarchy

Who controls such a sacred performance? While the appearance of the
Blessed Virgin Mary to a visionary medium follows well-established Christian
precedents, its form in the *cepakulam* concedes in significant ways to Hindu
patterns of spirit possession which is, for many clients, their only experience
of transcendence. The medium, her colleagues, and clients are located at the
threshold between two worlds of meaning and obliged to construct for themselves a coherent meeting place for expression of both traditions.

The work of Kathleen M. Erndl, in her study of Śeranvali, a popular
Hindu goddess of Himachal Pradesh (Erndl 1989, 1993), offers guidance for
appreciating the Hindu side of this tension. Erndl approaches the question of
control from three perspectives—theological, personal, and collective—and
affirms them all. From the theological point of view, this Hindu model un-
ambiguously asserts the divine patron's self-expression through the medium's
speech organs. It is the goddess herself who directs the possession, which is
the vehicle for her self-manifestation to her people. Her devotees' faith in her
enables the goddess's presence among them in a gracious form, and it is their
faith and yearning that induces her to appear (Erndl 1993, 133).

From the personal point of view, the possession performance is controlled by the cooperation of the one possessed, the medium. As described by
Erndl, "A common pattern emerges: the vehicle participates in the power of
the deity, at first seemingly unwillingly. But gradually she is able to gain
control over this power to a certain extent, to predict its coming, to prevent

it from coming at times, and to bring it on at other times. Idiosyncrasies in
the Goddess's behavior during possession seem to emanate from the vehicle's
personality" (Erndl 1993, 134). This ambivalence of person, and therefore of
control, is evident when Philomena, entering trance, speaks in the first person
alternately as Our Lady of Sorrows and as herself.

My own initial introduction to the sisters one Thursday afternoon in
June 1993, serves to illustrate the question of control from a collective perspective. Our first meeting was fraught with suspicion. I was guided to Lourdu
Mary's doorstep by a local diocesan priest who may have desired to gain
information for his superiors about the activities of the *cepakulam*. First I was
told that *Mātā* had asked to be excused for several weeks and was not expected to come that Friday or Saturday. After some courtesies and conversation, my guide desired to return to his own duties and asked that I leave with
him. I decided to stay and talk further. By the time I left, Philomena had
hinted that *Mātā* might well come at her usual time the next day, after all. It
seemed to me that either a decision had been taken to induce *Mātā*'s presence
the next day in spite of Her "reluctance" or the initial disposition to cancel
the regularly scheduled *āvi kaṭṭu* had been reversed. As I was to learn from
him later, Dr. Kumar had been summoned urgently from Salem immediately
after my departure.

Arriving the next day equipped with audio and video recorders, I was
met by a full house who had been advised that *Mātā* might—or might not—
come that evening. I had the distinct feeling that this was, at the same time,
a previously scheduled event being protected from my foreign incredulity as
well as one managed for my benefit. While it was not clear who exactly was
managing this event, audience participation and the quality of its response
was certainly critical to its effectiveness.

From the collective point of view, notes Erndl, the audience controls the
possession. The enactment of possession has a grammar located in anteced-
ent, accepted cultural meanings which are necessary to validate a vehicle's
genuine possession, as when *Mātā*'s influence shifted from Bernadette, to the
second seer, and ultimately to Philomena. The second medium's frenetic
exclamation, "*Makaḷē Cakāya*," seems, from a naïve outsider's viewpoint,
simplistically imitative of the sole available model, Bernadette. On the other
hand, because it addresses Sagaya *(Cakāya)*, it may indicate just how much
in control of the process Sagaya has been from the start.

Erndl characterizes the mode of communion between the human and
divine orders in the goddess religion she studies:

> Fluid boundaries between self, collectivity and the sacred are con-
> ducive to acceptance of possession phenomena. The audience, by
> interacting with the possessing deity, affirms its presence within the

vehicle, converting what without this interaction would be a disordered subjective experience into a public one (Erndl 1993, 133).

Underlying the fluidity of identity, which is ambivalent and indistinct in possession states, is the taxonomy of humans, spirits of the dead, and gods in south Asian cultures (Stirrat 1992, 86).[7] R. L. Stirrat reports how the Catholic Church in Sri Lanka has attempted to represent the gods as negative images or evil equivalents of the saints, but that this has unintentionally resulted in their incorporation into a single-graded continuum within the category of supernatural beings (Stirrat 1981, 188). Stirrat found that for Catholics in Sri Lanka the highest ranks of demons are populated by the "fallen angels" of the Judeo-Christian tradition, while indigenous gods such as *Shiva, Kataragama, Kāli,* and *Saman* are included along with fallen humans in an intermediate category. Beneath these two categories are the evil beings of the local tradition, resulting in a continuous, three-layered taxonomy of demons (Stirrat 1992, 89–90).

Similarly, Dr. Kumar was eager to qualify the nature of the Hindu gods as vouched for by all the *pēy.* Kumar assured me that he has interrogated *pēy* during exorcism and collected this evidence from the *pēy* themselves. According to these spirits, the Hindu gods are all *iranta āvi* (spirits of the dead) or, as Kumar interpreted the phrase, "fallen angels," and all evil spirits testify to this identity of the gods during the exorcism process. These *iranta āvi* are, he averred, corrupted angelic beings that have been let loose on the earth until the world ends, when they will again be bound. Unlike them, when humans die prematurely by malice or accident, they remain here in the world as *pēy* until their proper time comes; then they go back to God. *Civan* (Sanskrit *Śiva*) is said by the *pēy* to be Lucifer. "It's a pity," Kumar added forlornly, "that Hindus are going after fallen angels. "

The process I observed among Catholic Tamils of eclectically incorporating the gods and demons of the environing majority culture—which is, in fact, their own culture—closely resembles Stirrat's findings, with the difference that deities are ranked along with fallen angels rather than with deceased humans. If, in the Hindu or Sinhala Buddhist spiritual hierarchy, *pēy* or other malign beings can be driven out by a possessing deity such as a village goddess, it becomes equally possible, in the Catholic frame of reference, for a malign being to be displaced by a benign but more powerful spirit entity. This superior possessing deity is typically a popular Christian saint, such as St. Anthony, or the Blessed Virgin Mary herself.

The essential difference—perhaps the only significant one—between Hindu and South Asian Catholic possibilities of possession is that the Catholic model retains a Christian super-set of benign spirit entities. The malign spirit may be conceived not only as a "fallen angel" or Judeo-Christian devil, but as a Hindu deity as well (Stirrat 1992, 85; cf. Meyer 1986). In the Hindu view, it is quite appropriate for a goddess, especially, to be the purveyor of disease and distress precisely in order to evoke a worshipful response in her victim and the victim's community. The afflictive goddess may then later become "benign, a comforter and healer and a source of refuge for the afflicted" (Bayly 1989, 133).[8] In such a fluid reality where both gods and saints abide together, present to the popular religious consciousness, their properties are subject to exchange, and saints are enabled to possess mediums, as the gods have always done. When this happens, the medium is positioned ideologically to compete with the institutional Church in matters of salvation (Stirrat 1981, 185).

The Roman Catholic system for soliciting divine help in seeking salvation, mediated through the sacraments and priests, and for pragmatic assistance through the invocation of saints and seers, is a unitary system, each component complementing the other and together making up a comprehensive system of religious beliefs and behaviors. From the Church hierarchy's perspective, the official soteriological discourse is metaphysically as well as morally superior to the discourse concerning worldly affairs. The doctrine of the "Communion of Saints" asserts that, whether living or deceased, all Christians are alive to God, in the Holy Spirit, and may pray for each other (Tambasco 1984, 68–69). This is the foundation for the cult of the saints, in which living people appeal to the holy dead to intercede with God for them in prayer. Writing of Iberian Catholicism, William A. Christian views the chain of intercession as enabling: "There is not . . . a radical separation of the divine from the human. Rather there is a long helping chain that goes from the sinner to God, by way of the souls in purgatory, the saints, and Mary" (Christian 1972, 132).

In Tamil Catholicism, as in the Iberian Christianity from which it came, the saints are capable of acting at times in the domain of soteriology, and so of displacing the Christian God pragmatically, if not theologically, by incarnating themselves in, or through, humans in a modulation between practical and transcendental styles of being religious.[9] This is functionally consistent with the principle of the Incarnation of Christ in Jesus which, by mediating the gap between this world and the other, makes possible a novel kind of intimacy with the divine. It is just such personal proximity to a unique and intimate hierophany, but a contemporary one, that devotees crave.

Philomena's mode of petitionary communion responds both to this Catholic model of saintly presence to humans and to the Hindu model of relations documented by Erndl between a divine patron and her human protégé. It corresponds to relations between a Hindu goddess and her worshippers, through a human medium upon whom she "comes"—as distinguished from a demonic being who "rides" its victim (Erndl 1993, 106).

Women and Supernatural Power in Tamil Culture

A distinctive feature of the *cepakulam* is its emphasis on the exorcism of evil influences in the form of *cēviṉai* and *piḷḷicūṉiyam* inflicted by human beings through *māntirikam*, or sorcery.

Piḷḷicūṉiyam involves a *pēy*, the malignant spirit of one who has died before her or his time, who possesses a vulnerable person, distressing them emotionally and psychically. Women more so than men tend to be afflicted in this way. A *pēy* may sometimes speak through the victim, treating her or him as an oracle (cf. Obeyesekere 1981; Meyer 1986, 257–63). Such a possession state is ambivalent, for even as it causes distress within the victim's social circle, it offers important access to a state of being and knowing beyond this world. Often help from a saint or local deity will be sought through vows and trials of physical endurance to exorcise this malignant spirit (Moffat 1979, 219–89). Under the duress of exorcism the previously silent *pēy* will speak, identify itself, argue its case to continue its possession of the victim, and insist on changes in the social arrangements in which its victim lives (Obeyesekere 1981; Gold 1988, 36). A *pēy* may advocate in disturbing ways for its victim's best interests, and so become a radical instrument for her social empowerment. In a similar way, a goddess may possess a devotee to bring that person closer to herself in worship in just the way that *Mātā* comes to Philomena.

It is not uncommon for women who are survivors of family violence to assume possession states through which they become socially empowered (Obeyesekere 1981). After social victimization, and especially after suffering a wretched or untimely death, some women even today become objects of ritual propitiation and sometimes come to be worshipped as local patronesses (Blackburn 1985; Brubaker 1978; Dumont 1986, 435–39). The classical example of this type of apotheosis is Kannagi, heroine of the epic *Cilappatikāram* who, dying in distress and neglect, the victim of an appalling injustice, becomes a goddess patronized by royalty (Aiyar 1955; Comacuntaran 1977; Danielou 1961, 1965; MacPhail 1988, 1993; Parthasarthy 1992; Dikshitar 1978). While Kannagi loses her husband, Kovalan, to rash, royal injustice, Mary loses her son to an equally undeserved judicial execution. These two women, putative symbols of ideal Tamil and Christian womanhood, share much, especially the inauspicious status of the *amaṅkali*, the husbandless woman, in their moments of deepest crisis and loss.

The image of the unjustly suffering woman who is transformed through death into a fiercely protective, but equally fiercely vindictive goddess is persistently reinforced in the Tamil popular cinema, a primary medium for modeling values and roles in this culture (David 1983). Such a goddess continues to be represented in villages by a temporary festival icon formed of earth, by a pot (Meyer 1986, 235–37), or an entranced dancer. More permanent representations might be a tree, a well or pond, or a stone (Rao 1980, 54–63). More accurately, she is not represented by, but rather inhabits, such objects (Hiltebeitel 1988; Meyer 1986, 331–33). Through human suffering, victimization, and apotheosis (Egnor 1980, 13–19; MacPhail 1988, 59–71; MacPhail 1993), a distinctive kind of sacredness comes to be expressed through the humans who are possessed by these goddesses, once also human, as well as by dangerous and malign spirits (Caplan 1985, 113).

The boundary between the human and the divine thus remains indefinite. No clearly distinguishable, radical otherness is attributed to the divine as it is in the Semitic traditions of Judaism, Christianity, and Islam as framed by orthodoxy (Bayly 1989, 28; Stirrat 1992, 86). Tamil Hindu ideas about the sacred are set in and conditioned by this indigenous tradition of local patron deities, usually female, who appear to and communicate through the bodies of specially chosen worshippers (Weissman 1988). Human communities ritually acknowledge such protectors through periodic festivals and construct their collective identity through their relations with these predominantly female divine patrons. Petitioners desire intensely personal interaction with the goddess (Meyer 1986, 250–57; Younger 1980, 497) and approach her with reverence and trepidation (Schulman 1976) for the resolution of domestic, material, and social problems. They seek the goddess's insights and blessings which, they hope, will confer some advantage in the competitive employment and education markets of today's world (Younger 1980, 500–501). Such divine female patrons are called *ammans*.

In Dravidian India, an *amman* is a goddess who is independent of any domineering, deference-demanding husbandly god, one who acts through her own, nonderivative exclusive power. She is undomesticated, fierce, and combatively unpredictable, slaying demons, and expressing her will through ecstatic possession phenomena. The *amman* who is at once universal as well as patroness of multiple particular localities, simultaneously malefic and benign, becomes in the south Indian context, recognizable as an homology of the Blessed Virgin Mary. Mary likewise appears under a multitude of names and forms; her reputation for compassion may suggest to the Indian devotee a somewhat more certain grace. Represented also as more universal, with broader powers and a wider geographical scope than the *ammans*, St. Mary may not require quite the same pitch of ferocity to accomplish her cosmic work of sustaining order. Perhaps Mary is better at "keeping her cool" than are the *ammas*.

I detect two keys to understanding the Holy Mother, *Mātā*, as she exists in the Tamil conscience, and both are primarily affective. She fulfils two basic prerequisites in the sacred imagination for being a village goddess: first, she has suffered grievously and innocently. It is no accident that *Viyākula Mātā* (Our Lady of Sorrows) is one of India's favorite representations of the

Blessed Virgin. The second key is *Mātā*'s motherly constancy. More popular by far than the sorrowing mother in India is *Catā Cakāya Mātā* (Our Lady of Perpetual Help), depicted as the crowned Madonna holding the frightened Holy Child who, while rushing to her for comfort, has nearly lost his shoe. Even the Lord Himself seeks comfort in her, proclaims this image, evoking for many Tamils and other goddess-oriented Indians a distinct primacy for Mary in their devotional life. *Mātā*'s earnest and intimate concern for her devotees is profoundly attractive.

When pilgrims undertake an often arduous journey to one of *Mātā*'s shrines, they come yearning to feel her maternal, nurturing presence, to encounter her directly in human form, to see and hear her. They seek to encounter a sacred person, contacted and made present, not merely a verbal invocation that can be heard on any day in any church. When pilgrims visit shrines, it is commonly to bargain with the sacred for help with their pragmatic needs. To this end, offerings are brought, *nērttikaṭan* (*promesas*, sacred bargains) made, and practical results expected. When the expected result occurs, a thanks-offering, either of penance or of money, completes the transaction. An appreciation of the manner in which the Virgin pervades Tamil Catholic imagination, and of the kinds of transactions people make with her, are essential for understanding the symbolic roots of the *Kōvai Tūya Mariyannai Cepakulam*.

Authentication within the *Cepakulam*

In my reading of clients and events in the *cepakulam,* a restoration of balance and normalcy from a condition of life-disruption and confusion is the pragmatic goal. The "therapy" offered in the *cepakulam* is not a passive process of assimilating or adjusting to environing conditions, problems, and limitations as might be recommended by the pastoral representatives of the Church, but of radically dismissing and overcoming them by disempowering their effects. Undertaking the effort to alter habits, understanding, and intention must be done conscientiously, not as a mere enactment or exhibited cultural performance.

People bring their life situations and particular afflictions, seeking a radical remedy, and they arrive with patterned expectations that are recognized and validated by the seer in a formal, stylized response. Even oblique acknowledgment by the sacred specialist is a sign that the affliction is manageable and on its way to resolution. If such recognition fails, this is merely a sign of the depth of the difficulty, not of ineptitude on the part either of the medium or of the being possessing her, and a replay of the performance may yet bring about a resolution. A production of confidence in the *āvi kaṭṭu* is constantly going on, reinforced weekly by the testimonials of those who have been successfully exorcised and whose life-situations have been transformed.

Authentication of the record of success and of the actual presence of the Blessed Virgin are essential to the construction of Philomena's authority as seer. From the beginning, her austerity was accepted as a primary sign of authenticity, as was her helplessness—even her "absence"—during the possession trance. Philomena claims to know nothing and be able to do nothing when *Mātā* comes upon her, yet she seems able to invoke *Mātā*'s presence at will. Neither does it come upon her, as with Bernadette and the second medium, without her intentional cooperation. Both passivity and assertiveness are modes of her leadership style and both are intrinsic to it. Her assertive mode was more evident on my return to the *cepakulam* in 1997, when Philomena herself selected and vigorously led hymns before going into trance—perhaps mimicking the style of her elder sister, Sagaya.

Whatever may be the external factors in validating her authority, Philomena's authenticity is best affirmed by her diagnosis, in trance, of people's problems and her prescriptions for them. This, of course, depends on her "not being herself" at the point of entrancement when she first identifies the clients, then challenges them to assess how they had become vulnerable to arcane forces, and determines whether they had done so consciously or unconsciously. The presumption here is that evil forces in people's lives are essentially external to them, something "injected" into them by another's malice. The truth-force of exorcism derives from the mutual affirmation of medium and client, a convergence that takes place in a group process of rehearsed and repeatable events that reinforce both the confidence of new and old clients in the seer, and the seer's own confidence in the actuality and knowability of clients' problems. This production of confidence is essential for the success of the ritual enactment and its prescribed remedy.

Orthodoxy and the Construction of Meaning

The *cepakulam* has a further concern for authentication in its relations with the clergy, especially where an excess of enthusiasm may compromise its ability to construct its own authority. At the outset, in February 1990, when *Mātā* first came to Bernadette, a diocesan priest had become intrigued with this emergent Marian phenomenon. He began to speak publicly about the *cepakulam,* even while celebrating Mass, and would announce exactly where to find the sisters. He was warned by his superiors against saying that *Mātā* speaks in the *cepakulam*. But then even *Mātā* has given her own counsel for silence. Dr. Kumar testified to hearing *Mātā*'s message himself, "You need not be in a hurry. The time will come when the whole world will come

to know that I'm speaking here. My Son knows when it should be revealed."
All in the *cepakulam* appreciate *Mātā*'s warning that if her presence among
them comes to be widely known too early, they will be disturbed. The priest's
conversion and over enthusiasm had produced undesirable political pressures
on the *cepakulam* as well.

Cepakulam members are aware that, while hoping the benefits of their
spiritual healing work will become available to a wider public, overpubliciz-
ing their activities may induce Church authorities to investigate and perhaps
constrain them. None of the Christians involved deny the formal authority of
the Church's teaching in their lives as Catholics or wish to be alienated from
the sacraments. Still, the institutional Church remains an outsider to the par-
ticularity of their religious experience. They fear that the ordained clergy may
become jealous, possessive, and controlling of their own privileged access, be
they lay Christians or Hindus, to the Blessed Mother and her favors.

My unexpected arrival had produced considerable controversy resulting
in Dr. Kumar's immediate summons from Salem. Some *cepakulam* members
argued that I should be told nothing and permitted to witness nothing. I had
arrived with a priest, and it was certain that investigations would follow, with
questions from the Bishop, and a lot of disturbance. Clearly the *cepakulam*
members are apprehensive about losing control of their activities, hence their
insistence to me, fearing that my interests were journalistic, that nothing
about them should enter the popular print media, which might initiate an
enquiry by the diocesan authorities.

In the end, how to inform me about the *cepakulam,* and how much to
tell, seems to have been left to the discretion of Dr. Kumar, our cultural
mediator. I was generously permitted to attend the *āvi kaṭṭu* rites and to freely
tape the entire proceedings. I could converse with anyone, from central participants to first-time visitors, in Tamil and in English, and freely visit members' homes for extended private discussions. However, on my subsequent
visit in 1997 I was not permitted, on *Mātā*'s instructions, to videotape
Philomina in trance. This may indicate, in the impressive setting of Philomena's
new *"Cepa Illam,"* a greater confidence and assertiveness in the *cepakulam*'s
leadership.

Cepakulam leaders are vocal in their assertion that they have no overt
conflict with institutional Church authority in terms of doctrine. Dr. Kumar
and other *ūliyar* insist that nothing said or done among them departs from
Christian orthodoxy or makes any nontraditional claims. This is so even in
regard to exorcism, which is not only Biblical but is officially recognized in
the practice of appointing one priest in each diocese as the official exorcist,
even though the incumbent may not himself believe in spirit-possession.

Can the Church as magisterium, the repository of official doctrine, and
as local spiritual authority in the diocese be regarded as any kind of "baseline"

for the *cepakulam*'s functions? The answer is at once "yes" and "no." *Mātā* herself prescribes regular attendance at Mass in their parish church for her Catholic devotees. On the other hand, many of Her followers are Hindus, and a few are Protestant Christians who are not subject to Roman Catholic authority in doctrine or prescribed practice. Membership in the *cepakulam* is therefore not equivalent to Catholic identity for all; this is the core of the Church's apprehension concerning such phenomena, which blur the lines of religious identity, affiliation, and authority.

The *cepakulam*'s Marian focus, as declared in its mission statement, places it squarely in the "losing" camp at Vatican II, and their desire to avoid unnecessary contact with the Bishop's House speaks of expedient political considerations bearing wider implications for ecclesiastical authority and finance. In any diocese that actively promotes and materially benefits from established Marian shrines and devotions, new manifestations of St. Mary's active presence and initiative are often unwelcome. Such phenomena are regarded by the Church as a challenge if they are independently managed by lay Christians, and more so if managed by Hindus.

There is an active tension here between institutional orthodoxy and personalistic, localized religious experience. The *cepakulam* means to affirm Philomena's revelatory experiences, to encourage lay ministry, and to retain its exclusive right to manage and interpret *cepakulam* events, the eventual wider significance of which will be revealed in good time. To this end any putative challenge to orthodoxy or to ecclesiastical authority is carefully self-censored.

In its amateur theological discourse the *cepakulam* rests its case on the intercession, rather than on any independent powers, of *Mātā*, thereby guarding its claim to orthodoxy while promoting a cult of exorcism based on her proactive presence, advice, mediation, and empowerment. Their prayers are to the Persons of the Trinity, and the *cepakulam* principals never cease to exhort clients to attend Mass and participate regularly in the sacraments. The *cepakulam*'s process of constructing a meaningful world integrates a variety of cultural components. It combines a Christian plan of salvation that incorporates the presence of evil beings and sacred persons (both Hindu and Christian) and their actions among living humans. It involves the therapeutic process of expelling tangible, externalized evil from persons and places, enframing this process within the expression of distinctive Marian apparitional phenomenon. This is done without undermining the absolute priority and transcendence of the Trinity. All of these components reinforce a shared reality in such a manner as to produce effects of truth, authority, and credibility.

That such a combination is possible teaches us that no cultural construction is in itself improbable but only seems so from an outsider's construction of reality. Strategies such as we have seen here, developed for the construction within the *cepakulam* of official, hegemonic views, must produce their own reasonableness and legitimacy. History testifies to the tendency of the elite to appropriate the popular vision, to remake it and the subjectivity that produces it, so that even the eyes of common people come to see themselves through the replicas of the taxidermist's art. The irony of such appropriation is that the globalizing hegemonic vision often comes to be self-consciously represented as its antithesis, as the popular!

It is just such an identity—and meaning—destroying end that the *cepakulam* seeks to avoid. Its leaders must remain within and true to the Church, for saving Truth is there, but in the process of constructing limited authority, credibility, and a positive reputation for Philomena and the *ūḷiyar* they must avoid interference from any form of officialdom, ecclesial or secular, which might challenge the autonomy of their own vision or impose an external discipline upon them.

Notes

1. This is a report on continuing research on the construction of the identity and authority of religious specialists in the context of relations between Catholics and Hindus in Tamil Nadu. Materials were collected in 1993 and 1997. Pseudonyms have been used for the location and to protect the privacy of persons. Names of persons and places have been retained in their commonplace English spellings for readability, rather than, for example, the strictly transliterated *tirumati pā pilomīnā mēri*. Technical terms use the *Tamil Lexicon* transliteration. A version of this paper was read at the Faculty Research Seminar of the United Theological College, Bangalore, in February 1998.

2. Literally, "Coimbatore Holy/Immaculate Mary-Mother Prayer-family." The adjective *tūya*, according to the *Tamil Lexicon*, denotes "clean, pure, holy." The substantive *ūymai* denotes "purity, cleanness, immaculateness, holiness," connoting the purity for which Mary is reputed and is at the core of her holiness.

3. This account of events and opinions concerning the *cepakulam* is from personal observations, some recorded on videotape, and from private interviews at the home of Mrs. S. P. Lourdu Mary with Dr. S. Kumar, Mrs. K. Sagaya Mary, Mrs. P. Philomena Mary, and several clients on 25/26 June 1993 and at the home of Mrs. P. Philomena Mary with clients and *cepakulam* leaders on 19/20 September 1997. Interviews were audiorecorded in their entirety.

4. *Maraṇapāṭu* refers to the death-wounds of Christ on the cross, symbolized by five candles.

5. The sense here is "lord of *anpu, agape*; Christ."

6. *Cēviṉai* refers to malefic magical practices, in service to, or under the control of, a malefic master.

7. This perceived continuity of human and divine realms has also been reported in Spanish communities by Christian (1972, 132).

8. Many of Philomena's followers are and remain Hindus, unaware of canonical limitations and open to ever new revelations. They do not distinguish in Catholic fashion between practices that are "public," binding on all the faithful, and "private," not contrary to faith and valid for those who find them useful for devotion.

9. Mandelbaum (1966) distinguishes between a "transcendental complex" of religious functions concerned with ultimate purpose and a "pragmatic complex" generated to meet local and temporal exigencies. These modes are complementary; they overlap and converge, symbols transiting from one complex to the other (Mandelbaum 1966, 1177). Following Marriott (1955, 211–18), Mandelbaum writes: "A local godling may gradually be endowed by worshipers with transcendental attributes, and, conversely, a deity from the scriptural pantheon may be . . . transposed into a pragmatic spirit."

References

Aiyar Caminatha, U. V. 1955. *Cilappatikāram.* (6th ed.) *Cennai* (Madras) n.p.

Bayly, Susan. 1989. *Saints, Goddesses, and Kings: Muslims and Christians in South Indian Society, 1700–1900.* Cambridge: Cambridge University Press.

Blackburn, Stuart H. 1985. "Death and Deification: Folk Cults in Hinduism." *History of Religions* 24, no. 3: 255–74.

Brubaker, Richard Lee. 1978. "The Ambivalent Mistress: a Study of South Indian Village Goddesses and Their Religious Meaning." Ph.D. Dissertation. University of Chicago.

Caplan, Lionel. 1985. "The Popular Culture of Evil in Urban South India." In *The Anthropology of Evil*, ed. David Parkin, 110–27. Oxford: Basil Blackwell.

Christian, William A., Jr. 1972. *Person and God in a Spanish Valley.* Princeton, N.J.: Princeton University Press.

Comacuntaran, Po. Ve. 1977. *Cilappatikāram.* (3 vols., 1977, 1975, 1976). *Cennai* (Madras): The South India Saiva Siddhanta Works Publishing Society, Tinnevelly, Ltd.

Danielou, Alain. 1961. *Prince Ilango Adigal: Le Roman de l'anneau (Shilappadikaram).* Paris: Gallimard.

———. 1965. *The Shilappadikaram (The Ankle Bracelet).* London: George Allen and Unwin.

David, C. R. W. 1983. *Cinema as Medium of Communication in Tamil Nadu.* Madras: The Christian Literature Society.

Dikshitar Ramachandra, V. R., trans. 1978. *The Cilappatikāram*. 2nd ed. (1st ed. 1939). Madras: The South India Saiva Siddhanta Works Publishing Society, Tinnevelly, Limited.

Dumont, Louis. 1986. *A South Indian Subcaste: Social Organization and Religion of the Pramalai Kallar*. (*Une sous-caste de l'Inde du Sud.*) Trans. M. Moffatt, L. Morton, A. Morton, ed. M. Moffat. Delhi: Oxford University Press.

Egnor, Margaret. 1980. "On the Meaning of *Śakti* to Women in Tamil Nadu." In *The Powers of Tamil Women*, ed. Susan S. Wadley, 1–34. Syracuse, N.Y.: Syracuse University.

Erndl, Kathleen M. 1989. "Rapist or Bodyguard, Demon or Devotee? Images of Bhairo in the Mythology and Cult of Vaisno Devi." In *Criminal Gods and Demon Devotees: Essays on the Guardians of Popular Hinduism*, ed. Alf Hiltebeitel, 239–49. Albany: State University of New York Press.

———. 1993. *Victory to the Mother: The Hindu Goddess of Northwest India in Myth, Ritual, and Symbol*. New York: Oxford University Press.

Gold, Ann Grodzins. 1988. *Fruitful Journeys: The Ways of Rajasthani Pilgrims*. Berkeley and Los Angeles: University of California Press.

Hiltebeitel, Alf. 1988. *The Cult of Draupadi. Mythologies: From Gingee to Kuruksetra*. Chicago: University of Chicago Press.

MacPhail, Richard D. 1988. "Justice, Foreknowledge, and Fate in the *Cilappatikāram*." M.A. thesis. McMaster University.

———. 1993. "Injustice, *Anaṅku* and Apotheosis in the *Cilappatikāram*." *Journal of the Institute of Asian Studies* 11, no. 1: 18–27.

———. 1995. "*Śānti*'s *Līla*: Godbearing in India." Ph.D. Dissertation. McMaster University.

Mandelbaum, David G. 1966. "Transcendental and Pragmatic Aspects of Religion." *American Anthropologist* 68: 1174–85.

Marriott, McKim. 1955. "Little Communities in an Indigenous Civilization." In *Village India*, ed. M. Marriott, 171–222. Chicago: University of Chicago Press.

Meyer, Eveline. 1986. *Aṅkāḷaparamēcuvari: A Goddess of Tamilnadu, her Myths and Cult*. Stuttgart: Steiner Verlag Wiesbaden GMBH.

Moffat, Michael. 1979. *An Untouchable Community in South India. Structure and Consensus*. Princeton, N.J.: Princeton University Press.

Obeyesekere, Gananath. 1981. *Medusa's Hair: An Essay on Personal Symbols and Religious Experience*. Chicago: University of Chicago Press.

Parthasarthy, R. 1992. *The Cilappatikāram of Ilanko Aṭikaḷ: An Epic of South India*. New York: Columbia University Press.

Rao Ramachandra, S. D. 1980. *The Folk Origins of Indian Temples.* Bangalore: IBH Prakashana.

Schulman, David Dean. 1976. "The Murderous Bride: Tamil Versions of the Myth of Devi and the Buffalo-demon." *History of Religions* 16, no. 2: 257–63.

Stirrat, R. L. 1992. *Power and Religiosity in a Post-colonial Setting (Sinhala Catholics in Contemporary Sri Lanka).* Cambridge: Cambridge University Press.

————. 1981. "The Shrine of St. Sebastian at Mirisgama: An Aspect of the Cult of Saints in Catholic Sri Lanka." *Man* 16: 183–200.

Tambasco, Anthony J. 1984. *What Are They Saying about Mary?* Ramsey, N.J.: Paulist Press.

Tamil Lexicon. 1982. 7 vols. Madras: University of Madras.

Weissman, Lee A. 1988. "Who is *Paṅkāru?*" Paper presented at the Conference on Religion in South India, June 2.

Younger, Paul. 1980. "A Temple Festival of *Māriyammaṉ.*" *The Journal of the American Academy of Religion* 48, no. 4: 493–517.

CHAPTER 8

Charismatic Transgressions:
The Life and Work
of an Indian Catholic Healer

Mathew N. Schmalz

The Lotus Feet of Mr. Jude

One late autumn day, the Catholic healer Jude lay in bed in his apartment in the North Indian city of Varanasi.[1] His body was covered by several thick woolen blankets, and scarves were wrapped tightly around his head to protect him from the high fever he had contracted while ministering to his supplicants at a recent Catholic charismatic convention. When a knock came on the door in the afternoon, his wife opened it to an elderly man who asked to be led to "the lotus feet of Mr. Jude." Jude's wife politely explained that her husband was too sick to see anyone, but the man pushed his way past her and prostrated himself at Jude's feet. Reeling from his fever, Jude recalled that he could only manage a moan and a labored gesture of his hand. But this seemed to satisfy the gentleman, who departed after insisting that Jude accept a jar of mango pickles as a sign of his gratitude.

Several days afterwards, I was able to meet this earnest new supplicant when I accompanied Jude to a Christian *āśram* outside of Varanasi. The man, whom I will call Mr. Prakash, had recently retired from his job as a government clerical worker in Patna, the capital of Bihar. When I introduced myself to him, he greeted me in English and said in a loud voice, "See, I am a great sinner!" He then pointed down to his left foot which, along with his calf, was terribly swollen. He explained to me that he had come to the Radhasoami *āśram* in Varanasi and there had heard of "Mr. Jude" and sought simply to see him—to have his "*darśan*." That day, every time I attempted to talk with Mr. Prakash at length, he would politely rebuff me by saying, "Please, let me see Mr. Jude and go to his lotus feet." Such an intense desire to be near the teacher or guru is not only common but expected for Radhasoami devotees, who are often reported to compete with one another to gaze at their guru's visage. The very phrase "lotus feet" itself suggests that the feet of the guru rise unsullied from the ground like a lotus bud that grows up from the mud to blossom. Mr. Prakash told me that he felt peace when he looked upon Jude. There was need neither for confession nor counseling, since Mr. Prakash believed that he would find healing simply by being close to Jude and by touching his "lotus feet."

To understand a healer is both to listen to the various voices in the healer's own life and to understand the diverse contexts shaping the discourse of healing. With Jude, the importance of these two components come into sharp relief when viewing the intensity of Mr. Prakash's devotion. Jude finds himself, a Catholic south Indian, living in the north Indian city of Varanasi, a place sacred to Hindus throughout India. To minister to non-Christians, and especially to Hindus in their most sacred city, would mean carrying the Gospel to those who had yet to realize the power of Jesus' name. But Mr. Prakash's attentions also underscore how Jude's status as a healer resonates within distinctly South Asian cultural patterns and concerns, raising for Jude the disquieting possibility that it was he himself who was being defined by the surrounding Hindu culture. For Jude, the discourse of healing presents both challenge and opportunity because it is within the diverse contexts shaping his ministry that he must maintain his Christian voice.

To begin our discussion of Jude's life and work we will consider how Jude, a self-confessed alcoholic and rapist, repents his sins and gains the divine gift of discernment. In the process of this conversion, Jude moves along the horizontal and vertical axes of self to create what I will call a cruciform space of redemption. The structure of this transformation then becomes a template for Jude's efforts to heal, as he adapts his healing voice to the different contexts of his ministry. In his work with Hindu supplicants, we will examine how Jude relies upon indeterminacy and a particular construction of Hinduism to articulate a Christian discourse of healing. Moving next to his work with Christians, I will consider how he speaks with his most Indian voice when dealing with sexual sins and demonic possession. In the various contexts of his ministry, Jude creates a bricolage of healing that attempts to reshape the self by altering the boundaries that define it. Indeed, I will argue that Jude's effort to change the boundaries of the self emerges as an improvisational tactic to create a space for his Christian voice. But by shifting the boundaries that circumscribe the self, Jude's ministry derives its power as much from the act of transgression as from the hope for redemption.

A Cruciform Space

To understand the complex influences shaping Jude's healing ministry, we will begin precisely where Jude would have us begin—with the events leading to his own conversion. When Jude presents his life story, it initially appears as an organic whole, tightly organized by a Christian teleology culminating in his transformation into Jesus' slave. But this narrative is also shaped by Indian mythical tropes that give the story a deeper resonance than its explicitly Christian structure would seem to allow. By telling such a tale of redemption, Jude seeks not only to render his own conversion intelligible but also to frame a broader conception of human transformation. Central to this vision is a view of human existence as defined by shifting physical, conceptual, and moral boundaries. And so, Jude himself becomes redeemed in a two-fold move to realign the boundaries that define him as a sinner. As we will see later, it is the pattern of his own conversion that guides Jude's ministrations to his Hindu and Christian supplicants.

"My Dear Jesus, I Know How Much I Have Done Against You"

Jude was born into a family in a predominately Christian part of Kerala that had for generations belonged to the Syro-Malabar rite of the Roman Catholic Church. Even before his birth, signs foretold Jude's special gifts. When his mother was in her sixth month of pregnancy, the doctor discovered a tumor near her uterus. According to Jude, he was taken out of his mother's womb so that the malignancy could be removed. After the operation, the doctor pronounced the fetus dead and instructed the nurse to dispose of the apparently stillborn Jude. But "the mighty hand of Jesus" was there, and as the nurse took hold of the fetus, she realized that it was still alive. Jude was then put back into his mother's womb, for what he calls "the test."

When speaking of his childhood, Jude recalls how Catholic piety dominated his home life. For example, every evening his family would kneel down together to recite the Rosary. Jude himself maintained a spiritual diary in which he recorded his small attempts to imitate the way of the cross. Of course, he attended Catholic schools during his childhood and teenage years and recalls how the opposite sex seemed rather strange and foreign. After all, he comically interjects, he was surrounded by "a fence" of priests and religious during most of his young life in Kerala.

Jude managed to scale the clerical fence that confined him by earning a commission as an officer in the air force. He entered the military newly married but curious about the experiences possible outside matrimony. So he sought what he calls "the pleasures of the world," an endeavor made easier by the fact that he held the keys to the liquor cabinet in the officer's mess. He began to drink wine and carouse with friends. These friends, he recalls, soon brought him "to the outer world of pleasure." Sexual affairs with women followed, both with prostitutes and with the wives of fellow officers. Often dispensing with the charade of seduction, Jude would force himself upon women once he had them alone. In his own retrospective judgment, he became a murderer as well as a rapist, for he procured numerous abortions for his pregnant lovers. Although his "inner conscience" began to trouble him, the liquor soon drowned out such thoughts of repentance. Indeed, as he now reflects, there was no pleasure that he did not seek, no sin he did not commit, and no commandment he did not violate.

Jude's drinking became so intense that it led to his dishonorable discharge from the air force. Taking his wife and young son with him, he relocated to Bombay. Jude had money saved, so with some partners he began to produce and market an ayurvedic tonic for impotence called "Vivirex." He often displays testimonies to the product's success, with letters from India and beyond confirming its efficacy. For example, an eighty-five year old Muslim gentleman from Kenya wrote that after taking Vivirex he experienced his first "night-fall," or nocturnal emission, in decades. Jude claims that he made hundreds of thousands of rupees through this business, but one of his partners stole his money and left him penniless. Faced with bankruptcy and having to support a newly born daughter in addition to his wife and son, he shifted his family once more, this time to Varanasi in eastern Uttar Pradesh, where his wife had found employment as a nurse in a government hospital.

After he moved to Varanasi, Jude returned to the Catholic Church. By this time, Jude's "inner conscience," in his own words, had begun "to eat him." Unable to sleep at night and alone at home while his wife worked to support the family, Jude recalls that he began to feel "crushed" by the weight of his sins. To relieve this burden, Jude went to confession for the first time since he joined the military. Yet after admitting his guilt, Jude recalls that he still did not feel complete peace. So, upon the advice of his confessor, he became involved in the charismatic movement that had spread from south India to become a prominent part of the north Indian Catholic landscape.

When Jude became a charismatic, he embarked upon a personal regimen of prayer and fasting supplemented by regular retreats for spiritual discernment. While deep in prayer during one particular retreat, Jude claims he received a message from God to confess his sins before the crowd gathering for a public healing ceremony. But as Jude went to reveal his "black deeds," he realized that his wife, young daughter, and son were among the crowd. Jude hesitated for a moment because he knew how much it would hurt his children to hear about the sins of their father. Still, he felt compelled to "open" himself fully, and so he spoke before the entire assembly and recounted his affairs, his drinking, and his whoring. When he concluded his testimony and returned to his family, he recalls that he found nothing but love and forgiveness; a love and forgiveness that stood in stark contrast to the inner guilt still torturing him. Since he believed that he had "destroyed so many souls," Jude then vowed to commit his life to the conversion of sinners.

"He Got a Sinner like Me"

To fulfill his promise to redeem the fallen, Jude began to travel with a charismatic prayer group throughout Uttar Pradesh and Bihar. One day, he was attending a charismatic service at a Catholic mission in the Ballia District, about 100 miles north of Varanasi. While praying in tongues, Jude started making a noise, "Bagalā, Bagalā, Bagalā." He recalls that he paused and thought: "Bagalā, Bagalā, what it is (sic) 'Bagalā'?" Then it came to him: "A man named Bagalā is sitting here, he's with a stick in the church, and now Jesus is asking him to leave his stick and come to the stage." He told this to a priest who immediately announced this message to the assembled crowd. Truly, according to Jude, there was a man named Bagalā, and he cast away his cane and walked upright. This gift of prophecy and discernment found confirmation at a subsequent prayer service in northwest Uttar Pradesh. There Jude received permission to counsel those in need of healing. When the first person came to ask for his discernment, Jude found that he could immediately see into the supplicant's heart and reveal past events and sins. Jude recalls that he did not receive these "messages" as images or as thoughts that appeared in his mind before he spoke them. Instead, in a state resembling a kind of divinely inspired Tourette's syndrome, the words simply "came," leaving him no opportunity to pause and reflect. After that healing service, Jude's gift of discernment became an integral part of his healing ministry, for he would often confront his supplicants with their sins before they confessed them. To this day, Jude asserts, no one has ever publicly challenged his gift, and he points to the hundreds of written testimonies recorded in his notebook, all of which attest to his uncanny power to read the human heart. Jude admits that others have suggested that his ability might only be psychological, and he smiles, saying, "It may be." But he finally reflects, "I know Jesus' love, because he came in search of sinners, so he got a sinner like me."

Enfleshed by Sin, Embodied in Christ

In the story of his fall and conversion, Jude initially presents himself as a sinner divided from his own true self and from God. This sense of a self out of place emerges most clearly from the oppositions structuring his narrative. When he was taken out of his mother's womb, he was born but not born; considered dead, but in fact alive. When he permanently left the womb of his mother, his birth was then a rebirth. Jude contrasts "the outer world of pleasure," craved by his flesh, to the inner world of the spirit. Flesh exists as a thin membrane, easily permeable and crossed; but it also stands as an almost absolute barrier separating the individual from God. Flesh thus counters spirit, false self is juxtaposed to true self, and Jude's past life of sin opposes his present life of redemption. Jude was a man literally turned inside out, for his true self, as spirit, became external to the false "enfleshed" self that he had embraced.

In his narrative of redemption, Jude's divided self becomes unified by the very act of narration. Through public confession, elements that stood outside his true self become reintegrated in a narrative that emphasizes God's healing power. By admitting his sins before the Christian community, he once again enters the bounds of the Church that is itself the body of Christ. Through narrative, Jude also completes his journey from the outer world of the flesh to the "inner world" of the spirit, for in the very act of narration the boundaries of this "inner world" extend to envelope the outer. Spirit thus encompasses flesh and unifies the self by identifying it with the divine. The disparate elements of Jude's life then find coherence within a teleology fulfilled by his gift of healing and discernment. His rebirth from his mother's womb foreshadows his rebirth in Christ, his role as a healer of sexual dysfunction through ayurvedic preparations anticipates his work as a spiritual healer who diagnoses and heals sexual transgressions. Jude's conversion, however, is not a unique personal transformation. Instead, it is a way of acting in the world as a forgiven person, a healer whose power relies upon the ability of narrative and confession to redefine the boundaries that shape the self.

While public confession reunites Jude with Christ's collective body understood as Church, his divine gift of discernment reflects a special rela-tionship with the personal body of Jesus. Jude describes himself as Jesus' "slave," a term which St. Paul also uses to introduce his epistles. As a slave for Jesus, Jude speaks the words of Christ. In making this claim, Jude intends no hyperbole since he often reflects that if someone strikes him, it would be equivalent to raising a hand against the Lord. His embodiment in Christ is so complete that Jude's own body may also act as an empathetic medium of grace. At prayer services, when Jude receives a message that someone in the audience is possessed by a devil, he will begin a private ritual in which he first sympathetically becomes the demoniac through prayer and then marks his own body with signs of the cross to exorcise the demon. His belief in empathetic union with his supplicants also extends to substitution. For ex-ample, Jude once mentioned to me that when his arm was injured in a rick-shaw accident, he understood it as a sign that one of his supplicants had been healed. His body thus assumes the qualities of Christ's body by accepting wounds for others.

Echoes and Resonances

Jude's life story is consciously constructed as a Catholic charismatic tale of redemption. Accordingly, Jude emphasizes how his conversion reflects broad Christian themes, and the narrative itself seems almost totally bereft of specifically Indian elements, apart from Jude's brief discussion of his work in ayurvedic medicine. But in spite of its Christian teleology, aspects of Jude's narrative also recall Hindu, Jain, and Buddhist mythic tropes which themselves concern the boundaries that define human existence. Jude's miraculous birth, for example, evokes Indian stories of embryo transfer and thereby becomes a kind of mythic moment that orients the course of his narrative. In the *Harivaṃśa*, the baby Krishna was conceived in the waters of hell, in the womb of Kali, and then transferred to the womb of Devaki (Doniger 1975, 205). According to the Śvetāmbar tradition of Jainism, the king of the Gods, Shakra moved the embryo of Tirthankara Mahavira from his Brahmin mother into the womb of Trishala, a member of the ruling Kshatriya caste (Jaini 1979, 7). In both cases, natural boundaries were changed so that destiny could be fulfilled: Lord Krishna was removed from the womb before birth so that he could be saved, while Mahavira was transferred so he could become a spiritual monarch. Jude, of course, was removed from his mother's womb so that she could be saved but was brought back from death by Jesus' "mighty hand." One could also interpret this double birth as a twice-born image: Jude's first birth is a pure one, like that of the Buddha (Conze 1975, 35), through his mother's side, while his second birth is impure, through the vaginal canal. Such an interpretation might find confirmation in Jude's reflection that he was put back in his mother's womb for "the test"; a description that resonates with Hindu conceptions of the womb as a place of torment (Parry 1989, 498).

While Jude's life narrative is a weave of both Christian and Indian elements, it nonetheless has a general thematic coherence that holds its strands together. The key point in Jude's life is not his return to the Catholic Church or even his public confession. Instead, it is the bestowal of the divine gift of discernment and healing that orients his narrative and its attendant themes. Jude's ability to read the hearts of his supplicants culminates a spiritual journey from being enfleshed by sin to being embodied in Christ, for in becoming Jesus' slave Jude enters a special relationship with his Savior's body.

While admitting the deeply personal and even idiosyncratic aspects of his conversion, Jude would not consider his life story to be confined to such limited significance. Rather, he would argue that the story of his transformation has a broader import that speaks to how humans can change their lives. Through confession, Jude initially acts to reorient the boundaries of his self along a horizontal axis by rejecting the flesh, accepting the sins he once denied and rejoining the Christian community. Yet in this process, he also

170   *Mathew N. Schmalz*

empties or opens himself to be filled by Jesus. This final step is Jude's
decisive act of will, for here he moves along a vertical axis of self to establish
continuity with God. The "existential" or personal space that Jude creates for
himself then is cruciform, since his identity as a slave for Jesus extends both
vertically and horizontally to conform itself to the boundaries of the crucified
and risen Christ.

Sujata and Sita

Jude's life narrative not only authorizes his work as a healer but also
becomes a template for his diagnoses and healing ministrations. Recall that
Jude's first moment of transformation was his public confession. By establishing an appropriate relationship between flesh and the body, and by healing the rift between himself and the surrounding community, Jude moved
along what could be called a horizontal plane of self to shift the boundaries
of his identity. Using this initial move as a frame, we will consider Jude's
attempts to diagnose the afflictions of two Hindu women. Within this context,
Jude's effort to shift the boundaries of the self emerges not only as a therapeutic tool but as a tactical device that he can deploy to maintain his Christian identity in north Indian society. Relying upon both indeterminacy and a
tactical construction of Hinduism, Jude articulates a resolutely Christian conception of self-transformation. Yet, in spite of the apparent exclusivity of this
vision, an evocative overlapping of Hindu and Catholic symbols, as well as
a particular congruence of intents, allow a shared space for healing to emerge
between Jude and his north Indian supplicants.

Sujata's Silence

One evening a north Indian Protestant lawyer, whom I will call by his
professional title "Waqil Saheb," summoned Jude to minister to a young
Hindu woman. This young woman, henceforth "Sujata," was reportedly possessed by a "devil spirit." Waqil Saheb had earlier brought her to the Varanasi
Cathedral to meet Jude. But upon reaching the threshold of the church, Sujata
refused to enter and fled back to her home. Waqil Saheb took this as a sure
sign of possession. He also claimed that he had talked to the demon and that
it came from Bihar. Jude was less credulous and simply said, "Let's go and
take a look."

Waqil Saheb led us to a three-room dwelling near the Varanasi Cathedral. Like many of the houses in the area, it seemed a hasty construction of
brick and mortar with a roof of corrugated metal. When we entered the house,
a young woman, probably about sixteen, stood by the television. She had her

back turned, so it was difficult to see her face. Her mother was also present, as well as a younger brother. Her mother explained that Sujata would wake up in the night screaming that three men were coming to take her away. After having these dreams or visions, she would cry uncontrollably for hours. These three men, it seems, had recently died: two were "uncles," while the other one was a boy close to her own age. The family suspected that these men, since they had died unexpectedly, could perhaps still be lingering on earth in ghostly form. Alternatively, a single ghost, in Hindi a *bhùt* or *pret*, could be causing these visions and tormenting Sujata for its own mysterious purposes (on ghosts in Hinduism, see Gold 1990, 64ff; Parry 1990, 229ff).

Jude said, "Well, let me pray." Sujata meanwhile had not moved from her position facing the television. Jude moved close to her and, placing his hands upon her head, began to pray in Hindi: "Praise [you] Jesus, thank [you] Jesus." He continued for several minutes with Sujata still motionless. Jude then stopped and sat down on the couch. He remained silent for a moment and then asked the mother whether the family prayed together. The mother answered that they did not. At this point, Jude became more assertive and said that they should pray together since there was certainly no peace in the house. The mother then admitted that her husband was a drunkard who would often beat her and Sujata. Jude finally pronounced Sujata's problem to be psychological, not a possession requiring exorcism.

Waqil Saheb expressed disappointment with this diagnosis, insisting that the devil spirit was in fact attempting to humiliate him by its silence. Since he claimed that the ghost spoke when Sujata was sitting down, he enlisted the help of Sujata's mother and brother and forcibly turned Sujata around and sat her down on the floor. Waqil Saheb then commanded in Bhojpuri: "In the name of the Lord, I order you: speak!" He then started to jerk her head and struck her in the face several times.

At this point, Jude told Waqil Saheb to stop hitting Sujata and especially not to move her head. Jude then motioned to the mother to bring water, and he blessed it. Jude then began to sprinkle the holy water over Sujata while repeating in Hindi, "Praise you Jesus, thank you Jesus—bless this child, keep her from harm." But Sujata remained silent. Jude next offered his gold-plated cross for her to kiss. Sujata refused. The encounter ended there with Jude declaring that many miracles had happened through him and insisting that the family return for counseling.

Jude applied the pattern of his own self-transformation in order to make Sujata's silence comprehensible. He observed that she could not be possessed because devil spirits cannot remain silent before a slave for Jesus. He elaborated this diagnosis by arguing that the etiology of Sujata's symptoms lay in her past relationships. Jude said that the images of these three men were not apparitions of evil spirits but the echoes of a sin that had become externalized as a vision. He surmised that one of these men must have hurt her—or perhaps all three had harmed her in some way. This injury could have been something simple like not returning her affections or something worse, like physical or sexual abuse. Thus there was the initial sin, committed by at least one of these men, followed by Sujata's inability to forgive that was itself sinful. While Sujata believed that the specters of these men were following her, in Jude's judgment, the apparitions were reverberations of the sins connected to her relationships with them. The impact of Sujata's refusal to forgive became even more severe because there remained no possibility for a personal reconciliation with these men who were now dead and gone. Sujata's self was thus fragmented by sin, with elements that properly existed as part of her, divorced from her own self-awareness. In Jude's view, only confession could heal her by helping her to understand the impact of these sins upon her life.

Like Jude, Waqil Saheb also drew upon his own personal experience and cultural knowledge to understand Sujata's condition. But in maintaining that he had encountered a *bhūt* or *pret*, Waqil Saheb, as a native north Indian, drew upon a font of information that Jude, a south Indian, did not have. He spoke of a nasal sound coming from Sujata, and inquired about her avoidance of light, incense, and iron—all traditional signs of a malevolent, ghostly presence (Upadhyay 1991, 321). The claim that the ghost was from Bihar was particularly significant because a north Indian *ojhā*, or exorcist, would be very careful to discern the identity of the offending spirit and determine its caste and place of origin. Not only did Waqil Saheb express his concerns with these issues, he also focused upon more specific aspects of Sujata's demeanor. He attempted to contrast Sujata's willingness to sit on the tiled floor to her insistence upon standing at other times. He hypothesized that since she was possessed, the ghost could have feared the power of the earth, a force which the tiles blocked. Moreover, Waqil Saheb started to strike Sujata, a common way to deal with possession, pithily recommended in the Bhojpuri saying: *"Marala se bhūt bhāgelā"* or "a ghost flees from a beating" (Upadhyay 1991, 323). Yet for Waqil Saheb his encounter with Sujata was also a new experience, for he is a north Indian Protestant. He confided that he had never personally confronted a ghost before and was quite eager to see one now. While he agreed that these apparitions were indeed supernatural, he did not endorse the explanation that they had assumed such a form because they had died by violence or because their funeral rites were not performed properly. Instead, for Waqil Saheb, the young woman was under the power of the devil, although evidently in his view a Christian would counter satanic power in essentially the same way as a Hindu would fight demonic possession.

For both Waqil Saheb and Sujata's family, the answer to Sujata's presumed possession was not to develop a new narrative through confession but to transform the body and its constituent elements. For example, the family requested holy water, blessed by Jude, so that they could keep it at home and have Sujata drink it at regular intervals. This request almost certainly derives from the belief that water is a purifying or unmarking element that would cool the intense heat of Sujata's possession. Waqil Saheb's beating was also a way of directly countering the physical or somatic aspects of the presumed possession: it met force with force and attempted to drive the spirit from Sujata when it taunted him with silence.

But precisely because of her silence, a new space emerged for the expression of identity among Sujata and her would-be healers. For Jude, her lack of engagement challenged his power, and he countered by denying any supernatural influence upon her behavior: Sujata was under the power of sin, a sin that was objectified and seen as extrinsic to self. Jude wanted Sujata to accept responsibility for the sin and unify herself through confession. Sujata's parents, however, drew upon what could be described as Hindu conceptions of the body and sought healing through what they essentially saw as a transaction of fluids in Jude's use of holy water. Waqil Saheb relied upon his knowledge and memories as a north Indian and longed to be involved in fighting possession in a way that would have perhaps drawn the suspicion of many of his fellows in the Church of North India. Sujata's silence thus became a symbol. It displaced attention and expectation because it resisted definition. In doing so, it created a kind of cognitive vacuum that drew in a variety of practices, theories, and evocations that might otherwise seem to be quite incompatible.

Within the conceptual ambiguity surrounding Sujata and her symptoms, all the participants succeeded in encompassing her case within the boundaries of their own personal narratives. Even though Sujata did not respond to his ministrations, Jude still reaffirmed his own identity as a healer by successfully explaining her silence and the troubles afflicting the family. Waqil Saheb rediscovered a part of himself as a north Indian that his Christianity had encouraged him to abandon. In this confusing hurly-burly of healing, Sujata too asserted her own identity, for she controlled this discourse in and by her silence. In a family suffering from the violent effects of alcoholism, she was able to make herself the focal point of concern and, for a moment, to alter the boundaries that defined her position within the family.

Sita's Sin

Jude's confrontation with Sujata depended upon an indeterminacy and silence that freed the participants to imbue the encounter with their own meanings. Jude was able to make use of this silence to create a space for his identity as a Christian charismatic healer. Yet this shared space is an improvisational construct that can collapse as quickly as it is constructed. Such was the case in Jude's work with another supplicant later in the year, when the shared space they had created together seemed to challenge Jude's identity as a Christian charismatic healer.

One day I arrived at Jude's house in the late afternoon. He led me into the living room, where, sitting on the sofa, was an obviously middle-class couple. The woman, whom I will call "Sita," was dressed in a bright green and pink sari and engaged in conversation with Jude's wife. Jude then said, "I need to pray over this woman." So he prayed the Hindi Our Father and Hail Mary and was soon enraptured by the prayer of tongues. I looked at Sita and saw her eyelids begin to close ever so slowly. The rest of her body gradually grew limp, and she reclined to rest her head on the sofa. There she remained for the next fifteen to twenty minutes, until her husband revived her by gently shaking her shoulder.

While Sita was sleeping, Jude explained her case to me. She doubts everything, he said, she thinks people are out to poison her, she sees things in the windows and on glasses. Jude then stated emphatically, "She's totally mad." When Sita awoke, Jude decided to have her demonstrate a particularly perplexing aspect of her symptoms. Jude asked his wife to bring a stainless steel cup. Jude's wife gave the cup to Sita who began to look at it quite intently, her eyes fixing on it as she slowly turned it in her hand. Several times she would stop and run her fingers on the surface of the cup, as if tracing some sort of invisible line. Sita then stopped and remarked, "Well, this time I don't see anything." She explained that she would often see lines and shapes, most particularly the outline of feet, in glasses and wood panels. What she seemed to be saying was that the grain in the wood, or the scuffmarks made on the glass after cleaning would coalesce into an image—of feet, of a name, of eyes—that would have a malevolent import.

About a month later I was able to talk with Sita's husband about her troubles. They both had come from Bihar to Varanasi, where she found employment as a public health nurse while he was able to continue work in government service. According to her husband, Sita began to have problems several months earlier, when she started flying into rages in which she would throw pots and pans around the kitchen, sometimes striking him in the process. She would also say she saw things written on cups, windowpanes, and walls that she understood as signs that she had been cursed. She began to visit temples of Durga and Kali to offer fruit and sweetmeats. She then would take the offerings, now *prasād*, and consume them as an antidote to her afflictions. She would also insist that the temple priest tie a red string, called a *rākhī*, around her left wrist for protection. The goddess Durga is a fierce protector of her devotees and, as the vanquisher of the buffalo demon Mahisha, known for her power over evil. Kali's power is even more ferocious, and she is often depicted standing over the inert body of her consort Shiva. For Sita, such protection was surely necessary, for she alternatively blamed her condition upon actions of a demon and then upon the efforts of her own husband and a friend to poison her.

At the beginning of these episodes, Sita's husband learned that he had been transferred to another district. The friend, a female colleague at the hospital, had recently distanced herself from Sita. With the situation at home becoming intolerable, the family sought medical help from a psychiatrist at Banaras Hindu University. Sita's husband remarked that the doctor did not give a specific diagnosis but did prescribe a tranquilizer and trifluroperazine, an antipsychotic drug administered for a variety of conditions ranging from severe anxiety to schizophrenia. These prescriptions had provided relief for a time, but the drugs seemed to have lost their effectiveness. With nowhere else to turn, the family sought out Jude who, they hoped, could discern the cause of Sita's troubles.

I asked Jude his evaluation of Sita's condition and he replied, "You see, she is in a state of sin." Jude continued, saying that she had committed a sin against her body. He did not mention the exact nature of this sin—in his view it could have been something as simple as masturbation or an affair out of wedlock—but he did say that this particular sin occurred before her marriage. Because she had not confessed the sin, she remained in its thrall. More immediately, it was Sita's relationship with a female friend that was causing her pain. This friend, a colleague at the hospital, had become debilitated by arthritis and took a leave of absence. Sita began to take care of her friend by cooking for her, helping her bathe, and escorting her to the bathroom. During this time, a "boyfriend" made some appearances and, after inquiring about the finances of Sita's friend, suddenly asked her to marry him. When Sita questioned the motives of this suitor, her friend became hostile. In the room where Sita's friend was living there were many pictures of Hindu deities on the wall, and often during their conversations the woman's gaze would be drawn to these pictures and away from the conversation. The combination of all these pictures of Hindu gods and goddesses and the now overt hostility led Sita to believe that her friend was trying to curse her—something that she would try to counteract by going from temple to temple and consuming *prasād*.

Jude once again developed a diagnosis that emphasized the divisive effects of sin. Sita had committed a sin against her body, a sin that she as a non-Catholic had not been able to confess. While an unconfessed sin always festers within the individual, it can be elicited and given even greater power through the workings of memory and desire. Sita was a loving woman who cared for her friend and her family. But she remained frustrated in her desire for love: her friend turned on her, her husband was transferred, leaving her hurt and her need for love unfulfilled. Her sin against her body was motivated by similar feelings of denial and frustration, and thus there was a link between the previous sin of her flesh and her present emotional state. Like Jude before his conversion, she was bound to the flesh.

While Jude counseled Sita and formulated his diagnosis, a shared space formed around similar elements used in both Catholic and Hindu religious practice. An interesting aspect of the Catholic charismatic movement in north India is that it employs many practices that bear at least a superficial similarity to what it would label as "Hindu superstitions." Certainly for Sita, there were clear homologies between many of the accouterments of Jude's ministry and what was familiar in her devotional life. The Eucharistic hosts, consumed during Mass, resembled the *prasād* that she herself would take home after her visits to temple. Indeed, Sita felt invited to partake of the Eucharist, since in Hindi the Eucharist is called *param prasād*. And so, at public Masses, Sita would often approach the altar to accept the consecrated unleavened bread upon her tongue, only to be stopped by nuns positioned to prevent non-Catholics from receiving Communion. The *rākhī* she wore on her left wrist, a symbol of a vow she had made and protection she sought, appeared functionally very similar to the scapular, made of twine and brown cloth, often worn by charismatics as a sign of their devotion. The holy water that Jude would dispense also had its resonances. When he would pour Lourdes water from his Virgin Mary-shaped plastic decanter, Sita would accept the water in her hands, touch it to her lips and then run her hand over the part in her hair, much as she would accept water or milk that had been used to cool the deity at a temple. In his prayers for healing, Jude would lay his hands upon Sita and repeat the name of Jesus. Sometimes, he would give her a special blessing with his cross; a cross infused with the healing power of his recently deceased confessor. He would also softly massage her forehead and lightly blow into her face. Sita identified the name of Jesus as a particularly powerful mantra, while Jude's breathing into her face was the blowing of a blessing, or *duā*. This apparent combination of a variety of healing practices suited Sita quite well, since she and her family were pursuing all available means of a cure—from appealing to the Goddess, to consulting a doctor trained in psychiatric medicine, and finally to seeking help from Jude.

Although the counseling continued for weeks, problems began to emerge when Sita insisted upon continuing to go to a Kali temple near her home. Jude told me that Kali's image, black, smeared with blood, and bedecked with human skulls, exerted a demonic influence upon Sita's behavior. Jude's real difficulty with Sita became clear when she persisted in calling Jesus' name a mantra. Many charismatics consider mantras a Hindu superstition. Accordingly, Jude attempted to explain to Sita that the name of Jesus was not a mantra, even though by repeating it she would be delivered from her illness.

He also demanded that she stop taking medication and *prasād*. For Jude, the tendency to promiscuous sexuality that he identified in many women was mirrored in the Hindu promiscuous approach to belief and healing. By calling the name of Jesus a mantra and continuing to go to temples, Sita, in Jude's view, was cynically hedging her bets and refusing to rely exclusively upon the power of Christ.

While for Sita the difference between Christian and Hindu had little meaning, for Jude the distinction became crucial. Jude was attempting to help Sita to name or identify what properly belonged inside the boundaries of her own self. In fact, much of her case concerned the very act of naming and its implications. For Sita, the lines on a cup or the grain of a wooden window shutter would form images that she could name and identify as signs of the evil forces arrayed against her. Jude attempted to persuade her that the forms she saw belonged to no other name except her own, since they were the traces of her own sins. Yet when Sita used the marked word "mantra," Jude saw the crucial boundary between Hindu and Christian being ruptured and his own identity being challenged. Catholic charismatic healing in north India, and Jude's ministry in particular, relies upon improvisation. The blowing of the blessing, the use of holy water, and, most prominently, the repetition of Jesus' name are all practices that have their analogues in the surrounding non-Christian culture. But within the ambiguous symbolic interplay of charismatic healing, these acts become imaginatively marked as Christian, not Hindu. By explicitly suggesting a convergence between Catholic and Hindu practice, Sita unintentionally challenges the boundaries of Jude's identity as a healer, whose power comes exclusively from Christ. Boundaries are, after all, often constructed through the very process of naming, and Sita refused to recognize a crucial boundary between Hindu and Catholic that charismatics wish to construct and maintain, if only in the form of a name.

A Space for Redemption

What finally characterized Jude's encounter with both Sita and Sujata was a pervasive concern with the fragmentation of the self. For Jude, human wholeness and integrity become threatened by sin, most particularly by sins of the flesh, which invert the appropriate relationship that humans have with their true selves. For Sita and Sujata, the self was in constant need of sustenance; a sustenance provided by the words, water, *prasād*, and medication that respectively constituted integral parts of the therapies that they or their families sought. Often the differences between the Hindu and Christian worldviews have been characterized by distinguishing Christian conceptions of the unified "individual" with an unchanging essence, from Hindu conceptions of the "dividual," an entity constantly in flux and changing in its inevitable transactions with others (Marriot 1990, 17). Yet what brought Jude together with Sita and Sujata was precisely their collective concern for reestablishing a threatened or lost integrity of self. Underlying Jude's encounters with the two women was a conception of the self not as a purely psychological entity, but as an amalgam of body, flesh, and will. Accordingly, Jude's ministrations were often transactional in nature, since they relied upon infusions of grace or divine power through a variety of mediums such as holy water or his gold and onyx cross.

Jude's work with Sujata and Sita also seemed to draw its strength from a particular consonance of motives. For Jude, confession is central to conversion and healing because accepting personal responsibility for sin unifies the self. Hence, he remains concerned with what humans consider to be part of their own sense of identity, or, more simply, with what lies inside and outside the self. Sita's and Sujata's cases then resonated with these preoccupations of his ministry, for he saw both women unable to accept the parts of themselves that had experienced sin. Yet, for Sita and Sujata, the locus of conflict was not cast in such self-referential terms. Instead, their concerns seemed to be relational and involved the painful marginality they were experiencing within the lives of their families. Sujata had to endure the violence of her alcoholic father. Sita endured the hostility of a woman who was once her friend as well as the transfer of her husband to yet another job assignment, even though they had moved only recently. To this extent, the effect of Sita's and Sujata's apparent illnesses was certainly aggressive, for their troubles most certainly shifted the balance of power within their respective families (on possession and gender in South Asia, see Freed and Freed 1964; Obeyesekere 1977). Both women were able to find a voice for their feelings through Jude, who, by his very presence, exposed what their families attempted to conceal.

Jude also found expression for his own concerns and identity as a healer, since with both Sita and Sujata he was able to adapt to the context and improvise a discourse of healing. In Sujata's case, her own silence became a symbolic pivot around which a variety of practices and interests revolved. With Sita, elements such as holy water or the repetition of Jesus' name became centers of overlapping Hindu and Catholic evocational fields—fields that only became disjoined when she used the marked word "mantra." Jude's efforts to change the boundaries of the self thus emerge as tactical interventions to create a space for his healing voice. As he moves through urban Varanasi, Jude modulates his healing voice to match the rhythms of his supplicants and the strains of his own personal narrative. Although his healing ministrations did not reach the harmony he sought, they nonetheless became quite compatible with Sita's and Sujata's anger toward the boundaries that defined their positions within their families. A redemptive space was created in these encounters—what Michel de Certeau (1988, 117) might

call a "polyvalent unity" of "contractual proximities"—made possible by a
congruence between Jude's healing practices and the expectations of the two
women and their families. Through a convergence of practical logic and
tactical intent, Jude, Sita, and Sujata all managed to create new personal
spaces that provided refuge from the afflictions of their daily lives.

North Indian Improvisations

In his own story of redemption, Jude moves from a horizontal axis of
self-definition to what can be described as a vertical axis of self to establish
continuity with God. For Jude, the body becomes an evocative referent in this
transformation because it often becomes a crucial barrier between humans
and the Divine. Not only does an awareness of the flesh tempt sin, but the
body itself records the traces of sin. In what follows, we will consider Jude's
account of counseling sessions involving the diagnosis and healing of sexual
transgressions. Unlike with Sita and Sujata, where Jude's Christian identity
was most strongly expressed, it is here that Jude speaks in his most distinctly
Indian voice by initially drawing upon conceptions of the body prevalent
within the broad sweep of South Asian culture. Within these contexts, Jude's
healing ministry emerges not as a seamlessly Christian form of self-expression,
but as a very north Indian bricolage.

"The First Sin is So Beautiful, So Soft"

As Jude was traveling with a prayer group to a Christian community in
Bihar, he had a premonition. "We are going to Sodom and Gomorrah," he
said out loud to his companions. They laughed, Jude remembers.

It was hot, terribly hot, Jude recalls, with the dry hot wind called the
lū blowing. On the second day, he began his counseling and his first supplicant was a twelve-year-old girl. She had a pain in her stomach, and he
asked her, "Do you know the reason for this pain?" Since she did not know
the reason, Jude asked her, softly, "Are you using your body for others?"
She was indeed using her body for others, and the pain the girl was experiencing resulted from that "sin." Other children came to him. One eleven-
year-old could not urinate because her vagina had been so bruised by sexual
contact, and there were many more like her. These were the children of
bonded laborers, raped and sexually exploited by the landlords of the district to "repay" debts that their parents owed. These debts were passed from
generation to generation, since no family could ever pay back the interest.
Trapped in virtual slavery, these children had no choice but to hand over
their bodies to the landowners.

Jude refers to the children's rape and exploitation by the landlords as a "sin" that both the landlords and the children were committing. In making this rather disturbing observation, Jude seems to understand sin as an objective entity like a disease that somehow becomes separate from human intent. Even though the children were forced into these sexual acts, their exploitation opened them to sin by tearing away their shame. Since these children had also seen their parents having sexual relations, they had begun to understand how the flesh could bring pleasure. So they started to experiment with one another, discovering, according to Jude, that "the first sin is so beautiful, so soft." The taste of the initial sin, especially a sexual one, is so sweet that the sinner is inevitably drawn into a web of violation. In an intriguing conflation of images, Jude observes that while the first sin initially appears as a "sweet fruit," eventually "it will ripen, it will burst" and, like an abscess or boil, spill its poison into the body of the sinner.

In presenting such a physical conception of sin and its effects, Jude evokes a vision that owes much to ayurvedic conceptions of the body. Recall that Jude was involved in the production and marketing of Vivirex, an ayurvedic tonic for male sexual vigor. Within ayurvedic theory, sexual dysfunctions are usually attributed to a blockage of the humor *vāyu* by or in seminal fluid (Dash 1984, 180; Jaggi 1981, 132). According to Francis Zimmerman (1979, 19–20), the body in this conception has a pervading "unctuousness," there is "no anatomy," only channels through which vital fluids pass. Ayurvedic treatments clear the body channels and nourish the tissues, thereby producing an "internal smoothness" and "external plumpness" (19). Accordingly, when Jude speaks of the effects of sexual transgressions on these children of bonded laborers, he emphasizes their somatic manifestations. Jude here considers the body as a point where the physical and moral overlap, a central element in ayurvedic conceptions of the body (17). Sin can also be transferred to a fetus in the womb, for that is how the children first experienced the sins of their parents. This is eminently possible, according to ayurvedic theory, because the fetus passes through a "bi-cardic stage" of development in which it not only shares the heart of its mother, but her actions and longings as well (Kakar 1982, 245). In recognizing these similarities, it is also important to realize that Jude was not formally trained as an ayurvedic doctor, or *vaidya*. He has surely never read the *Caraka Samhita* or other central ayurvedic texts. Instead, he was a front man, a marketer for a product promoted as ayurvedic. Accordingly, what emerges in Jude's discussions of the body are traces and fragments of an ayurvedic worldview and its vision of health and well-being. Hence, when Jude likens sin to a boil or tumor that hardens and bursts, it recalls Margaret Egnor's (1978, 52–55) account of an ayurvedic doctor who would attribute many illnesses to "hardening matter" obstructing blood and other bodily fluids. In

Jude's somatology, sin occludes the flow of grace as it ripens or hardens in the body. Confession then is not only a narrative that unifies the self, but an emetic that clears channels in the human body for the action of grace. Sin is indeed somatic, since a redeemed person does have an internal smoothness without the tumors and eruptions of sin.

A Tale of Two Sisters

On a winter day, Jude was once again counseling at the Catholic *āśram* outside of Varanasi. Although Mr. Prakash, the Radhasoami devotee, never appeared, Jude was occupied with a number of female supplicants who had come to see him. I was walking back and forth in front of the room where Jude was counseling, when he emerged leading a noticeably dazed and unkempt young woman. He returned her to the charge of her mother and cried loudly in Hindi, "She's all right, she'll be fine!" At that point her mother let her go, and the young woman walked into a tree. Then another woman entered the room with Jude, and a few moments later I heard a scream followed by a fusillade of obscenities in Bhojpuri: "Mother fucker! Don't touch me! Sister-fucker! Bastard!" Jude then swung open the door and invited me in.

I entered the room and saw a woman in an orange sari writhing on the ground. She was perhaps fifty-five to sixty years old, with her gray hair knitted into a tight braid. She was first in a fetal position from which she would often strike out into the air or, if the timing was right, at her earnest exorcists. Jude, cross in hand, was praying over her vigorously in Hindi, "Praise you Jesus, thank you Jesus, we love you Jesus, remove this devil spirit—in Jesus' name I command you." The woman started to thrash more violently, rolling around on the ground. Jude called for holy water, which another charismatic supplied, and began to sprinkle it over the prostrate woman. Slowly her cries and spasms reduced in intensity and then stopped. She sat up and pulled part of her sari over her head, smiled, and walked out of the room.

The next woman who entered the room appeared to be in her mid-forties. She was wearing a deep purple sari with a white, yellow, and black floral pattern. On her chin was a tattoo of three dots which was to protect her from the evil eye (*nazar*) and also marked her as a member of an untouchable caste. Jude raised his hands and placed them on her head and began to pray. At the touch of his hands, she began to inhale deeply through her nose and then to bark like a dog. When she started barking, Jude took his hands off her head, drew back his right hand and slapped her in the face. He then pointed at her and said, "This is a daughter of God—leave her!" The barking continued, and he slapped her again saying, "Stop this play acting!" This seemed to quiet her somewhat, although the heavy breathing continued. Jude then asked for the holy water and began to sprinkle it over her, repeating the now familiar refrain, "Praise you Jesus, thank you Jesus." The woman's barks gradually subsided, and her breathing became steady and unlabored. Jude gave her the cross and asked her to kiss it, which she did several times, as she cradled it in both hands as a precious object.

These three cases that Jude encountered in rapid succession demonstrate how much his ministry had become integrated into a north Indian pattern of the healing of possession. The young woman who Jude first treated constituted a classic case of possession. As Veena Das (1985, 189) observes, within Hindu culture great care is exerted to present the female body as a bounded and enclosed system: hair is tightly braided and oiled, and bangles and anklets symbolically close bodily extremities. Such "presentations," Das also maintains, not only reflect the containment of women by the social system but are also designed to protect women from ghosts and witchcraft (Das 1985, 189). The young woman Jude treated had distinctly unkempt hair and a disheveled sari, signifying perhaps how the boundaries of her body had been violated by the malevolent spirit who had taken control of her. Such a ghostly manifestation most certainly occurred, according to north Indian standards, with the woman who next came to see Jude. Although she did not sing or prophesy, her spasms, shaking of the head, striking out and, of course, her use of obscenity were are all culturally marked signs of possession, and a familiar sight in temples and shrines in Uttar Pradesh and Bihar.

Jude, of course, provided a Christian interpretation for his supplicant's verbal and physical assaults. The rage the demon was expressing—through insults and curses—was the rage it felt at confronting the power of Jesus. Yet, in spite of his effort to bring them into a Christian framework of interpretation, these possessions followed north Indian Hindu patterns. The third woman who entered was possessed by a *bhūt* or *pret,* as she pulled down the border of her sari and loosened the braids of her hair to have Jude pray over her. In doing so, she almost invited possession for she left bodily boundaries open. Jude responded to the presence of the demon in typical north Indian fashion: he struck his supplicant in the face, something that he refused to do with Sujata, and he sprinkled holy water over her. So the encounter between Jude and these possessed women became a transfer of fluids and marked substances. When the two women, who were in fact sisters, left the *āśram,* they asked Jude to bless a container of water that they had brought with them. He agreed and placed his hands on the stainless steel container, filling it with his healing power.

A North Indian Bricolage

To be a charismatic healer is not only to claim the ability to discern afflictions and to move beyond space and time through the vehicle of divinely inspired speech. Perhaps even more importantly, to be a charismatic healer is to claim the ability to improvise. From his confrontations with Sujata and Sita to his encounter with the three women, we have seen how Jude acts out crucial themes in his personal narrative through an improvised discourse of healing. In his work with his Hindu and Christian supplicants, we have also seen how the Indian, Catholic, and personal elements shaping his life assume differing combinations, as Jude endeavors to establish and maintain a space for his own identity as a charismatic healer. In the confident, but always adaptable, claims that mark his counseling and works of healing, Jude finds his redemption continually confirmed. Yet to argue that Jude's effort to change boundaries is an attempt to create a space for his healing voice is not to say that his is a static, unchanging, identity. When he drew back his hand and slapped his female supplicant, Jude was doing more than simply translating his healing methods into a north Indian idiom and conveniently transgressing a personal boundary he had set not that long ago, when he chided his friend Waqil Saheb for striking the young woman, Sujata. Instead, when the palm of his hand was met and accepted by the woman who had come to him for healing, Jude was emphasizing how he himself had become a north Indian healer and his ministry a north Indian bricolage of healing.

Charismatic Transgressions

While Jude's charismatic ministry is an improvisational effort to maintain his Christian voice within north Indian culture, there are nonetheless consistent themes that structure his healing and counseling. Sexuality in particular assumes a prominent place in Jude's own recollections of encounters with supplicants who sought his discernment and guidance. At a charismatic prayer service in a large north Indian city, Jude recalled that he confronted a woman with a particularly shameful sexual sin that he had discerned she committed. His female supplicant then wrote her testimony in Hindi for Jude to preserve:

> When prayers were being made over me, the words that were being said seemed to be only for me. Everything that was going on in my life was revealed. I am very happy now that I know how much Jesus loves me—that he wants me in every way, that he wants my entire body, my entire body, my entire body only for himself and in his service, he will forgive me, forgive me, forgive me and not give attention to my weakness. Forgive my weakness, Jesus, forgive, forgive, forgive. From my foul heart, from my weak heart, I give you thanks Jesus because you will stay with me and give me only

love and will continue to love me. I pray that I overcome my temp-
tations so that Jesus may stay with me.

Jude's initial ministrations in this case emphasized characteristically
Christian themes. He urged her to offer her body, and her flesh, to Christ in
His service. By loving the body of God, and by having one's own body loved
by Him, the flesh of the body is transformed, and sensuality itself becomes
a means for reaching the divine. If, as some have argued (Laing 1969), the
human sense of embodiment provides a crucial awareness of continuity over
time, Jude joining with Christ's body establishes a continuity beyond the
boundaries of time. Indeed, by urging his supplicant to empty her heart of
filth, to be filled by Christ, penetrated and purified by His Word, Jude attempts to bring her closer to the incarnation, which itself spans the distance
between humans and God.

But there is something more underlying this counseling session than
conventional Christian imagery. When Jude described his initial revelation of
his supplicant's sin, he referred to it as "the opening of the sinner"—a confrontation that revealed what she did "in secret" in order to prove that God
also sees what "each person does in the dark." And so Jude "opens" his
sinning supplicants, to be penetrated by the word, understood both as his
word of discernment and as Christ, the embodied Word. It is here that Jude's
charismatic ministry becomes not simply an improvisational discourse of
healing, but a distinctly charismatic form of transgression.

In his discussions of his "past life," Jude quite explicitly portrays himself as a transgressor, a rapist, and a violator of women. Although he has
renounced his past bondage to the flesh, one could argue that he remains a
violator in the act of confronting his female supplicants with their presumed
sins. Veiling and other restrictions placed upon female behavior, in addition
to positing a dangerous female sexuality, also assume a predatory sexual
instinct among men. Just as a woman would perhaps irreparably damage her
reputation if she met alone with a man, so too would the man often be subject
to some level of social censure, at the very least in the form of rumor. In spite
of these general cultural restrictions, Jude not only meets alone with both
married and unmarried women, he also touches them when he lays his hands
upon them for healing. What is more, he hears the intimate details of their
sexual lives and, he claims, often confronts women with their sins. The sins
he claims to reveal are sexually explicit and bizarre: a nun having intercourse
in the sacristy, for example, or, in a case he related to me, a woman mastur-
bating by penetrating her vagina with candles. Such images are all quite
striking and would seem provocative, even perverse, if mentioned within
exclusively male company: to mention such matters in the presence of women
would be unthinkable. And so, in raising sexual issues so openly with women,

Jude crosses the cultural boundaries that often divide the male and female realms within Indian society. Indeed, if we accept his own description of these encounters, it is Jude himself who becomes the transgressor by actually reenacting his fall into the flesh by aggressively examining his supplicants for their sexual transgressions. His work itself then becomes a test in which he continually meets temptation, a temptation which he may implicitly acknowledge in his frequent statements that while a woman could appear nude in front of him, he still would not touch her. To this extent perhaps, Jude's divine gift was bestowed as much to alleviate the afflictions of the healer as those of the supplicant.

One day Jude was counseling Prema, the younger sister of Waqil Saheb, the lawyer who had introduced him to Sujata. Prema had been so crippled by polio that she could only move by literally crawling on the ground. Obviously without any prospects for marriage, she had remained housebound for years. But Jude resolved to take her out of the house to prayer meetings in Varanasi and counsel her. He would often pray over her and gently massage her twisted legs. He prayed for healing and urged her to meditate upon the legs of Jesus which were themselves broken on the cross. He then asked her to forget about herself and reminded her of his own personal prayer to Jesus, "Whatever you give me to suffer, I will suffer, for you suffered everything for me." Yet losing herself in prayers for others was only part of her healing, since Jude said that she must also learn how to forgive. But Jude elaborated his observation in a strikingly unexpected way when he said, "She needs to forgive God for making her the way she is." Here, Jude does not mention will and sacrifice, which are elements of a Christian language of power. Instead, his words are pregnant with the realization that all of us, even those like Prema who suffer terribly, finally have no claim on the way life goes. In the end, Jude is saying, we can only confess and pray for mercy. Just as we must forgive ourselves and one another, so too must we forgive God. Perhaps Jude is implying that it is precisely by forgiving God that we learn how little depends upon sacrifice and how much depends upon mercy. If this is so, then it is because forgiving God is itself a transgression.

Notes

1. In November of 2000, I returned to India eager to see "Jude" once again. A week before I arrived, Jude died of kidney failure. I have retained his pseudonym in this essay and have also chosen to retain the original style of presentation that reflects the nature of my research with him. Although I do not address the subject in this chapter, my relationship with Jude was complex, and I have specifically reflected upon the friendship we shared, and the methodological issues it elicits, in "American Catholic, Indian Catholics" (Schmalz 2001) and in "On Method and Narrative" (Schmalz

and Gottschalk forthcoming). This essay draws from research presented in my doctoral thesis "A Space for Redemption: Catholic Tactics in Hindu North India," Ph.D. Dissertation, The Divinity School, The University of Chicago, 1998. Portions of this essay have been presented as "A Slave for Jesus: Portrait of an Indian Charismatic Healer" at The Conference on South Asia, The University of Wisconsin-Madison, 10/96 and as "Sins and Somatologies: Sexual Transgression and the Body in Indian Charismatic Healing," American Academy of Religion Annual Meeting, San Francisco, 11/97. I would like to thank Peter Gottschalk of Southwestern University for organizing both of these panels. Fieldwork for this paper was conducted between January 1995 and May 1996 and was supported by grants from the United States Doctoral Dissertation Research Abroad Program (Fulbright-Hays) and the American Institute of Indian Studies (AIIS). I would also like to thank Professors Wendy Doniger and McKim Marriot of the University of Chicago and Professor Thomas Csordas of Case Western for reading initial drafts of this paper. Finally, thanks to Kristin, Anna, Maxi, and, of course, to my friend "Jude" and his living memory.

References

Conze, Edward. 1975. *The Buddhist Scriptures*. New York: Penguin.

Dash, Vaidya Bhagwan. 1984. *Diagnosis and Treatment of Diseases in Ayurveda, Part III*. New Delhi: Concept Publishing.

Das, Veena. 1985. "Paradigms of Body Symbolism: An Analysis of Selected Themes in Hindu Culture." In *Indian Religion*, ed. Richard Burghart and Audrey Cantlie, 180–207. London: Curzon Press.

De Certeau, Michel. 1988. *The Practice of Everyday Life*. Translated by Steven Rendall. Berkeley and Los Angeles: University of California Press.

Doniger, Wendy. 1975. *Hindu Myths*. New York: Penguin Books.

Egnor, Margaret. 1978. "The Sacred Spell and Other Conceptions of Life in Tamil Culture." Ph.D. Dissertation. University of Chicago.

Freed, R. S., and S. A. Freed. 1964. "Spirit Possession as Illness in a North Indian Village." *Ethnology* 3: 152–71.

Gold, Ann. 1990. *Fruitful Journeys*. Berkeley and Los Angeles: The University of California Press.

Jaggi, O. P. 1981. *Ayurveda: Indian System of Medicine*. Delhi: Atma Ram and Sons.

Jaini, Padhmanabh. 1979. *The Jaina Path of Purification*. Berkeley and Los Angeles: The University of California Press.

Kakar, Sudhir. 1982. *Shamans, Mystics and Doctors*. Chicago: University of Chicago Press.

Laing, R. D. 1969. *The Divided Self*. London: Penguin Books.

Marriot, McKim. 1990. "Constructing a Hindu Ethnosociology." In *India Through Hindu Categories,* ed. McKim Marriot, 1–39. Delhi: SAGE Publications.

Obeyesekere, Gananath. 1977. "Psychocultural Exegesis of a Case of Spirit Possession in Sri Lanka." In *Case Studies in Spirit Possession*, ed. Vincent Crapanzano and Vivian Garrison, 235–94. New York: Wiley and Sons.

Parry, Jonathan. 1989. "The End of the Body." In *Fragments for a History of the Human Body*, ed. Michel Fehr, 491–517. San Francisco, Calif.: Zone Books.

Parry, Jonathan. 1990. *Death in Banaras.* New York: Oxford University Press.

Schmalz, Mathew. 2001. "American Catholic, Indian Catholics: Reflections on Religious Identity, Ethnography and the History of Religions." *Method & Theory in the Study of Religion* 13: 91–97.

Schmalz, Mathew, and Peter Gottschalk. Forthcoming. "On Method and Narrative or How a Textualist Gave Birth to Two Ethnographers." In *Notes on a Mandala: Essays in Honor of Wendy Doniger*, ed. Laurie Patton and David Haberman. New York: Seven Bridges Press.

Upadhyay, Krishnadev. 1991. *Bhojpuri Lok Sanskriti* [Bhojpuri Folk Culture]. Illahabad: Hindi Sahitya Sammelan.

Zimmerman, Francis. 1979. "Remarks on Conceptions of the Body in Ayurvedic Medicine." In *South Asia Digest of Regional Writing, Volume 8: Sources of Illness and Healing in South Asian Regional Literature*, ed. B. Pfeiderer and G. D. Sontheimer. Heidelberg: South Asia Institute, Heidelburg University.

PART III

∾

Visionaries and Missionaries:
Redefining Religious Authority

CHAPTER 9

Redemptive Hegemony and
the Ritualization of Reading

Eliza F. Kent

In a collection of stories set in his mythical Minnesotan hometown, Garrison Keillor bemoans the lack of visual splendor in his family's ritual life when compared to the local Catholics. Keillor's family belonged to a Protestant sect, the Sanctified Brethren, that was, as he says, "so tiny that nobody but us and God knew about it," and so ritually impoverished that their weekly celebration of the Sabbath consisted of sitting together in silence on folding chairs in his uncle's living room (Keillor 1985, 101–2). The Catholics of Lake Wobegon, on the other hand, celebrated their holy days with gusto. Keillor writes enviously of the Catholic ritual style:

> Everything we did was plain, but they were regal and gorgeous—
> especially the Feast Day of St. Francis, which they did right out in
> the open, a feast for the eye. Cows, horses, some pigs, right on the
> church lawn . . . I stared at it until my eyes almost fell out, and then
> I wished it would go on much longer. . . . I wasn't allowed inside
> Our Lady, of course, but if the Blessing of the Animals on the Feast
> Day of St. Francis was any indication, Lord, I didn't know but what
> they had elephants in there and acrobats (Keillor 1985, 103).

A similar stylistic divide distinguishes Catholic and Protestant ritual life in south India. Keillor's voracious appetite for a richly sensual ritual style would go as unsatisfied in the services of the Church of South India as it did in Lake Wobegon. Flowers, incense, and brightly decorated images are notably absent from much CSI (Church of South India) liturgy. Instead of flowers, incense, or images, CSI ritual practice is animated by the Word: sung, spoken, or haltingly read off the page, recited from memory

191

at rapid-fire pace in the formal Tamil of public debate and the political platform or drawn out in dramatic fashion in colloquial, spoken Tamil. In this article, I want to draw attention to the place of reading—particularly women's reading—in the ritual lives of CSI Christians. But to do so we must turn our gaze from public, institutional liturgy to the people and practices at its margins. Since women are very rarely active as ministers in the CSI, I will focus here on the ritualization of reading by Christian women in the evangelical practices that take place outside the physical boundaries of the church.

In using the term "ritualization," I draw on Catherine Bell's reconceptualization of ritual as defined not by essential qualities, but by a style of practice that employs diverse behavioral tactics or strategies to distinguish prosaic action from its sacred or value-invested counterpart (Bell 1992, 7–8, 89–92). In a comprehensive reevaluation of the study of ritual, *Ritual Theory, Ritual Practice,* Bell responds to the work of a broad range of social theorists from Emile Durkheim to Pierre Bourdieu, all of whom see a relationship between ritual and the organization of hierarchical social relations. Bell too understands ritualization as a strategy of power, but not one by which power is imposed by the powerful on the weak. Discarding substantive definitions of power, Bell sees at work in ritual the operation of what she calls "redemptive hegemony," a phrase that seeks to describe how people reproduce relations of domination and subordination through practice. Redemptive hegemony exists "as a practical consciousness of the world" that when translated into action shapes the actor's sense of the field of possibilities confronting him or her, thus providing the context for meaningful action in the world. Bell writes,

> Although awkward, the term 'redemptive hegemony' denotes the way in which reality is experienced as a natural weave of constraint and possibility, the fabric of day to day dispositions and decisions experienced as a field for strategic action. Rather than embracing an ideological vision of the whole, it conveys a biased, nuanced rendering of the ordering of power so as to facilitate the envisioning of personal empowerment through activity in the perceived system (Bell 1992, 84).

Ritualized reading involves a redemptive appropriation of the dominant ideology of the Church of South India insofar as it structures the way people, even those most marginalized from the centers of power within the CSI, negotiate for themselves a more or less secure position within the overall social field without disrupting the dominant social order. The specific

mode through which ritualized reading works, I argue, is through the de-
ployment of widely recognized forms of authoritative speech. In the ideology of the CSI, literacy holds pride of place as the means for both spiritual
and material upward mobility. Deeply influenced by the atonement theology of nineteenth-century Christianity as transmitted by English and American missionaries, the crux of the Christian message as manifest in CSI
liturgy and literature is the redemptive sacrifice of Jesus Christ, whose
death created the conditions necessary for the salvation of even the most
reprobate sinner. On a spiritual level, literacy gives one personal access to
the holy Scriptures, through which one approaches the salvific understanding of the true meaning and power of Christ's death. On a material level,
it is by mastering the technical skills of literacy that one gains access to the
institutional networks of power created by the Church (e.g. CSI-run churches,
schools, hospitals, nursing homes, orphanages, etc). In the following pages,
I analyze how Christian women reproduce the gendered and classed power
relations of the CSI Church, even as they use the symbols of authority
properly deployed by the official Church leaders to enhance their own prestige and their own reputations for virtue and spiritual prowess. There may
be forms of silent reading that one could see as ritualized, but I am interested here in reading out loud, a performative, public form of reading that
is "ritualized" insofar as it is differentiated from other, more prosaic forms
of reading, and structures relations of domination and subordination between people.

In order to establish the centrality of this form of speech within the CSI,
I first discuss the importance of reading out loud in the public services of one
church that I attended in Madurai, Christ Church, the spiritual home of a
medium-sized congregation near the Railway Colony in the southern part of
the city. I then examine the kind of interactive reading that characterizes the
work of Bible women, salaried agents of the Church whose office originated
in nineteenth-century western women's missionary organizations and who
now occupy a fairly humble place in the CSI leadership. My focus is on one
particular Bible woman, Muttammal, a seventy-year-old widow and mother
of three who was one of my main informants when I was conducting fieldwork
in Madurai in 1996. I conclude with an analysis of one of the pedagogical
tools used by Muttammal (and other Bible women) in her evangelical and
educational work, the Wordless Book, a four-page blank book whose multi-
colored pages she uses to explain core Christian teachings. This simple device, I argue, enables a kind of ritualized reading that seeks to convey to the
nonliterate the capacity of literacy to gain one access not only to the salvific
power of the Christian scriptures, but also, by extension, to the benefits of
modern, secular literacy.

Ritual Life within the Church of South India

First it is necessary to provide some historical background information
on the CSI itself and the place of ritual within south Indian Protestantism.
The relatively spare quality of CSI ritual life can be traced to the fact that the
Anglican, Lutheran, Baptist, Presbyterian, and Congregationalist missionaries
who brought Protestant Christianity to India from England, Germany, and the
United States in the eighteenth and nineteenth centuries took a dim view of
any ritual practices that appeared to derive from the Hindu (and, less frequently, Muslim) pasts of converts. Unlike their Catholic counterparts, who
had a complex but generally more tolerant attitude towards popular religious
practices that drew upon elements of local religious traditions, Protestant
church leaders vehemently discouraged the growth of syncretistic practices.
Protestant missionaries tended to resist local efforts to assimilate preexisting
popular Hindu religious practices into church liturgy and assigned such practices to the category of "superstition." What was identified as superstition
varied over time and across the different missionary societies. What stayed
consistent, however, was the missionaries' (and later Indian church leaders')
assumption of authority to distinguish between superstition and knowledge,
where "superstition" consisted of forms of understanding regarded as outmoded and retrograde, and "knowledge" generally referred to forms of understanding grounded in Christian faith or Western science.

The process of categorizing different varieties of practice intensified in
the second half of the nineteenth century, as large numbers of the so-called
low castes entered the Church through group conversion. These poor and
largely uneducated converts were thought to be particularly attached to superstition. At this time, many missionary societies coordinated their efforts to
establish firm categories for discriminating among religious, superstitious,
customary, and caste-based practices. Missionary conferences made one declaration after another to distinguish between those customs that were harmless and those that were harmful to Christian faith, and resolved to root out
the latter while tolerating the former (Forrester 1980, 71; Estborn 1959, 8,
33–39). These conferences continued even after the Indian mission was, with
considerable effort, transformed into a Church.

In 1947 the departure of the British from Indian political life coincided
with a corresponding withdrawal of foreign missionaries from their positions
of dominance within the Church leadership. The Church of South India was
the result of a large ecumenical movement to unify into one body all of the
Protestant churches that had been founded by different missionary societies.
In the end, virtually all of the different Protestant sects merged into the CSI,
except for the Lutherans, who remain a separate Church to this day. The
discouragement and desanctification of popular religious practices coincided

with a corresponding elevation of literary practices; in particular, Western-style education and composition of hymns and songs, and evidence of piety demonstrated through familiarity with scriptural texts were highly valued.

Literacy, Speech, and Authority within the Church of South India

The gift of volubility is a highly prized skill in Tamil culture. One would say of someone of good character, "He speaks nicely" (*Avaru nallā pecuvāru*). This emphasis on oral linguistic competence is connected no doubt to the pride in their language for which Tamils are justifiably renowned. Additionally, however, it stems from a tradition of oratory in which facility with formal speech functions as an important marker of status and prestige (Bate 1999). Tamil is a diglossic language, with two different but interrelated forms of the language. Broadly conceived, the two divisions of the language are spoken Tamil and "high Tamil." Spoken Tamil, *pēccu valakku Tamil*, is the language of colloquial speech and varies considerably according to region and the class and social location of the speaker. High Tamil, known as *centamil* or *uyirvalakku pēccu*, is a formalized spoken form of the language that closely follows the pronunciation of written Tamil. The ability to speak clearly in *centamil* is one of the most significant if unspoken criterion of status in the Church, dividing those with formal education from those who lack it. It is the sine qua non of public speech performances in Tamil Nadu. While demonstrable competence in *centamil* in itself does not guarantee an audience, the absence of such competence guarantees that one's authority will be compromised.

A prominent feature of much of the ritual life of Christ Church is *centamil*'s elevation to special status and the closely related practice of reading out loud. At the beginning of a typical Sunday Sabbath service, the opening hymns would be sung from the CSI hymnal. The hymns collected here are for the most part eighteenth- and nineteenth-century English, German, and American songs translated into formal Tamil and sung, more often than not, according to a slowed-down version of the Western tune. The ability to sing from the hymnal itself is a test of the congregation's functional literacy, although the hymns are sung slowly enough and with enough repetition that one does not necessarily have to know how to read in order to sing along. *Centamil* is also prominent in the formal liturgy, the CSI order of service, which follows the Anglican liturgy rather closely. The CSI order of services, delivered by Rev. David, Christ Church's resident pastor, was a virtuoso performance in rapid-fire *centamil* presumably read off the page but more likely committed to memory after repeated practice. Rev. David was able to get through the recitation of the Nicene Creed in a matter of seconds, producing a sort of wall of sound that resembled to my ears nothing more than the chanting of priests in a Hindu temple—the same periodic, rhythmic emphases, the same haste to get through a body of text in the most economical manner, the same deadpan emotional delivery.

Rev. David's facility with the difficult language of the CSI liturgy is evidence of his own hard work within the educational institutions run by the CSI and, I would imagine, contributed to his rapid rise within the social worlds governed by it. Born a Hindu, with the name Kannan, his father died when he was ten, leaving his mother a widow with five children. David, née Kannan, was the second child. Evidently he was a constant source of grief to his mother, who was unable to manage his prodigious energy and curiosity. When he was older a District Inspector of Schools took him off his mother's hands and enrolled him in a Christian school where he did very well. Though initially relieved, his family grew increasingly unhappy as Kannan became more involved with the Christian aspects of school life. Because of his association with Christians at the school, Kannan's family began ostracizing him even before he had formally converted. In the perception of Kannan's family, as in that of many south Indians, Christians were to be avoided on account of their low social and caste status. When he came home to visit, they served him meals on a banana leaf, which could be easily thrown away. They set aside a special cup for him as well, cleansing and purifying it with cow dung after he had eaten. In spite of this treatment, or perhaps because of it, David eventually ratified his commitment to Christianity by being baptized.

The background of Rev. David's wife, Mary, contrasts sharply from that of her husband insofar as she is the product of a family of five generations of pastors. She too is very well educated, having earned an M.A. She knows some English but is more comfortable speaking in Tamil. A mother of two children and an ordained CSI minister, she travels fifteen miles to her job as the principal of a CSI elementary school for girls. In addition to these responsibilities, she carries out her role as pastor's wife with admirable tact and skill. On Wednesdays she presides over the women's prayer meetings and is actively involved with other aspects of "women's work" within the church. For example, she was a speaker at the Madurai Diocese's annual celebration of the Annunciation of Mary, an event organized by a cohort of educated, middle-class Christian women to highlight and provide a venue for women's leadership within the church.

Women's participation in CSI church services provides special opportunities for the display of competence in language use. In the Sunday services of Christ Church, as in the majority of CSI churches in Tamil Nadu, men sit on one side of the sanctuary, and women sit on the other. Unlike women worshippers in Hindu temples, Christian women do not adorn their hair with flowers nor wear on their foreheads the circle of colored *kumkum* powder or adhesive-backed colored paper, the *poṭṭu*, or mark of auspiciousness without which Hindu women, unless widowed or grieving, do not leave the house. During the service, they cover their heads with the ends of their saris, a gesture done with extra assiduousness when taking Communion. While the pastor or guest speaker, who is almost always male, addresses his homily to the congregation, he sprinkles his sermon with Biblical proof texts. At each reference to a biblical verse, there is a pregnant pause and a flurry of hands passing over the pages of Bibles until one voice shouts out the content of the verse—demonstrating in one stroke her (or less frequently his) facility with the Bible, level of literacy, and command of the formal, written Tamil in which the Tamil Bible is composed. It is an intensely competitive moment, as the winner strives to bring her voice to bear on the collective moment.

Women's Literacy and Community Prestige

The question arises, why do women thrust themselves into the spotlight in this way when they are excluded from many other parts of the service? Why do preachers encourage women to display their facility with the Bible and their level of literacy by reading aloud in the church? In some conservative Indian churches women reading aloud from the Bible in this way might be a source of contention, perhaps considered a contravention of the Pauline injunction against women teaching men in church. But here, women's voices are elicited and encouraged. This is so, I would argue, not because of a liberal and deliberate transgression of the taboo against women teachers, but rather because women's literacy has been for a long time a widely recognized sign in India of the advanced state of a community. India possesses a long history of conceiving of women's literacy as an index of the level of "development" of a community. This history is rooted in nineteenth-century colonial efforts to spread women's education (oftentimes through the mediation of missionary schools and literacy drives) and extends into the present day in the paradigms provided by international development programs and institutions such as the World Bank and the United Nations.

Inspired by the populist efforts of English and American Methodists, Protestant missionaries in India envisioned a direct progression from general literacy to Scriptural literacy, and thus to religious conversion and moral and social improvement. Women's literacy held a special place in this scheme insofar as women were believed to be especially stubborn obstacles to the modernization and Christianization of India's subject population. In the publications that promoted women's missionary work in India, images of women reading served as poignant symbols of the progressive nature of Christianity in India. One of the first American women missionaries dedicated to the training and supervision of rural Bible women in the Madurai District urged her readers to support the mission with this image of the challenges faced by her students: "Think of a woman out in the field holding a stick in one hand with which to drive away the birds from the ripening grain, and in her other hand a book from which she is learning a lesson" (Chandler 1910, 340–41).

Female religious specialists known as "Bible women" were key instruments in the dissemination of literacy and Christian teachings among women in nineteenth-century India. Usually literate or semiliterate women who were themselves converts to Christianity, Bible women accompanied foreign missionary women in their visits from house to house, introducing women to the virtues of the Christian faith (and the "dangers" of non-Christian faiths) through reading lessons, sewing and knitting lessons, hymns, and conversation. The concept of training local women to act as intermediaries can be traced to revivalist missions in Britain whose aim was to bring about the moral and spiritual regeneration of working-class communities. The most celebrated leader of this movement in England was Mrs. Ellen Ranyard, an influential evangelist who recruited from among London's industrial urban poor. She was born in 1810, the daughter of a cement maker (Prochaska 1980, 126). In her efforts to bridge the social distance between her fellow evangelists, for the most part educated and middle-class women, and their target audience, mill workers and factory girls, Ranyard was motivated in part by anticlerical sentiments. As she wrote, "the people are tired of what they call "parsons" and "humbug" (Williams 1993, 47). She was inspired by missionary emphases on "native agency" and in turn inspired many who sought to contest the monopoly on church leadership enjoyed at the time by educated, middle-class men. What the people needed, she felt, was a new kind of agent, "a woman of their own class who could speak as they spoke, understand their difficulties and be as it were like themselves, only transformed by her faith and her Christianity" (Williams 1993, 47).

Instead of class differences, Bible women in India were employed to overcome the vast linguistic, religious, and cultural differences that separated Western missionary women from their charges. And yet, they occupied a decidedly low position in the hierarchy of the missions. They were to carry out the laborious day-to-day tasks of teaching, while the Western missionary "ladies" would come once a week or every two weeks to evaluate and supervise the progression of the work. Leaders of women's missionary societies in India strongly encouraged the training of Bible women, in part, no doubt, to relieve themselves of the physically uncomfortable work of walking around in the sun from house to house or village to village (Haggis 1998). Pitman wrote,

> It is a judicious outlay of strength and time to train, at each centre
> of mission-operations, as many native Bible-women as can be found

fit for the work. Being natives they can bear the heat of the climate better, understand the feelings of the people and the modes of daily life far more, and feel a sincere sympathy for their sufferings—not deeper or more true perhaps, than that cherished by English missionaries, but a sympathy born of actual experience (Pitman [n.d. before 1906], 38).

The importance of Bible women within the Church as intermediaries between culturally and linguistically distinct groups has continued into the present day, even as their status has diminished due to various social forces.

The period subsequent to the union of the different Protestant missionary societies in 1947 witnessed a sharp decline in the numbers, funding, and influence of Bible women. This was due in part to the withdrawal of their main patrons and raison d'être, the Western women missionaries for whom they acted as intermediaries, and also due to the professionalization of women's work in the Church. Fueled by women's greater access to secondary and higher education, this trend towards professionalization did not bring about an increase in prestige or salary for Bible women. Rather, Bible women, who were often not educated beyond the primary level, were considered unskilled and unpolished members of the Church community, socially just a few steps above their illiterate, rural, and imperfectly converted students. Though the office has not become altogether defunct—several dioceses and independent churches continue to maintain a department of Bible women's work—it has become for the most part a form of low-paid social work. However, when out of the rigid surveillance of their middle-class patrons, Tamil Bible women can still exercise some degree of local influence, as the following description of Muttammal's career seeks to demonstrate.

Muttammal, Bible Woman

Muttammal has worked as a Bible woman for the congregation of Christ Church for several years. It is not clear exactly how long she has received a salary from the church, but she testifies that she has been there longer than any of the ministers. In the first of many apparent status reversals, she declared during one of our interviews that she had trained all four of the previous pastors sent to Christ Church by the diocese (Muttammal, 1996b). From a non-Brahmin, high-caste background (*Piḷḷai*), Muttammal was raised a Christian by parents who converted to Christianity before she was born. Because she was not educated beyond the second standard, her claims to authority lie not in her formal education, but in her extraordinary piety and her long years of experience as an evangelist. She knows the Bible backwards and forwards, as we would say in English, or "*suttamā*," "cleanly," as the

Tamil idiom goes. The verses of the Bible, which she manipulates so skill-fully in her teaching work, are "written on her heart" (*manasile eluntatu*).

Muttammal began her ministry at the instigation of a vision. As a wid-owed mother of three small children, she struggled to support her family with earnings from an *idli* stand that she set up on a sidewalk in Madurai town, selling to passersby the steamed white cakes made from fermented rice and lentil flour which are a staple of the Tamil diet. Her life was dominated by financial worries, and many a night she was unable to sleep because of her agitation. One night, as she lay awake until midnight reading from the Bible and praying, she dreamed or saw that Jesus came to her in the form of the bishop, Leslie Newbigin (an English clergyman who was elected bishop of Madurai and Ramnad in 1947 and Bishop of Madras in 1965), and pulled her up by the hand. When she asked Jesus why, He said that He himself was pulling her up, and that He wanted her to dedicate her life to spreading the Gospel. As she told the story to me and my research assistant, she cited Isaiah 41:13: "I, the Lord your God, take you by the right hand; I say to you—do not be afraid." From then on, she said, she was not troubled by financial worries; God himself provided for her.

At first her ministry grew directly out of her *idli* business: she would distribute Bible verses to her customers along with *idlis*. Whether these verses were written down or recited orally along with the transaction I don't know. Muttammal did indicate that to the extent that she knew her regular customers, she strove to match the words to the person, selecting verses that would have some personal relevance. To meet the particular concerns of her customers with an appropriate verse required not only extensive knowledge of Scripture (to avoid repetition), but also a certain talent for improvisation, the capacity to respond immediately to a person with an empathic, fitting response.

Muttammal used her intuition and empathy in other forms of ministry as well. Some years after her midnight conversion experience, she received a mark on her hand, in the clear shape of a cross, which she understood to be a sign that she had received authority to heal. She recounted many stories of having healed people suffering from what psychoanalysts would consider hysterical symptoms: a boy whose eyes were tightly shut, a man whose body was completely bent backwards and rigid.

Approximately ten or fifteen years after her conversion experience, Muttammal began working for the Church on a more formal level. She un-derwent the brief course of training that the CSI offered for the preparation of "women workers" and continued her evangelical, healing, and teaching work under the supervision of those in charge of women's work, usually the wives of bishops or other leading churchmen. She traveled throughout the villages surrounding Madurai, teaching basic literacy skills and spreading the Christian Gospel along with information about health, hygiene, child-rearing and so forth. When I met her she had been working for many years in her current position, as Bible woman for the congregation at Christ Church. The pastor, Rev. David, and his wife, Mary, both well-educated professionals, treated her with a great deal of respectful affection. But for them, it seemed, she was a kind of female counterpart to the sexton—a person of limited means, who carries out the menial chores necessary to the smooth functioning of the church. They demonstrated no small amount of paternalism towards her, indicating to me that they took care of her out of gratitude for her having taken care of their children. However, from another point of view, the Bible woman is a figure, like the sexton, whose location at the interstices between the faithful and the church leadership can be a source of considerable power. I observed that after Sunday services, prayer meetings, and fellowship meetings, Muttammal received a great deal of respect from the women in the church, especially those with less than middle-class means and only primary school educations. At a picnic sponsored by the church on the occasion of its anniversary, several women with the thin faces and thin saris of the Indian underclass came and touched her feet.

At the interface between the laity and the official Church, Muttammal is a purveyor of the kind of folk Christianity that people usually associate with Indian Catholicism. Though she never departs from the Protestant emphasis on the Word as the primary vehicle for the message of Christ, she adapts it to the local context. The teaching that she engaged in during her years as an itinerant evangelist consisted largely of story-telling. One of the stories she told me to illustrate her kind of evangelism offered an explanation as to why Jesus left the world after coming here once to save it. In the context of her village itineracy work, it served as an answer to the kind of objection that a Hindu villager would be likely to make in response to hearing the story of Jesus' life. This is my paraphrase of her story, which she told to me in colloquial Tamil, repeating key phrases at intervals.

> One day a boy who was tending his animals by a village tank (*kuḷam*) decided to go swimming. When the people on the shores called out, "Don't go out too deep!" he didn't hear them. Then, he went under the surface of the water. Three times his head sank beneath the surface of the water and rose up again. The people on the shore said, "Didn't we tell you that it was deep? It is your own stupidity that led to this." While he was drowning they said, "Come on out, boy. Get up and come ashore. Aren't you able to come out?" As his head broke the surface of the water for the last time a king [*rājā*] happened to come by. He wore the clothes of a king. The minute he saw the boy, he cried out, "*Aiyō!* A boy is drowning in the tank." Without a moment's hesitation, the king plunged directly into the filthy

water to save the boy, even though it meant getting his fine silk
garments dirty. He lifted the drowning child out of the tank, placed
him face down on the ground and stroked his back until all the water
that had entered his nose and his ears drained out. He did that until
the boy finally opened his eyes (Muttammal 1996a).

Muttammal interrupted her story at this point and barked out, "Psalms 40:1!"
directing me and my research assistant to this verse. At the time I had no idea
what she meant, but Kavitha, my research assistant, knew. She pulled a Bible
out of her bag, and together we turned from book to book looking for Psalms.
Our inability to locate the book of Psalms among the onionskin thin pages of
the Bible was a clear sign that Kavitha, though a born CSI Christian, was not
a very regular churchgoer and that I was a woefully inadequate representative
of American Christianity. Still, it was an uncanny experience, to leaf through
the pages of this large, cumbersome book and then to feel the relevance of
that verse, as I clumsily read aloud in formal written Tamil: "I waited, waited
for the Lord. He bent down to me and heard my cry. He brought me up out
of the muddy pit, out of the mire and the clay; He set my feet on a rock and
gave me firm footing." After emphasizing the last phrase of this biblical proof
text for her narrative, Muttammal continued with her story, which itself had
no biblical precedent. After the king had revived the drowning boy, the boy
fell down at the feet of the king and begged to be allowed to serve him, and
follow him to wherever he was going. "No," said the king, "you must stay
here. I am going back to my palace where I am going to make a place ready
for you. I will come back to get you." Muttammal clinched this culmination
of the narrative with another proof text and sat back while Kavitha and I
struggled to locate it and read it aloud. It was, appropriately, John 3: 13: "No
one ever went up into heaven except the one who came down from heaven,
the Son of Man whose home is in heaven."

   One way to approach this form of interactive Bible reading is to consider how Muttammal tailors Christian teachings to her Indian audience. In
part she directs her story to her specific audience by filling her narrative with
details evoking the local context—the *kuḷam* or manmade lake where animals
are watered, and the *rājā*, a figure around whom innumerable relationships of
dependency, love, and loyalty can be imagined. Muttammal also attends to
the core Christian concept of Jesus as a *savior*, as one who literally comes
down to earth to save people drowning in sin. As she emphasized in her
narrative, " 'Who do you think pulled you up?,' said the *rājā* to the boy, 'I
myself pulled you up.' " The theme of redemption expressed through this
metaphor of physically pulling someone up recurs repeatedly in Muttammal's
discourse, as we saw earlier in the story of her being called to become an
evangelist. One could explore at great length the significance of this meta-

phor for Muttammal, as for many impoverished and socially marginalized Christians in India who seek and perhaps find a means of advancement or "upliftment" in Christianity.

To me, however, what is even more significant about this style of inter-action is how the act of reading is used to create a particular relationship between the teacher and the student. Kavitha and I stood, in a way, for students unfamiliar with the individual books of the Bible and with the ar-chaic-sounding, formal language of the Tamil translation of the Christian Bible. Muttammal established a distinctly hierarchical relationship between herself and us through her virtuoso performance of her extraordinary scrip-tural literacy. In this example of the ritualization of reading, the display of vastly different degrees of familiarity with the text serves to hierarchize the participants, separating the sheep from the goats, as it were, in the scale of relative familiarity with the written word.

To accredited Church leaders, the charismatic authority of religious spe-cialists like Muttammal is the object of either scorn, ridicule, or wary appre-hension. I spoke with one CSI pastor, Rev. Paul, who undermined the authoritative stance taken by Bible women like Muttammal by emphasizing their socially stigmatized status. He observed that Bible women were fre-quently widows or abandoned wives. In his experience, they were often poor and uneducated, with knowledge of only a few passages of the Bible. Their most important roles within the church, he said, were as servants within the pastor's house or as counselors who visited lonely women. In addition, though, they could serve as a substitute for the pastor on his visiting rounds to the homes of the congregation. CSI pastors are, in general, very active in their ministry. They (or their assistants) are engaged in a constant round of home visitations to pray for God's merciful intervention in the event of a death or illness, as well as for his blessing on the occasion of special events such as birthdays or retirements. Rev. Paul observed that Bible women may some-times receive food or clothing from the people whose homes they visit, a fact, which, if true, underlines their socially and economically dependent condi-tion. When I asked him about some Bible women's claims to healing powers and other spiritual gifts, he dismissed them. "These women are so poor and uneducated," he said, "that they sometimes claim these gifts for themselves. For instance, they will pray very loudly over someone and claim the gift of ecstatic speech." In spite of this stark appraisal of the role of Bible women within the Church, the pastor went on to say that some of the minor figures within the Church hierarchy, such as sextons and Bible women, have in fact "come up in the world" to the point where they have opened their own rival churches (Paul 1996).

The official leaders of the Church may scoff at the claims of a Bible woman such as Muttammal, but in the company of nonliterate, or newly

literate individuals from her own social class, Muttammal appears a powerful, engaging, and highly empathic figure worthy of respect. She makes the
central narratives of Christianity accessible to newcomers to Christianity and
wins their trust and respect in part by wielding the central symbol of Protestant Christian religious authority—the ritualized reading of the Bible. Although clearly existing at the outer fringe of the Church hierarchy, Muttammal
fully engages with the specific limits and possibilities of her own particular
niche in the overall hierarchical order of the CSI. Negotiating the boundaries
between the Church's institutional authority and those whom it would embrace, she utilizes its primary symbol, the Bible, as a value-laden object and
as the source of highly valued speech, to enhance her own prestige in the eyes
of her social inferiors and, additionally, extends the influence of the Church
into new terrain. Whether or not Muttammal actually commands the techniques and capabilities that ritualized reading refers to, however, raises another issue, to which I will return shortly. As Pierre Bourdieu, and more
recently, Bruce Lincoln have convincingly shown, authority does not depend
on the actual talents or skills of an agent so much as the ability to convince
her audience that she has such talents or to persuade her audience to act as
if they believe that she does (Lincoln 1994, 1–13).

The Wordless Book

This insight into the construction of authority is borne out in another
form of ritualized reading that Muttammal engaged in, a form of reading that
employed a book that was not, in fact, the actual Bible. Muttammal once
showed me her copy of the Wordless Book, one of the tools that she used in
her teaching and proselytizing work in the villages surrounding Madurai.
This pedagogical device has a long legacy in the Protestant Church in India.
As early as 1898, references to it describe a four-paneled piece of fabric or
paper that served as a very simple prop to illustrate the Gospel message. Four
square pieces of cloth or paper, colored black, red, white and gold, were
stitched or glued together along one side to form a "book" of sorts. Each
"page" stood for one component of the core Christian message, which could
thus be communicated in an economical fashion to a diverse audience. As
Muttammal demonstrated, black represented the state of sinful souls dark-
ened by transgressions, known and unknown, against the laws of the Christian God. Red stood for the blood of Jesus, which was spilled for the
redemption of human sinners and was able to wash away the sins of humanity. White represented the state of the soul after a person had accepted Jesus
as the one true savior, who rose from the dead and thereby conquered both
sin and death. Finally, gold represented heaven, where Jesus had a place

reserved for every person who accepted him as the Savior and genuinely repented of their sins.

The Wordless Book that Muttammal showed me in 1996 was tiny, a small paper pamphlet small enough to fit in your hand, suggesting an intimate venue for teaching. As described in the annals of nineteenth-century missionaries, the Wordless Book could be as large as a flag, capable of attracting the attention of a large crowd if necessary (*Proceedings* 1892, 282; Carmichael 1918, 18). While ostensibly designed to assist nonliterate audiences in understanding the Christian message, the book also probably helped missionaries compensate for their frequently inadequate training in local languages. This potentially embarrassing aspect is elided in missionary anecdotes that extol the capacity of the Wordless Book to dispense with the trappings of language altogether. In one 1898 report from Tirunelveli, the teacher of a Church of England Zenana Missionary Society school for deaf children once quieted an unruly village Sunday school class by enlisting the help of one of her deaf students. Miss Swainson wrote, "One of the dumb girls was told to explain by signs the 'Wordless Book' which was being shown, and all that the heathen children learnt that day was from her" (*Proceedings* 1899, 121). Such missionary accounts attest that the Wordless Book was helpful both for nonliterate teachers and audiences, reminding one of the scrolls and story boards used throughout India for disseminating religious stories and doctrine among nonliterate groups. Like these tools, the Wordless Book appears to transcend the need for written language, yet the device nevertheless retains its form as a book. Why?

At first glance, the Wordless Book is a fairly dull symbol. Without a live performance of reading to accompany it, its meaning is almost totally obscure, its appearance totally uninteresting. Even when read, it exhausts its meaning as soon as one arrives at the conclusion of its allegorical rendering of the Christian kerygma. Yet, the fact that it must be "read," performatively, allows us to extend its meaning. In this colorful abstraction of a book, the "words" on the page, normally written by pen or printed in ink, are replaced with plain fields of color. The message normally conveyed by script is now conveyed through the energetic verbal witnessing of the "reader." When the supports necessary for a literal act of reading fall away, the complex religious and social meanings of literacy in the Indian Christian context come to the fore.

In a sense, the colored pages of this "book" play on the theological notion that the revealed Word of God contained in the pages of the Christian Bible was not necessarily the literal speech of God addressing his people, but rather a message carried by writings that were felt to have a divine origin (Graham 1987, 121). The promise held out by Christian educators in India, as elsewhere, is that through the painstaking process of learning to read, one gains direct access to those writings and the message they contain. One can then make sense of the revealed word of God in the context of one's own life. Thus, the Wordless Book is in this sense an inducement to learn to read so as to gain direct access to the salvific teachings of God for oneself.

But that is not all. Even as the ritualized reading enabled by the Wordless Book sets reading the Bible apart from and above other forms of reading through a process of abstraction and reduction, it sets reading itself above other forms of action. Insofar as Protestant conversion in India has, arguably, consistently been accompanied by a drive towards "modernization," the allure of scriptural literacy has been and remains bound up with secular literacy, and thus with aspirations of upward social mobility. Following this point of view, readings of the Wordless Book witness to the power of books. They extend the promise held out by Christians in India from the time of the missionaries, that literacy can reveal avenues not only into fresh worlds of religious thought, but also into new opportunities for employment or advancement within the many institutions governed by Indian Christians.[1] Whether that promise has, in fact, been fulfilled is a topic this paper cannot take up.[2]

One point I wish to return to is the considerable irony in the fact that Muttammal herself never actually reads in any of the ritualized performances of reading that I describe. The construction of her authority as a bearer of Christian knowledge, it seems, does not depend on her literally demonstrating that she can read. It is possible, moreover, that such a display would have diminished her authority, by reducing reading the Bible to any old prosaic form of reading words off a page. Indeed, the authority of the Bible woman is generated precisely by virtue of her location at the juncture between the literate and nonliterate (or minimally literate). Through her ritualization of reading with the aid of pedagogical devices such as the Wordless Book, she offers nonliterate audiences a taste of literacy's capacity to open new vistas of religious meaning and social power. In her more interactive reading performances, a Bible woman situates herself as the bearer of valuable knowledge. By directing readers to passages that confirm their expectations, which she herself has raised, she induces in them an experience that ratifies her authority. Through her facility with biblical texts, a Bible woman wields a power not unlike that of divination. Provided her students are beginners at Bible study, for whom the combination of a book, a chapter, and a verse does not immediately call up a memory of a particular text, the Bible woman can reveal that a seemingly random combination of elements has an unexpected relevance to one's own condition. Like a diviner with a set of cards, the Bible woman makes the meaningless point towards the meaningful, causing a confusing journey through the pages of a Bible to resolve itself into certainty with a kind of shock that makes the import of the words and her authority seem indubitable.

Muttammal's ability to persuade her audience of the relevance and importance of the Christian message of universal salvation is, in my estimation, considerable. Yet, her relationship to the institutional authority of the Church is by no means that of a usurper. She does not attempt to undermine the patriarchal structures of Church leadership by the assertion of an alternative, specifically feminine or nonelite form of leadership. Catherine Bell's understanding of ritual allows us to see the complexity of Muttammal's relationship to centers of power within the CSI, for while Muttammal does seem to reproduce the relations of power that privilege elite, educated members at the expense of nonelite, illiterate members, she does so while garnering for herself a measure of empowerment and autonomy. She does not override the control over public, institutionally based authority held firmly by the male clergy, nor does she share their power the way that the more educated and "respectable" pastor's wife does. Instead, through her skillful manipulation of the central ritual of reading out loud from the Bible, she draws on the authority of the Church to establish her own coterie of followers and achieve a level of power and self-respect that can be seen, in multiple ways, as redemptive.

Notes

1. This is a perspective that one cannot assume is shared by all audiences of a performance of a ritualized reading of the Wordless Book, as literacy represents many different things to different people. See, for example, studies on literacy programs for women in India by Saraswati and Ravindran 1982. Also see Rockhill 1987.

2. For a more thorough investigation of this issue see Caplan 1989.

References

Bate, John Bernard. 1999. *Metaittamil: Beauty and Power in Tamil Speech and Society*. Ph.D. Dissertation. University of Chicago.

Bell, Catherine. 1992. *Ritual Theory, Ritual Practice*. New York: Oxford University Press.

Bourdieu, Pierre. 1977. *Outline of a Theory of Practice*. Cambridge: Cambridge University Press.

Bourdieu, Pierre and Loic J. D. Waequant. 1992. *An Invitation to Reflexive Sociology*. Chicago: University of Chicago Press.

Caplan, Lionel. 1989. *Religion and Power: Essays on the Christian Community in Madras*. Madras: The Christian Literature Society.

Carmicheal, Amy. 1918. *Ponnammal: Her Story.* London: Society for Promoting Christian Knowledge.

Chandler, John S. 1910. *Seventy-Five Years in the Madura Mission: A History of the Mission in South India under the ABCFM.* Madras: American Madura Mission.

Estborn, S. 1959. *Our Village Christians: A Study of the Life and Faith of Village Christians in Tamilnad.* Madras: Christian Literature Society.

Forbes, Geraldine H. 1986. "In Search of the 'Pure Heathen' Missionary Women in Nineteenth-Century India." *Economic and Political Weekly* 21, no. 17: WS-2–WS-8.

Forrester, Duncan B. 1980. *Caste and Christianity: Attitudes and Policies on Caste of Anglo-Saxon Protestant Missions in India.* London: Curzon Press, Ltd.

Graham, William A. 1987. *Beyond the Written Word: Oral Aspects of Scripture in the History of Religion.* Cambridge: Cambridge University Press.

Haggis, Jane. 1998. "'Good Wives and Mothers' or 'Dedicated Workers'? Contradictions of Domesticity in the 'Mission of Sisterhood,' Travancore, South India." In *Maternities and Modernities: Colonial and Postcolonial Experiences in Asia and the Pacific*, eds. Kalpana Ram and Margaret Jolly, 81–113. Cambridge: Cambridge University Press.

Keillor, Garrison. 1985. *Lake Wobegon Days.* New York: Viking Press.

Lincoln, Bruce. 1994. *Authority: Construction and Corrosion.* Chicago: The University of Chicago Press.

Muttammal, J. (1996a). Personal interview by the author, Madurai, South India, 24 February.

———. (1996b.) Personal interview by the author, Madurai, South India, 5 March.

Newbigin, Leslie. 1960. *A South Indian Diary.* London: S.C.M. Press.

Paul, Rev. [pseudonym]. 1996. Personal interview by the author, Madurai, South India, 30 March.

Pitman, Emma R. [n.d., before 1906]. *Indian Zenana Missions: Their Need, Origin, Objects, Agents, Modes of Working, and Results.* London: John Snow & Co.

Proceedings of the Church Missionary Society for 1898–1899. 1899. London: CMS House.

Prochaska, Frank K. 1980. *Women and Philanthropy in Nineteenth-Century England.* Oxford: Clarendon Press.

Rockhill, K. 1987. "Gender, Language and the Politics of Literacy." *British Journal of the Sociology of Education* 8, no. 2: 153–67.

Saraswati, L. S., and D. J. Ravindran. 1982. "The Hidden Dreams: The New Literates Speak." *Adult Education and Development* 19: 183–88.

Williams, Peter. 1993. "The Missing Link: The Recruitment of Women Missionaries in some English Evangelical Missionary Societies in the Nineteenth Century." In *Women and Missions: Past and Present Anthropological and Historical Perceptions*, eds. Deborah Kirkwood, Fiona Bowie, and Shirley Ardenev, 43–69. Oxford: BERG Publishers.

CHAPTER 10

Missionary Strategy and the Development of the Christian Community: Delhi 1859–1884

John C. B. Webster

Popular Christianity represents a new and very challenging theme for historians of Christianity in India. During the nineteenth and first half of the twentieth centuries these historians tended to adopt an "Our Mission in India" approach to their subject. This concentrated attention almost exclusively upon the work of missionaries and virtually ignored the emerging Indian Christian community, as well as the kind of religious life that was evolving within it. Even the more general histories of James Hough, Sir John Kaye, M. A. Sherring, and Julius Richter concentrated upon the missionaries and their work rather than upon the Church as a social or even religious entity with a history of its own. In many respects this paralleled the broader equation of modern Indian history with the history of the British in India during the same period (Webster 1979, 88–102). One can see among historians living in India a shift in emphasis during the decades following Indian independence. In 1973 the Church History Association of India explicitly stated in the guide-lines for its forthcoming multivolume history of Christianity in India that this history was to be viewed not as the eastward extension of Western Christianity, but as the history of the Indian Christian community within the context of Indian history (A Scheme).[1] This significant and difficult paradigm shift required adopting a social history approach to the subject. The other more recent trend, perhaps most apparent among historians living outside India, has been a broadening of the earlier mission history approach to focus not upon the work of missionaries so much as upon their religious, cultural, ideological, and political encounters with the people of India (e.g., Powell, Copley, Kawashima). A history of popular Christianity in India would require combining the priorities and methods used in these latter two approaches (e.g., Bayly 1989, 241–463).

211

This is not easily done because the sources, most of which were produced by missionaries, focus attention upon the missionaries themselves, their work, their issues, and their encounters. By comparison, they contain very little information concerning the history of the Indian Christian community, and even less about its developing religious life.[2] In the case of this essay, there is material in the sources that serves to highlight both the reality and the importance of popular Christianity, but not enough detail to provide answers to many of the questions one would want to ask about it. Thus this essay must serve as an illustration of both the promise and the frustrations of writing the history of popular Christianity in India.

The following tells the story of an attempt to recreate and then expand the Christian Church in Delhi during the years after the sepoy mutiny and widespread revolt against British rule throughout much of north central India in 1857. This is a story of two missions that had been in Delhi prior to 1857 and which, over the next twenty-five years, adopted in some respects similar and in other respects divergent strategies to carry out the task of mission. While the records the missionaries have left behind create the impression that their strategies, methods, and activity were primarily responsible for shaping the Christian communities they brought into existence, what is striking in this case are the ways in which the emerging Indian Christian community in Delhi came to shape missionary strategy. Moreover, and significantly for our purposes here, it was precisely at this point that one can see the vital role that popular Christianity had to play.

Christianity had been late in coming to Delhi and was very slow in getting established there. The Jesuit Mughal Mission had come and gone without leaving a continuing Christian community behind. Those few Christians who were there at the outset of the nineteenth century were outsiders, attached to the armies either of the Marathas or of the various freebooters who roamed the region. In 1803 the British captured Delhi and became the protector of the Mughal emperor, but the first missionary to establish residence in the city and provide a continuing mission there, the Rev. James Thompson of the Baptist Missionary Society, arrived only in 1818. Thompson concentrated his efforts more upon disseminating the Christian message as widely as possible throughout the surrounding region rather than upon establishing a Christian church in Delhi itself. Consequently, his converts in the city were few. He died in 1850, and his replacements arrived in 1856. The other mission in Delhi, that of the Society for the Propagation of the Gospel (S. P. G.), had been started in 1852 at the instigation of some British residents in Delhi and in response to the baptism of two high-caste converts. Their first missionaries arrived only in 1854. Thus both missions were very small in number and only newly established when on May 10, 1857, the sepoys, who had mutinied at Meerut the previous evening, arrived in Delhi and deliberately sought out every European and Eurasian as well as every Indian Christian they could find. They killed all of the missionaries and most of the converts. Those few who hid, fled, or both, were severely traumatized when they reassembled in Delhi after the British recaptured the city in September 1857. It took time for fresh missionaries to arrive and begin the process of rebuilding. Because they offer such interesting contrasts, the Baptist and S. P. G. stories will be treated separately, starting with the more innovative Baptists and then moving on to the larger S. P. G. enterprise before arriving at some conclusions.

I

The Baptist Missionary Society chose the Rev. James Smith to reestablish their mission in Delhi. Smith had originally gone out to India in 1841 as a regimental schoolmaster for the East India Company. Five years later he was teaching at the Baptist school in Agra. He remained in Agra, where he also had oversight of the Christian colony in the nearby village of Chitoura, until his furlough during 1857 and subsequent posting to Delhi. There he became the senior and most influential Baptist missionary on the spot, while others came and went. When he reached Delhi in March 1859, he found only a few Baptist converts who had survived the 1857 revolt. However, he began preaching in earnest and discovered that there was considerable interest in Christianity, especially among the Chamars. By the end of 1860 he had already baptized ninety-four people (*Annual Report 1860*, 6), a number far in excess of the total baptized by his predecessors during the entire forty years the Baptists had been in Delhi! Of the sixty-five people baptized in 1860, thirty-three or just over half were Chamars, six were Hindus belonging to other castes, nineteen were Muslims, and seven were Christians belonging to other churches (*The Missionary Herald*, September 1861, 584). The converts were organized initially into four congregations in Shahdra, Purana Kila, Daryaganj, and Paharganj, each with its own pastor (ibid., 582).

Smith's initial strategy was to preach in many of the bazaars of Delhi and its suburbs, to baptize relatively quickly many of his initial inquirers, and to develop local congregations where the converts lived rather than gather them together in one central location with one central church. However, it was the nature of this significant, early "post-mutiny" response that gave shape to the Delhi Christian community and to the strategies adopted by the missionaries in the years ahead. For one thing, the community was predominantly Chamar. The Chamars were a caste of leather-workers, whose occupation was considered so unclean and polluting as to make them untouchable to caste Hindus and, to a lesser degree, among Muslims as well. Whether living in the slums of Delhi or on the outskirts of the surrounding villages, they were poor, illiterate, and involved in local networks of caste-based, patron-client relationships upon which they were totally dependent for their survival. Smith noted that many had joined the Kabir Panthis, Rai Dasis, and other *panths* (religious sects) whose teachings against idolatry gave them an affinity to Christianity and made their members receptive to Christian teachings (ibid., 583; *Annual Report* 1863, 5). However, Smith failed to see what was for the Chamars an even more powerful affinity, namely that these *panths* and Christianity were socially egalitarian, explicitly rejecting the caste hierarchy, which placed the Chamars close to the very bottom of Indian society. Both initially and subsequently most of the Baptists in and around Delhi were Chamars (*The Baptist Magazine,* January 1861, 49; *Annual Report* 1872, 9).

The other important characteristic of this new Baptist community was its instability. The statistics are somewhat unclear, perhaps because of overlapping reporting dates, but it is obvious that there were a lot of people both entering and leaving the Baptist congregations during the early and mid-1860s. For example, a report in 1862 stated that while sixty-six had been baptized, seventy-five had been excluded (*The Baptist Magazine*, May 1862, 325). The reasons for this instability varied. Disappointment at not getting some direct economic benefits from conversion led some to leave. Persecution, especially by patrons who deprived converts of the jobs or regular custom on which they depended for a livelihood, was another. Some were excommunicated for "gross immorality," and some simply lost interest. However, the main reason seems to have been that the discipline not only of regular Sunday worship but also of giving up practices connected to their former religion proved to be unacceptable, especially when this meant that they could not join unconverted relatives in celebrations that involved "heathen rites."[3] Chamar converts were not socially boycotted by their own families and caste members, as were Muslim and caste Hindu converts, but failure to participate in such celebrations strained relationships and could lead to such a break.

Baptist mission policy during this period gave high priority to the development of independent and self-sustaining churches (Stanley 1992, 148–56). In this Smith fully concurred. However, whereas the Society's concerns were primarily financial (ibid., 148), Smith's were shaped by the cultural context in which his evangelistic work was being carried out and his newly formed congregations were emerging. His earliest published comments express a desire that the congregations discipline their own members (rather than leave it up to the missionary) and manage their own affairs (*Annual Report* 1863, 4; *The Baptist Magazine*, September 1865, 637). He found paid evangelistic workers to be ineffective and local congregational initiatives stifled by mission assistance (*The Missionary Herald,* September 1864, 637–38). Although he did not articulate it in this way at the time, it is apparent that to Smith "independence" meant freedom from the dependency inherent in patron-client relationships, including those between the mission society and missionary, on the one hand, and the converts and congregations, on the other.

Finally on November 5, 1868, drastic action was taken. After repeated conferences on the subject during the course of the year, a large meeting was held at which the Baptists decided to sign a kind of "declaration of independence" and elected a *panchāyat* or managing committee to oversee the affairs of the churches. All thirteen paid evangelists "agreed to take no more Mission pay after the 1st of January 1869, but to depend on their own labor, under God's blessing, for the support of themselves and families" (*Annual Report* 1868, 5; *The Missionary Herald*, February 1869, 117–19). Smith himself "heartily joined, or rather led the way, by renouncing [his] own salary."[4] This action did not apply to the teachers in the schools the Baptists had established, as their work was considered full-time and thus could not be done on a voluntary basis. It also did not preclude the possibility that congregations would want to have and support full-time pastors of their own.

In his report for that year Smith gave three reasons for this decision. The first was that people became evangelists for the pay and not for the sake of Christ. This had a very corrupting influence upon the quality of their moral, spiritual, and community life. The second was that payment placed evangelists in a servant-master (client-patron) instead of brotherly relationship to the missionary. Thirdly, it also put the evangelists in the awkward position of being "paid propagators of Christianity" in the eyes of others. "The people to whom they preach, are also continually asking them in public how much salary they obtain by their evangelistic labours; nor can the European Missionary protect them from such taunts and insults. It is not that any one objects to the payment or support of religious teachers, for the practice exists all over the land; but it is the fact of their being hired by aliens, to propagate an alien religion, and that too the religion of their conquerors and rulers" (*Annual Report* 1868, 4–5). Underlying these specific reasons was the burning conviction that Christianity was still an exotic thing that had not and would not take root among the people in that part of India until the prevailing dependency upon foreign patronage was removed.[5] Moreover, Smith had positive evidence from his experience in Delhi that the desired alternative was possible. In an earlier report he had described a Chamar convert who, for him, was a model of what an Indian evangelist should be.

> An old friend, Seetal Das, was at the service; he had just returned from a month's wandering in the villages, and told me the Gospel was spreading rapidly, and in several of his old villages the people had expressed a desire for baptism. I asked him why he did not

baptize them? He replied that he was afraid to do so. I urged him to
take his New Testament in his hand, and losing sight of man, obey
God. I should so much rejoice to see such men breaking loose from
the Missionaries, go forth preaching the Gospel, baptizing and form-
ing Churches. . . . Seetal Das is not paid by us, but goes over hundreds
of miles of country, sowing broadcast the seed of the Kingdom, and
the people everywhere feed him; he is an evangelist of the most primitive kind (*The Baptist Magazine*, September 1866, 593).[6]

The initial response to this experiment was, according to Smith, positive.
In writing his report for 1868, Smith stated that "it has already developed
new life and energy among the native Christians. Men who have been away
from all secular labour for years, have recommenced work in earnest. Some
are shoe-making. Several have taken contracts on the canal works, where
they regularly keep up Christian worship; and two or three have obtained
situations. The punchait [*panchāyat*] meets weekly for the transaction of
business" (*Annual Report* 1868, 6). A year later, three or at times four of the
original thirteen paid evangelistic workers spent most of their time itinerating
and preaching in the villages where they were given not only an attentive
hearing but also free food and lodging (*Annual Report* 1869, 5). The 1870
report was not written by Smith, who was away, and was not so sanguine.
The objects of reform had not been met, and attendance at Sunday worship
had fallen off in the Delhi as well as the Paharganj, Purana Kila, and Shahdra
congregations to the point where twenty-eight members were excluded during the year (*Annual Report* 1870, 4–6). On the other hand, voluntary evangelism was bearing some fruit. Chuni, who, like Seetal Das, had been touring
the villages, reported that:

The people, in almost every place, fed him, and sometimes gave him
a few pice to help him on his way. He was ill in one place, and the
Zamindar not only supplied him with food, but nursed him like a
good Samaritan, and when he was able to leave, gave him something
for his expenses on the road. In one large village he baptized a
convert in the presence of a number of people, and several others
will probably be baptized on his next journey. At first the people
said that he was paid by some European missionary; but when they
found he was no man's servant, their admiration was at once manifested, and they said he was the first who had thus come out to them
with the news of Christianity (ibid., 8).

In fact, at the first General Missionary Conference held at Allahabad over the
New Year of 1872–73, Smith was to become a staunch advocate of evange-

lism by such people of "the *faqīr* class," for they were the ones who had launched the great religious movements in India, and their (i.e., Kabir's) verses were "stamped on the minds of the people," having been passed down from one generation to the next "among a people totally uneducated" (*Report of the General Missionary Conference*, 242).

After eliminating paid evangelists, the Baptists' next step towards "independence" was to make "public worship subservient to family religion." This step followed naturally upon the earlier one and also served to rectify the problem of poor church attendance.

> ... our efforts have been devoted to the establishing of small assemblies in the middle of the houses of the converts, wherever they exist, thus bringing our instruction, as far as practicable, within hearing of the women and children, with a view of reverting to the old apostolic plan of the church in the house. In this way we are not without hope of getting rid of the difficulty there is in securing native pastors; for whilst we have no man properly qualified to take charge of a large church, yet many are fully capable of superintending these smaller assemblies, and leading them in their devotional exercises. Our brethren thus keep up twenty-one weekly services, according to a plan drawn up by themselves. About one thousand persons are in attendance at these meetings, and I anticipate results from them of far greater magnitude than we have ever realised in Delhi before (*Annual Report* 1872, 8).

In 1872 a Baptist missionary from Calcutta reporting on the Delhi mission noted that while the Delhi Christians could not measure up to the orderliness of British congregations or even of Indian congregations dependent upon foreign funds, there was an "unquestionable vitality" among them that promised well for the future (ibid., 9–10).

In fact, during the 1870s, Smith seems to have become fully committed to "low-caste work" primarily among the Chamars. He increased the number of primary schools in the *bastīs* or neighborhoods where the groups of converts were meeting. He even used his position as Secretary of the Delhi Municipal Committee to get partial funding for the schools from the government, arguing that since the low castes were not allowed into the government schools, the government had a duty to provide assistance for the schools which they could attend. These began by using the Bible and other religious materials in order to teach reading; over time they introduced more and more elements of the standardized government curriculum. In 1877 the Baptists closed their Central School in which English was taught and concentrated exclusively upon their *bastī* schools (*Reports on Popular Education* 1877–78,

71). In 1879 the Inspector of Schools reported that there were 582 pupils in these schools of whom ninety-seven were Christians, 469 low-caste boys and sixteen Hindus of "higher caste."[7] In like manner the Baptists began medical work in Delhi in part because Chamars were not being given proper medical attention in government dispensaries (*Annual Report* 1875, 73). The one exception was the Baptists' zenana work directed at the higher castes rather than at the Chamars; the result was that Chamar women did not receive the missionary attention Chamar men did, and so almost all of the Chamar converts were men.[8]

By 1878 a new pattern of congregational life seems to have developed, as was apparent from the report of a special deputation sent from England to investigate the Delhi Mission and deal with the charges made against Smith by some of his fellow Baptist missionaries outside Delhi.[9] The earlier "small assemblies" or "house churches" seem to have grown to the point where they now met in the school rooms the mission had rented or purchased within the *bastīs* where their converts lived. Prayer meetings, which were very well attended not only by the converts but also by their neighbors in the *bastī*, were held on Sunday and week-day evenings after people had come home from work. The deputation reported twenty-eight of these, each of which held two to seven meetings weekly;[10] it attended sixteen meetings at which there were from forty to 140 people present. At these *bastī* meetings much time was devoted both to prayer, in which the local converts often took a lead, and singing of "thoroughly Evangelical" songs to "native" tunes. The deputation found the singing, at times accompanied by musical instruments, to be "as a rule, loud, sometimes boisterous, and accompanied by much bodily exercise" (*Report on Mission Work in Delhi,* 23). A message was also given either by one of the preachers or by a missionary who happened to be present. Judging from the attendance and quality of participation, these open-air *bastī* meetings, rather than the more formal Sunday services in the church and chapels, seemed to have become the focal points of the community's devotional life. Since they were open to all, they were also proving to be so much more effective in evangelizing the local population than bazaar preaching that the missionaries were considering dropping the latter.

The deputation also found that the congregations connected with the Baptist Mission had 465 members of which 315, or nearly three-quarters, plus another 462 "nominal Christians" and 240 "inquirers" were connected with these school-based *bastī* meetings (ibid., 49). There was a central *panchāyat* which met weekly, as well as local *panchāyats* for each of the congregations. Despite being drawn from the poorest portion of the population, Baptists contributed both money and labor ("which had been considerable in repairing mission chapels and schools") to support the overall effort. The deputation pointed out that, "Besides this, during the last few years the people have wholly provided a school or chapel in three places. In four others, they have provided everything except the straw and bamboo for the roof. In one, they have helped much by giving labour; in another they have purchased ground at a cost of Rs. 25; while at Subzi Mandi the place now used was purchased at a cost by the people of Rs. 115. They have now in hand Rs. 83 towards building a chapel (ibid., 24.) The Mission also listed thirty-three preachers, of whom nineteen were teachers paid by the Mission and concentrating primarily on *bastī* meetings, two were paid by the native church, and the rest relied on independent means of support (like Seetal Das) or supported themselves by full-time work in another occupation (ibid., 57). Thus the deputation was satisfied that the Baptists in and around Delhi had taken some significant steps towards attaining that "independence" Smith had sought.

Smith left Delhi in 1884. The pattern of church life based on the *bastī* meeting and the *panchāyat* continued on beyond his departure. Preachers had been meeting on Saturdays to share and develop sermons for the coming week's *bastī* meetings (*The Missionary Herald*, July 1882, 212). By 1883 three of the congregations had chosen their own pastors; the Central Church supported theirs fully, while the others chose school teachers (*Annual Report* 1883, 83). *Panchāyats* faced the problem of finding marriage partners for the next generation of Christians, since marriages with Hindus and Muslims, whose marriage regulations were considered more lax, were forbidden (*Annual Report* 1881, 9; *The Missionary Herald*, July 1882, 213). At the time he left, an estimated two thousand people were attending *bastī* meetings weekly, the church was growing, and the "field" of the Delhi Mission was expanding to the point that the human and financial resources of the Mission were severely taxed (*The Missionary Herald*, October 1881, 422).

There is no doubt that James Smith had a clear-cut strategy for the attainment of the goals of his evangelistic endeavors. It was his staunch advocacy of his strategy that got him in trouble with his fellow missionaries. Yet his strategy and methods were the product not of abstract mission theory but of intense experience with and commitment to the particular people who had responded to his preaching in and around Delhi. These were the poor in general and, specifically, the Dalit Chamars. His strategy was dictated not only by what he perceived their needs to be—disciplined commitment to Christ, independence, education, medical attention—but also by the positive role models they provided—Seetal Das, the *bastī* meetings, the *panchāyats*—which demonstrated what they were capable of doing, being, and becoming. Smith was a paternalist—an admirer bestowed upon him the very un-Baptist title of Bishop of Delhi (*The Missionary Herald*, January 1883, 9)—but he was a guiding and inspiring rather than controlling paternalist, and so Christianity was able to take root in the *bastīs* of Delhi and be shaped by the people who lived there. In short, Christianity had become, as he had hoped, "popular" in style and ethos, so much so that within a few years his successors were to complain that it was entirely too Chamar. It had become, in their view, encapsulated within the Chamar caste with its virtues and shortcomings. They were thus convinced that the Church needed converts from other sections of society in order to provide greater diversity of views and feelings, to become stronger and more self-supporting, to be less identified in the public mind with the Chamars, and thus be capable of reaching out to other sections of society (*Annual Report* 1889–90, 44–45).

II

Inspired by the baptism on July 11, 1852, of two high-caste converts, Professor Ram Chandra, a professor at Delhi College, and Dr. Chaman Lal, Assistant Surgeon of Delhi, some British residents of Delhi were able to persuade the Society for the Propagation of the Gospel to start a mission directed especially towards the elite who had received a Western education. Its missionaries were to be "of a superior kind . . . learned as well as devout" ("Delhi," 3) and a school was to be the centerpiece of their work. After the devastating events of 1857, the S. P. G. sent three new missionaries there. The first reached Delhi in February 1859, and the one who was to become the most important during this period, the Rev. Robert W. Winter, arrived in 1860.

The mission school started prior to 1857 was revived by a convert, Theophilus Qasim Ali, even before these missionaries arrived. The school, the small congregation, and the process of learning the language kept the missionaries occupied during their first years in Delhi.[11] Preaching was done by catechists, one of whom had instructed a group of Chamars in Shahdra in preparation for baptism, only to have them decide in the end to join Smith and the Baptists (*Report of the Incorporated Society for 1859*, 103; *The Mission Field*, June 1860, 134). Nonetheless they did receive two high-caste converts, who had come under the influence of Ram Chandra in 1859. Chander Lall, who had been a student of Delhi College and was working at the government treasury office in Delhi, was one of twelve baptized that year, all of whom were either Muslims or high-caste Hindus (*Report of the Incorporated Society for 1859*, 104). The other was Tara Chand who was originally from Delhi but was baptized at Agra. He went on to study at Bishop's College in Calcutta, returned to Delhi, and was ordained a priest in 1864 (*Report of the Incorporated Society for 1865*, 115). The Rev. Lala Tara Chand occupied a special status in the Delhi mission, virtually equal to the missionaries, which no other Indian pastor during this period enjoyed.[12]

The methods developed by the S. P. G. missionaries during the 1860s were designed to reach out to the elite of Delhi. Their St. Stephen's School was one of two in Delhi that prepared students for the Calcutta and Punjab University entrance examinations, and for a short while (1864–1865) it held college classes as well. The S. P. G. also addressed religious controversy through their preaching and their Urdu monthly begun in 1867 called *Mowaiz-i-ookba* ("Admonitions related to the Other World") (*Report of the Incorporated Society for 1863*, 93; *Report of the Incorporated Society for 1867*, 106; *The Mission Field*, April 1869, 112).[13] When they began work among women, it was by starting a female normal school for women of good caste (*Report of the Incorporated Society for 1863–64*, 99), as well as separate schools for Hindu and Muslim girls.[14] The normal school was soon divided, so that a separate one for Muslim women could accommodate some of the *begams* (married Muslim women) from the old royal family. From these schools women's work was expanded into visiting the *zenanas* of respectable families and holding classes in them (*The Mission Field*, August 1865, 151). In 1873 a female medical mission was started (*Report of the Inncorporated Society for 1873*, 68). It is difficult to measure the success of this elite strategy, which gained renewed emphasis when the Cambridge Mission to Delhi was established in 1877. The number of converts baptized each year was small, and their caste backgrounds were not always given. In 1873–74 Robert Winter calculated that 40 of the 186 adult Indian members of the community were of either high-caste Hindu or Muslim parentage (Western cited by Alter and Jai Singh 1961, 37).[15]

Meanwhile a small congregation of Chamars was emerging near Delhi Gate under S. P. G. auspices. At first a catechist instructed them almost daily and conducted separate Sunday evening services for them. A small school with twelve to fifteen boys was also started among them. This small group of Christians faced some difficulties right from the outset. They were turned out of their houses because of their new religion and then, in 1863, out of the room they used for classes and worship by its Muslim owner. They then put a straw shed on the roof of one of their new houses and used that instead (*The Mission Field*, August 1863, 187; *Report of the Incorporated Society for 1863*, 93). Poverty and indebtedness required them to work for their creditors on Sundays. They also had to redefine their relationship to their fellow Chamars.

> The heathen Chaniars [*sic*] have a custom of sacrificing a goat, and offering it, together with corn, & before some idol, and then all collecting together, and making a common feast. In this feast, though, of course, not in the sacrifice, the Christians have hitherto joined; but now their own consciences have begun to teach them that this is wrong, directly contrary to the rules of the Apostles,[16] and therefore making them unfit for the Holy Communion, which none of

them have as yet, for this reason, received (*Report of the Incorpo-rated Society for 1883*, 93).

From this base at Delhi Gate the work among the Chamars expanded, so that in 1868 the catechists performed systematic home visitation. As a result many Chamars came under instruction for baptism and attended church regularly (*The Mission Field*, May 1868, 130). A year later Bible women were also visiting Chamar women to provide daily instruction for them and for their daughters (*The Mission Field*, August 1869, 236).

In the mid-1870s the number of Chamar converts increased quite dramatically. Of the 186 Christian adults Winter listed in 1873-74, eighty-three or about forty-five percent were "weavers and Chamars" (Western). There were twenty-three men baptized in 1875, of whom twenty-two were Chamars and one was a Muslim (*Report of the Incorporated Society for 1875,* 15). Conversions spread from the city to the villages as Delhi converts got their rural relatives interested in their new religion (*Report of the Incorporated Society for 1876*, 16). In 1878 between three and four hundred were baptized (Bickersteth 1878), the largest of any one year, and in 1879, forty-three of the fifty-three adult baptisms were of Chamars (*Report of the Incorporated Society for 1879*, 24–25). The missionaries attributed these increases to the fact that Chamars were not orthodox Hindus,[17] to the loose hold that caste had over them, to their improved condition under British rule, to the better treatment they received from Christians, and more specifically to the influence of the schools and worship services in their *bastīs* (*The Mission Field,* May 1875, 151; Bickersteth 1878).

Yet the "place" of this growing number of Chamar converts remained the same as when they were only few in number. Despite considerable expansion among the lowly Chamars, S. P. G. thinking about the development of the Church (as about its evangelistic mission) continued to be elitist, socially hierarchical, and centralized. At the end of 1869, a year after the Baptists had taken their most radical step towards self-support and "independence," the S. P. G. Delhi Mission decided, with the same end in view, to start a Native Pastorate Fund to which each member was to contribute a portion of their income, as well as to hold bimonthly meetings of all communicants "for a free discussion of any question which might be of interest to the whole body" (*The Mission Field*, May 1871, 141). In 1871 they began implementing a plan to increase the number of paid evangelists in their employ (Winter 1874). In 1875 they divided the city into eight parishes each under a head catechist accountable to the mission; each congregation had a local *panchāyat,* consisting of two elected members and a third appointed by the mission to "advise the local catechists, make arrangements for the services, settle petty disputes and exercise a useful influence upon the unconverted neighbors" (*The Mis-*

sion Field, June 1877, 184: September 1877, 381–82.) "The work" was seen as directed towards three separate categories of Indian humanity: "the men of the better classes, the secluded women of the same, and third, the low-caste people of both sexes" (*The Mission Field,* September 1877, 383). Schools were divided into those "for the higher and middle orders" and those for "the lower orders" (ibid).[18] All of this, whether church structures or outreach work of various kinds, was closely supervised by the missionaries and then, by 1880, placed under a Mission Council, comprised of all the missionaries plus Rev. Tara Chand and chaired by Winter, rather than remaining under him as an individual or as the senior missionary (Winter 1880).

In December 1883 the Native Church Council, evolved from the earlier bimonthly meetings of communicant members and chaired by Winter as senior missionary, decided to prohibit betrothals and marriages with non-Christians, as well as the use of other than Christian rites for life-cycle rituals. Offenders had their names posted and were denied "*huqqa-pānī*" (fellowship) until they repented publicly and paid a fine (*The Mission Field,* October 1884, 316–17). The mission also purchased four sites in the city on which Christians might live somewhat free of the "heathen influences" to which they were subject while scattered throughout the city.[19] The conditions set for living in these Christian *bastīs* were "that the members of the families . . . be baptised persons, that all Sunday labour be stopped, and that they avoid all attendance at non-Christian marriages and other ceremonies" (*The Mission Field,* October 1884, 318).[20] These regulations were aimed primarily at the Chamar converts, since the others were outcasted upon conversion and so could neither intermarry with nor attend the ceremonies among their unconverted caste fellows anyway.

These regulations increased pressures upon Chamar converts to choose between their Christian and their caste fellowships (*birādarīs*) and produced a major crisis in 1884. The Chamar converts in Daryaganj, led by their *chaudharī* (leader) decided to break their connection with the Chamar *birādarī.* In this they were strongly encouraged by the missionaries who believed that this would raise the low "spiritual state" of the Chamar Christians, whose Christianity was only nominal, and thus remove a major stumbling block hindering the evangelization of the rest of the city (Lefroy 4–5). To that end, in June 1884 some leading Chamar converts called a meeting of the leaders of the entire section of the Chamar community to which they belonged, some 250 in all, despite the opposition of many other Christian Chamars who did not wish to be put on the spot.

> The first move was on the part of our catechist, who gave a short *resume* of the events which had led to the present meeting, and thanked them for having all responded to the summons, and then

called on our chaudri and the other men to do their part. This they
did simply and well. Standing up they one after the other expressed
their appreciation of the comfort which they had enjoyed, and the
consideration they had met with in their old connection, but regret-
ted that they had now reached a point in their new life as Christians
which made it impossible for them to continue on the old terms of
fellowship, and they therefore wished to say that for the future,
while they were, and always would be, glad to reckon many individuals as personal friends, they would have nothing to do with the
Chamar Brotherhood, as such; they would not recognize its authority or attend its meetings (Lefroy 1884, 77).

This was well received for its frankness and sincerity, but that did not
end the meeting because the Chamar leaders wanted to "sift out the Christians." This they did by having each one raise a pot of Ganges water to their
foreheads or face ejection from the *birādarī*. Five men paid obeisance in this
way, but then a young *chaudharī* declined, and his followers stood firm with
him. However, since the Chamar leadership did not press for the immediate
exclusion of those who refused to honor the Ganges water, the division between the Christians who were in and those who were out of the Chamar
birādarī was not as clear and total as anticipated.[21] The following March, the
Bishop of Lahore, when confirming fifty-seven candidates, remarked, "There
appeared to me a marked improvement both in the number and solemnity of
the worshippers—a result which might fairly be expected from some searchings
of heart in one or more of the Chamar congregations in Delhi, which had led
to a greater separation of not a few of the members of the Christian flocks
from heathen worship and practices, of which the taint was not yet wholly
cleansed" (*Report of the Incorporated Society for 1885*, 7).

This has been depicted as one of the defining moments in the history of
the S. P. G.'s Delhi mission. The issue at stake for the missionaries was the
purity of the Church, purity being seen as freedom from corrupting "heathen
influences." It is ironic that it was the Chamar converts who posed this issue,
not because they were considered polluting in Christian as in Hindu society—
the missionaries were quite clear about that[22]—but because theirs was a caste
that did not automatically excommunicate and socially boycott members who
underwent Christian baptism. The issue for the Chamar converts can only be
surmised. As Winter indicated a short time later, they probably perceived
Christianity as a *panth,* like the *panths* associated with Kabir or Rai Das,
popular among Chamars, which they could believe in and belong to without
losing caste membership and without its interfering with their domestic or
caste customs, even if these involved a certain association with idolatry (*The
Mission Field,* December 1887, 365; Alter and Jai Singh 1961, 34). In addi-

tion, it should be pointed out that Christian Chamars could not attain genuinely equal status with other converts as fellow communicant members of the Church without making the kind of break with the past those in Daryaganj made. Those were the rules laid down by the Church authorities, and they had no choice but to embrace them or accept a permanent secondary status within the Christian Church and community.

The evidence, circumstantial as it is, does suggest that whereas the Baptists sought to encourage the development of popular Christianity in and around Delhi, the S. P. G. sought to discourage it. The S. P. G. certainly wanted converts, and their methods certainly resembled (perhaps even imitated) those of the Baptists, but the spirit behind their actions was more controlling than liberating. One gets a glimpse of this in the differing ways the two missions talked about worship among converts, the very heart of popular Christianity. The Baptists had prayer meetings in the *bastīs*, which they took pride in and described in some detail; the S. P. G. conducted "simple and short services" adapted to the requirements of the people there (*The Mission Field*, September 1877, 385), although the *bastī* Christians took their own services when the mission staff could not (*Report of the Incorporated Society for 1875*, 16). The language used suggests that these services were not spontaneous or ex tempore but were probably "read" from a modified form of the *Book of Common Prayer*. The Baptist delegation commented upon the *vitality* of worship in the *bastīs*; the Bishop of Lahore appreciated the *solemnity* of Chamar participation in S. P. G. worship. It seems that whereas James Smith was eager to have his Chamar converts develop their own ways of being Christian, the S. P. G. missionaries were more concerned to bring their Chamar converts into conformity with churchly ways. While this may have been very stimulating to elite converts like Professor Ram Chandra and Rev. Tara Chand, it probably reinforced among the low-caste Chamar majority within the Church the passivity inculcated by the caste system. It has also left us with little direct evidence of their forms of popular Christianity.

III

The Baptists and the S. P. G. began to rebuild their respective churches after the devastations of 1857 at virtually the same time. Each brought to the task their own Baptist and Anglican images of what the Church ought to be like, the legacy of their own past experiences in north India, as well as their own emphases and strategies in mission. Some of the correspondence to their home offices back in England suggests they were rivals who were quite critical of each other's methods rather than friendly collaborators. James Smith was inspired by a vision of the Gospel taking root in north India, and once having done so, spreading to embrace the whole land. To achieve this he sought to plant and nurture churches of the people who would take their own initiatives in spreading the Gospel. His strategy laid emphasis upon "independence" or more specifically, decentralization of power, congregational initiative, and lay leadership. The S. P. G.'s mission was directed primarily but not exclusively towards the evangelization of Delhi's elites and incorporating them into a Church in which power was more centralized and which relied upon clerical initiative and leadership. Smith saw Christianity as an alien thing and gave priority to having it owned and, in a sense, domesticated by its adherents, despite the risks involved. The S. P. G. was less concerned about Christianity's exotic nature in north India and paid more attention to having converts conform to Christian standards set by the proper Church authorities. Both remained committed, almost to the end of this period, to encouraging converts to continue living in their own neighborhoods and among their own people, so as to exercise a Christian influence upon them.

It is difficult to assess the impact these differing strategies had upon the development of the Christian Church in Delhi because the inner dynamics of the Delhi Christian community are not described in the records the missionaries left behind. Did these strategies produce the desired and anticipated results? The Baptists pointed to their *bastī* meetings and the self-support accomplishments of their local panchāyats to justify the rightness of their strategy. The S. P. G. pointed to some of its illustrious converts, as well as to the decision of the Daryaganj Christians to justify theirs. Was the evidence both cited symbolic of broader developments within these two sections of the Christian community or were they, in each instance, exceptional cases? Perhaps the evidence is both symbolic and exceptional at the same time.

While the examination of missionary strategies does provide a helpful tool in understanding the development of the Delhi Christian community during the postmutiny period, it is inadequate by itself. Missionaries could not dictate who would respond to their Gospel, who would thus come to comprise the Christian community and Church, or what they would bring with them when they entered it. The S. P. G. set out to evangelize the elites, and yet at the end of this period the baptized believers were predominantly, if not overwhelming, Chamar! Not only was this contrary to missionary design but, as it happened, those converts were allowed by their caste fellows to remain part of their *birādarīs,* something unthinkable among the elites the S. P. G. sought. Because of these continuing ties, the Chamar converts posed strategic problems for the missionaries that the elites did not. In like manner, the Baptists had a very unstable community, with converts moving in and out at an uncomfortably high rate, as well as poor church attendance among those who remained. One might say that the missionaries were facing considerable resistance from their converts, until they discovered that their converts found *bastī* meetings not only more convenient but also more congenial focal points for their common devotional life than the regular church services. Moreover, it was the positive example of the free-moving, independent, and highly effective Seetal Das who provided at least some of the inspiration for the important strategic decision to do away with paid evangelists.

In both instances missionary strategy had to confront the reality of the popular Christianity of newly won converts. Whatever their original aims and however they may have felt about them, both the Baptists and the S. P. G. ended up with predominantly Chamar churches. James Smith not merely encouraged the development of popular Christianity among his congregations, but he even embraced it as the means by which all of India would be evangelized. The S. P. G. missionaries were more leery and cautious about popular Christianity in their congregations. In their view only a "purified" and "uplifting" Christianity would commend itself to India as a whole. If measured solely in terms of converts won during this period, both approaches appear to have been equally successful.

IV

Around Christmas in 1889 a *faqīr* (muslim mendicant) from the Punjab appeared in the Chamar *bastīs* of Delhi, preaching against beef-eating and promising that if the Chamars would form themselves into a Hindu *panth*, they could be assured of a social status equal to that of other castes. The Chamars of Paharganj took the lead, and soon the movement spread to other *bastīs* as well as to the nearby villages. At first Christians were welcomed only on the condition that they refrain from eating beef, but after winning over a considerable following, the *faqīr* declared that members of the *panth* could not associate with Christians. Thus the Christian Chamars found themselves facing strong social pressure to renounce Christianity in order to be part of the new *panth*. Despite the strenuous efforts of the missionaries and mission workers, many—including some catechists—gave in, offering this explanation. "Sir, you live there, we live here; our neighbours, our relations, our masters, our creditors, all with whom we have anything to do, are compelling us to yield; if we don't, they will fine us, sue us for debts whether true or false, hate us, ostracise us, bitterly persecute us, making it impossible to live!" (*The Missionary Herald*, September 1890, 329).

Both the Baptists and the S. P. G. were hard hit. Herbert Thomas reported in April 1890 that only seventeen of the seventy-four Chamar Baptists resident in the city had been able to resist, and that George Lefroy had told him that among the S. P. G. Christians only those Chamars living in Christian *bastīs* had withstood the movement (ibid., 330). Winter's account, written in

August 1890, was much briefer but told essentially the same story. The dilemma Chamar Christians faced was "Heathen Society intercourse and influence versus Christian intercommunion and a deliberate choosing of Heathenism *as a life*—though they maintained that they still hold the doctrines of Christianity rather than the life of the followers of Christ" (Winter 1890). James Smith, who happened to be in Delhi at the time, wrote that Chamar Christians had begged him to break the movement, and he probably could have done so, but chose not to. "It was the same thing over again, they looked to me to do their work, and I declined to do what they knew *they* ought to have done." Other Chamar Christians, however, he found "full of fire and confidence, holding well together" (*The Missionary Herald*, September 1890, 332). Almost ten years later an S. P. G. pastor reported that the *faqīr* had subsequently disappeared, having "gathered all the money he could" and "leaving his followers pretty much or entirely where he had found them." Only thirty-five to forty S. P. G. Chamar families were still Christian (Ghose 1898, 35). There was no massive return to Christianity among earlier converts, although some restorations did take place, nor any significant conversion movements of Delhi Chamars to Christianity after the *faqīr* had left.

A major consequence both of this "time of testing" and of James Smith's departure from Delhi was that the Baptist missionary strategy in the years following came to resemble that of the S. P. G. Smith's successors did not share his vision—their reports resemble those of the S. P. G. with whom they worked more closely than they had in Smith's time. In 1959–60 James Alter and Herbert Jai Singh conducted an intensive study of the Church in Delhi, examining the oldest Baptist and S. P. G. congregations there with some care. In their account, the Christians had become, and functioned as, a separate, distinct Indian community. Identification and relationships with the Chamar *birādarī* were no longer issues in the Church. Isolated and contained, what social influence the Christian community still had upon the surrounding society at any level was exercised through individuals or institutions rather than through more traditional hereditary ties.

Notes

1. To date five books in this series have been published; the first three volumes cover the history from the beginning up through the eighteenth century, and the two others deal with northeast India and Tamil Nadu, respectively, in the nineteenth and twentieth centuries.

2. One who has concentrated upon the history of Protestantism in north India cannot but be impressed by (and even jealous of) the wide range of source materials, including "a vast array of shrine histories, devotional texts and local legends," as well as European sources Bayly drew upon to write her history (Bayly 1989, 243).

3. In 1862 the missionaries reported that of the seventy-four people in Purana Kila who had been baptized in 1859, only eleven remained. The others did not simply "go back" but in the missionaries' estimation "never entirely *forsook* their former heathen habits." The vast majority seemed to have laid down two conditions for continuing to attend Christian worship, both of which proved to be unacceptable. "These were, 1st that we should grant them liberty to enjoy and practise all the heathen rites of their clan and caste, and 2nd that we should recognize them *as Christians, should they need* a recommendation occasionally, to help them through any difficulties they might get into. On these terms, they were willing to favour our services with occasional attendance, but could not promise to be regular" (*Annual Report* 1862, 7). Other discussions of the problem of instability may be found in ibid., 6; *The Baptist Magazine,* May 1862, 325; ibid., March 1864, 188.

4. He expected to live off donations from friends and congregations in England instead, but did not offer this as an example that other missionaries should follow (ibid).

5. Ibid., 3–7. "We are sure to present Christianity in an Anglicized form and garb, and this it is that repels and disgusts the Native more than the fundamentals or essentials of the Gospel. A purely Native organization, freed from European dictation and aid, would necessarily adapt itself to the genius of the people, and avoid that which comes so directly in contact with Native social habits and modes of thought" (*The Missionary Herald,* February 1869, 118).

6. By "primitive" Smith obviously meant close to the New Testament model.

7. "Most of these schools contain a few boys who can read fluently, but not with intelligence, the meaning of difficult words not having been explained to them. In a few cases a little arithmetic and geography had been taught" (*Report on Popular Education* 1878–79, 66).

8. In 1890 Smith's successors pointed out this discrepancy *(Annual Report* 1889–90, 41).

9. These included making exaggerated and, in essence, false claims about the achievements of the Delhi Mission, as well as about "the moral condition of the Delhi Church." What seems to have made these charges so serious was not only Smith's strong advocacy of his own methods (with their results as evidence of their superiority to those generally used) as well as the equally strong opposition of his Baptist colleagues to them, but also the bad feelings these disagreements had generated *(Report on Mission Work in Delhi).*

10. There seems to be a discrepancy between the numbers listed in this report and those given in an appendix on schools, meetings, and membership in which twenty-four schools are listed and twenty-two of these held from one to seven meetings a week *(Report on Mission Work in Delhi* 23, 49).

11. According to their annual report for 1862 neither Winter nor Skelton, the first to arrive, had begun public preaching because of these other responsibilities *(Report of the Incorporated Society for 1862,* 148).

12. In 1880 the Delhi Mission Council included all the missionaries and Rev. Tara Chand but none of the "native pastors" (*The Mission Field*, August 1880, 241).

13. The monthly ceased publication in 1870 or 1871 (*The Mission Field*, May 1871, 143).

14. A normal school was a school for training teachers.

15. This number is probably on the low side because fifty were listed as "Christian born" without any indication of their parents' backgrounds.

16. The "rules of the Apostles" pertain to eating food that has been offered to idols (Acts 15:20, 29; I Corinthians 8).

17. "Most of them are not orthodox Hindus, but followers of some one or other of the modern Hindu reformers, as Ramanand, Kabir, Dadu, etc., whose teaching was much purer than that of the other Hindus" (*The Mission Field*, May 1875, 151).

18. The reference here is to social orders rather than to levels of education (e.g., primary, middle, and secondary schools), as a comment later in the essay makes clear.

19. Lefroy said that this decision was made in response to the pleas of some of the converts themselves (*The Mission Field*, March 1885, 72).

20. Lefroy lists the conditions as "(1) To observe Sundays as a day of rest. (2) To use Christian rites exclusively at times of birth, marriage, and death. (3) To abstain from the use of charas" [a drug similar to opium, inhaled when smoking a *huqqa*] (*The Mission Field*, March 1885, 72).

21. This account follows that of George Lefroy, who was present and an eyewitness, in a letter to Canon Wescott dated 8 September 1884 and published in Lefroy 1884, 70–81.

22. Two incidents illustrate this. One was their obvious approval of a community-wide meal, organized by Professor Ram Chandra, at which Christians from high- and low-caste backgrounds ate together (*The Mission Field*, May 1871, 141–42). The other was their delight in the fact that the Chamar *chaudharī* from Daryaganj had won a close election to the Church *panchāyat* because it "helps put into practice what we often confine to words, that the whole congregation, low and high, form one body with, relatively to its own concerns, equal rights and claims" (*The Mission Field*, October 1884, 316).

Bibliography

Alter, James P., and Jai Singh, Herbert. 1961. *The Church in Delhi*. Lucknow: Lucknow Publishing House.

Annual Report of the Delhi Mission, Branch of the Baptist Missionary Society. 1860–1870.

Annual Reports of the Committee of the Baptist Missionary Society. 1867–1918.

A Scheme for a Comprehensive History of Christianity in India. *Indian Church History Review* 8, 1974 (December): 89–90.

The Baptist Magazine. 1861–1866.

Bayly, Susan. 1989. *Saints, Goddesses, and Kings: Muslims and Christians in South Indian Society, 1700–1900.* Cambridge: Cambridge University Press.

Bickersteth, Edward. 1878. Letter to Mr. Bullock, October 16.

Copley, Antony. 1997. *Religions in Conflict: Ideology, Cultural Contact and Conversion in Late Colonial India.* Delhi: Oxford University Press.

Ghose, S. 1898. "Work amongst the Chamars." *Delhi Mission News* (July): 35.

Kawashima, Koji. 1998. *Missionaries and a Hindu State: Travancore 1858–1936.* Delhi: Oxford University Press.

Lefroy, G. A. 1884. *The Leather-Workers of Daryaganj: An Occasional Paper of the Cambridge Mission to Delhi* n.p.

The Mission Field. 1858–1892.

The Missionary Herald. 1859–1918.

Powell, Avril A. 1993. *Muslims and Missionaries in Pre-Mutiny India.* Richmond, U.K.: Curzon Press.

Report of the General Missionary Conference held at Allahabad, 1872–73. 1873. London: Seeley, Jackson and Halliday.

Report of the S. P. G. Cambridge Mission in Delhi and South Punjab. . . . for the Year Ending December 31st, 1885. 1886. Allahabad.

Report on Mission Work in Delhi: Report of Revs. John Aldis and Wm. Sampson. 1878. Deputation appointed to visit North-Western Provinces.

Report on the Indian Mission of the General Secretary, Baptist Missionary Society 1889–90.

Reports of the Incorporated Society for the Propagation of the Gospel in Foreign Parts for the Years 1857 through 1918.

Reports on Popular Education in the Punjab and Its Dependencies, 1860–61 through 1880–81.

Society for the Propagation of the Gospel. 1858. "Delhi." *Quarterly Paper No. CIV* (April).

Society for the Propagation of the Gospel. Files of "Calcutta Letters Received" and "Letters Received Asia." n.d. n.p.

Stanley, Brian. 1992. *The History of the Baptist Missionary Society 1792–1992*. Edinburgh: T&T Clark.

Webster, John C. B. 1979. "The History of Christianity in India: Aims and Methods." *Indian Church History Review* 8 (December), 88–122.

Western, F. J. 1950. "The Early History of the Cambridge Mission to Delhi." Unpublished ms.

Winter, R. R. 1874. Letter to Mr. Bullock, June 9.

Winter, R. R. 1880. Letter to Mr. Tucker, June 9.

Winter, R. R. 1890. Letter to Mr. Tucker, August 26.

CHAPTER 11

Dalit Theology in Tamil Christian Folk Music:
A Transformative Liturgy
By James Theophilus Appavoo

Zoe C. Sherinian

vānattila vāṟuhiṟa pettavarē sāmi–om
The divine one, our parent living in heaven,
pēr veḷaṅga vēṇuñcāmi viḍutalai varavēṇum
Let the meaning of your name be understood as 'let there be freedom!'
ottumayā oru olaiyil sēndu tiṟṟum sōṟu
Give us daily the 'oru olai' food that is shared
nittanittam keḍaikkaṇumē pettavarē sāmi
In unity O, divine parent.

In this spoken (*pēccu*) Tamil folk version of the Lord's Prayer, the Dalit[1] composer/theologian Theophilus Appavoo proclaims the meaning of God's name as freedom (*viḍutalai*) thereby defining Christianity and Christian indigenization as the action of liberation.[2] His strategy of Christian indigenization is to re/construct a valued cultural status for low-caste Christians (and non-Christians) by reclaiming their folk music and rural culture for use in Christian liturgy. Appavoo's theological strategy suggests that Christian indigenization of music necessitates use of a musical system, as well as religious and cultural content, that allows for a recreative process of adaptation and manipulation for Dalit people's own liberative theological and social use.

Christian theology in India has multiple manifestations that reflect the cultural diversity of Christians and ultimately the diversity of Christianities. Dalit theology is one of several forms of indigenous Christian theologies expressed through music, a phenomenon of religious transmission that has existed in Tamil Nadu since its first contact with Christian missionaries as early as 1535. Christian music used by Tamils today is a complex mixture of

233

European, American, Brahmanical, Indian cinematic, and Dalit flavors that have been sautéed in the oil of cultural contact over four hundred years to create not one, but a variety of musical and socio-religious styles: Western, Carnatic (indigenous classical), light (film or popular music), and folk. The most dynamic manifestations of Tamil Christian indigenization today continue to be the creation and transmission of Tamil theological perspectives through indigenous music; Dalit Christian theology has found its voice in folk music.

This essay presents a case study of Reverend James Theophilus Appavoo, a Protestant Dalit composer/theologian of the Church of South India (CSI), who has created a musical theology of liberation. Appavoo is one of the most influential and prolific Christian composer/theologians in Tamil Nadu today. He not only communicates a Dalit theology through sermons and written treatises but, as I will demonstrate, he musically actualizes and disseminates it through songs and liturgies—a significant strategy within the field of Dalit theology.[3]

The term "Dalit" reached Tamil Christian theologians and Christian activists by the mid-1980s and led to the development of a body of literature on Dalit theology. The earliest theological/academic use of the term Dalit in south India was at U.T.C. (United Theological College) Bangalore in April 1981 by A. P. Nirmal. Kottapalli Wilson used it in 1982 in his *The Twice Alienated Culture of Dalit Christians*. The CSI Bishop M. Azariah first brought the term to an international forum in 1984 to raise international Christian concern about the contemporary problems of Dalits. One of the most striking problems for Christian Dalits is that the government does not afford them the same degree of compensation (quotas in government jobs and educational seats) as "Hindu" Dalits because of their religion. In 1994 Bishop Azariah led the march to Delhi to fight for compensatory rights—affirmative action and quotas in education and government jobs—for Christian Dalits equal to those offered to "Hindu" Dalits.

Caste differentiation and prejudice continues to be practiced in the Protestant Churches, while its meaning has been recontextualized within the Christian subculture. My informants claimed that today caste distinctions affected elections for bishops, church pastorate committees, and Student Christian Movement leaders, as well as job preferences in Christian institutions, admission into choirs, seminary selection and financial support, decisions about whether one would invite another Christian into their house for a meal, and individual choice of music.

Dalit Christian music attempts to address oppressions that particularly plague the lives of Christian and non-Christian Dalits in villages. "Untouchables" are still given tea in differentiated tumblers at village tea stalls and forced to draw water from wells away from those near the upper-caste houses.

Dalit women in many villages carry water daily from government wells, often a good distance from their *ceris* (colonies). Basic infrastructure services like access to clean water, electricity, and phones are often denied or delayed in Dalit communities. Dalit men and women are most often employed as manual laborers in construction or agriculture. In urban areas Dalits are assigned the menial jobs of cleaning toilets and removing garbage.

The composer Theophilus Appavoo is of the ex-untouchable Paraiyar caste;[4] however, unlike the majority of Christian and non-Christian Paraiyars who are landless agricultural laborers, his family has lived in urban areas (Vellore and Cuddalore in Arcot district) for the past four generations, benefiting from middle-class employment and Christian education.[5] His musical journey began with his family who performed and highly valued Carnatic music—a phenomenon among some lower-caste families that reflects their musical Sanskritization. By reflecting on his experience of casteism in urban churches as a boy, and observing oppressive caste practices in rural areas as a priest, Appavoo has developed a theoretical critique of the hegemonic cultural values transmitted and reinforced through indigenized Christian Carnatic music used among a primarily lower-caste Protestant Christian community.[6]

Appavoo teaches at the Tamil Nadu Theological Seminary (TTS) in Madurai, a Protestant seminary with a rich musical environment where theology has become "singable" in multiple styles (Thangaraj 1990, 109–18). Within this environment, the folk music composed by Appavoo stands out not only for its beauty, rhythmic vitality, and theologically powerful lyrics, but also for the way it has generated excitement and inspiration among the pastoral and lay communities. While doing fieldwork (1993–94), I observed the transmission network generated by TTS. Students, faculty, and lay people learned, recomposed, and ultimately became carriers of Appavoo's message through his songs. As a "student" in this community, I too was moved not only by his message, but also by his theo-musicological position that folk music is the form of Tamil Christian music with the greatest potential to empower and liberate Dalits from caste and economic oppression.

Appavoo's theological purpose is to change the values of this world that divide people, bringing to fruition what he understands as the "kingdom values" of love, equality, and justice between all in this world today, not exclusively in heaven or at some indefinite time in the future. Appavoo never advocates conversion to the institution of Christianity, but to these "kingdom values." He works toward socially empowering the oppressed regardless of religion and changing the values of those who oppress, especially those Christians who continue to practice casteism. He believes that this goal requires radical action on all social and cultural levels.[7] He advocates beginning this process with the practice of poor people eating communally: practicing *oru olai* (literally "one pot"), a daily "Eucharistic" lifestyle of sharing food and the labor necessary for its production. *Oru olai*, then, is modeled on the communal labor and eating practices of the Indian joint family and used by many Dalit communities during festivals. It is also in tune with the values and practices of the early Church community.

Because Appavoo believes Christianity should be a means for social liberation, he theorizes that Christian indigenization of music should involve the use of local music and cultural perspectives. The adjective "Christian" is an essential defining characteristic of the musical, theological, and social method he has undertaken to create indigenized Tamil Christian music. He distinguishes between "Christian indigenization," which he understands as a method of liberation for the economically and socially oppressed, and "indigenized Christianity," which in India historically reflects the methods of Sanskritization, colonialization, Westernization, and translation. To "indigenize" Tamil Christian music necessitates reversing the hegemonic dominance that Brahmanical and Western cultural/musical forms and lyrical content have had on Christian music.[8] Because at least 75 percent of Tamil Christians come from the Dalit and Sudra castes, and a majority live in rural villages, Appavoo argues that folk music is the most meaningful and liberative due to its content and language, its participatory nature, and because it is easily transmitted to these people.[9]

Whether indigenization as cultural synthesis is destructive or constructive depends on its motivating purpose and the power dynamics between outside "missionaries" and indigenous people, and among indigenous groups. Appavoo asserts that if the purpose of synthesis is to destroy or replace the egalitarian nature of local religions, it is neither positive nor liberative. He maintains that Western missionaries destroyed the empowering practices of local religions by labeling them "devil worship" and, with rare exception, only chose to indigenize Christianity using the religious content of Brahmanical Hinduism.[10] In contrast, "Christian indigenization," according to Appavoo, is liberative in instances when 1) people reflect on and include their experience in the music, 2) they develop self-esteem by proudly reclaiming folk Dalit culture and identity, 3) they resist the tendency to internalize the hegemonic Brahmanical and Western cultures, and 4) they struggle together (in ritual, action, and performance) against multiple oppressions.

In Tamil village religions, empowerment occurs through transphysical rituals of "possession" by the *sāmi* (deity). The village deity possessing or "coming upon" a villager allows even the weakest members of the community to gain power both physically and emotionally. Emotions such as anger and fear are not pacified but rather channeled into action. The key to inducing this possession is the power of *parai* drumming.[11] Yet, the *parai*, and the drummers who play it, are more commonly thought of as polluting by upper castes because the drum is a necessary ritual accompaniment for upper-caste funerals.[12] Appavoo's most radical act of musical indigenization has been to bring the *parai* and its driving syncopated rhythms into a Christian liturgy that reclaims it as valuable and worthy rather than associates it with pollution (considering it *kōccai* or denigrated). Through reclaiming the content and form of folk culture, Appavoo similarly reclaims Dalit status as nonpolluting and esteemed.

The use of the folk form in the Tamil Church and in the larger hegemonic culture in which anything "folk" is considered to be degraded, represents significant subversive protest and marks an important first step in Appavoo's goal for a Dalit cultural revolution.[13] Folk music for Appavoo is music that is economically and socially accessible, draws on community skills, is potentially recreative, treated as unauthored, and orally learned. It uses spoken language and a musical syntax with which poor and oppressed people are facile. He furthermore reclaims rural musical moods, instruments, stylistic devices, agricultural metaphors, and elements of Dalit religions and politics. Appavoo has discovered through his own work with Tamil villagers that a message of Christian liberation is not as easily and powerfully spread through other "indigenized" Christian styles such as classical south Indian (Carnatic), Western hymnody, and some popular (film style) Tamil Christian musics. As communication mediums, these styles are oppressive to poor Dalit Christians because they reflect the culture and values of the higher-caste/class defined society, and moreover are rarely pedagogically accessible.[14] For example, Appavoo argues that transmission of Carnatic music is inherently limited and difficult; it is an individual art that does not facilitate community participation, unity, or protest to change society; and it cannot encode anger effectively but instead pacifies. The key to the difficulty of its transmission is its nature as a performance art controlled by class and caste elites.[15] Appavoo contends that if the message of a song has meaning to Dalits, if it is politically and spiritually empowering, it will spread quickly (Appavoo 1993, 75). If it is not meaningful, its message and style will either be changed to become powerful, or it will die a natural death from lack of use.

History and Context of Indigenized Tamil Christian Music

Since the early sixteenth century, music has played a primary role in the process of indigenization and the expression of each "new" mode of Tamil Christianity in its specific historical context. Translation and vernacularization of the Christian message into Tamil dialects and musical styles were central to the conversion process. Throughout this history, language and musical style continued to be markers of local identity as well as cultural and aesthetic values. Music became a means for theological transmission, while particular styles of music transmitted the aesthetic and social values associated with Sanskritization, Westernization and Dalitization. Music then became a means for expressing and transmitting indigenized theology as well as contextualizing Tamil Christian identities.

As local and foreign players changed throughout history, so did the dynamics and complexity of indigenization.[16] Beginning in the eighteenth century, different denominationally-based mission societies were involved with different Tamil groups—divided by caste, class, geography, and theological identity—creating a variety of indigenized Christianities in Tamil Nadu. The dynamics between missionaries and native groups took on specific qualities of power and valuation. Several factors played a role in creating these dynamics including the religio-cultural ideology of each mission society, the reasons for conversion and indigenization of each local Tamil group, as well as the influence of individual culture brokers. These social dynamics were in turn expressed through the resulting indigenous styles of music; particularly through the dynamics of linguistic and stylistic transmission, the values and cultural perspectives encoded in each style, and the degree of empowerment and passivity associated with each.

Although the Tamil Christian population today is relatively small—three million or 5.81 percent of the total state population (Grafe 1990, 2)—the support for the use of one music style over another often reflects the historically constructed identities and theological stances of particular Tamil Christian subgroups (Sherinian 1998, 193–291).[17] A brief description of the historical relationships between these social and musical categories will help to illuminate the context in which Appavoo has created his folk music liturgy and the meaning of its indigenization and reception.

Tamil Protestant Christian music can be divided into three major categories: Western hymns sung in European languages, Western hymns translated into Sanskritized Tamil, and indigenous classical, folk, and popular songs. Protestant missionaries brought their hymnody and instruments with them to India, musical representations of both their theology and cultural baggage. Most urban Christians learned this repertoire. Some lower-caste Christians have continued to use English-language hymns accompanied by organ and four-part harmony as a symbol of class mobility and an expression of agency against local elites. They associate themselves with colonial powers and Westernization in an attempt to shed the stigma of untouchability. Yet in the process of musical adaptation, they internalize the foreign and elite cultural ideology, rejecting Tamil village culture as "heathen" and "degraded."

Western hymns translated in the eighteenth century into highly Sanskritized Tamil, called *pāmālai* and *ñaṉappāṭṭu*, retained their English or German tunes and meters, rendering them meaningless to most Tamils. *Pāmālai* continues as the hegemonic music genre sanctioned by priests and lay officials in contemporary urban CSI and Lutheran churches, particularly by those concerned with maintaining the cultural values, Western aesthetics, and liturgical traditions inherited by the missionaries.

Indigenous Christian music sung in the vernacular, using local musical styles, poetic forms, and instruments, express culturally contextualized Christian hermeneutics as well as social hierarchies. Caste division among Christians played a core role in the process of indigenizing Christianity.[18] Caste distinction, then, manifests itself not only in daily relationships between Tamil Christians, but also in theology, liturgy, and music. Upper-caste identity has been most strongly encoded in classical indigenous song styles. The Catholic missionaries in the seventeenth century constructed an indigenized Christianity culturally and musically identified with Brahmins in hopes that conversion of these social/religious elites would lead to a trickle-down effect on the lower-castes. The Roman Jesuit missionary, Robert de Nobili, who worked with Brahmins in Madurai from 1606, did not consider the Christian principle that all people are equal before God to be contradictory to the social hierarchy of caste (Thekkedath 1982, 214).

The Lutheran missionaries at Tranquebar and Tanjore in the eighteenth century accommodated the upper-caste Vellala's determination to retain caste and their indigenous theology of pluralism.[19] They allowed for caste separation in seating and reception of Communion. As part of this accommodation, they also embraced the Carnatic Christian compositions of the famous Vellala (upper-caste) Christian composer/poet Vedanayagam Sastriar as the primary source for indigenized Tamil Christian music. Over 100 of Vedanayagam Sastriar's Christian kīrtanai, a three-part song form using classical Indian modes and time cycles, were compiled into the first Tamil Hymnal in 1853 by the American Congregational missionary Edward Webb.[20] The missionaries then disseminated the kīrtanai to the rural lower-caste Christian population who had minimal previous exposure to this elite form. This resulted in indigenization as Sanskritization, or elite cultural "Hinduization," for lower-caste village Christians who continue to use kīrtanai as their primary liturgical song genre.

Many of the Protestant missionaries since the nineteenth century have worked hard to eliminate caste identity distinctions, often requiring their upper- and lower-caste converts to sit together at love feasts.[21] Most did not, however, recognize the upper-caste and class values encoded in Carnatic music. Instead, missionaries, along with upper-caste elite Tamil Protestants, continued to support Carnatic music as the only form of indigenized Tamil Christian music considered acceptable for church liturgy.[22] Furthermore, because of the early establishment of caste practices by the Lutheran Vellalas and postindependence power struggles within the Protestant (CSI and Lutheran) Churches, caste has remained a category of identification and hierarchical social differentiation within the Tamil Christian communities.

In postindependence India, middle-class educated Tamil Christians, many of them theologians, combined elements of Carnatic music and de-Sanskritized or *sen* (pure) Tamil to create songs and liturgies, called *tamil isai vari pāṭṭu*.[23] While these replace the Hindu theological content and Sanskritized Tamil of the *kīrtanai* with a progressive Tamil Christian theology, the language and poetic metaphors of literary Tamil continue to reflect the values and cultural experiences of middle- and upper-class, highly educated Tamil Christians. Literary Tamil remains inaccessible to, and unreflective of, the lower-class members of the lower-castes. Furthermore, the musical performance is even more classicized than the contemporary *kīrtanai*: the message is more liberating, but the linguistic and musical medium of transmission remains elite.

Since the 1950s, indigenous Christian popular or light music, which fuses elements of Western pop music with Indian folk and light classical music, is often used by Tamil evangelists. However, it has faced official Church resistance because its style is too closely associated with secular themes in films. Many liberation theologians also feel light music pacifies people because its tunes and rhythms are used to attract masses of poorer people, yet it fails to address the issue of social oppression. Evangelists ask the people to have faith in order to find salvation in heaven, a message that helps maintain the status quo in a culture that is dominated by the ideology of caste karma.

The development of a Tamil Christian music that both addresses the social needs of poor village Dalits, the majority of Protestant Christians, and transmits a liberative message in a musical style that positively reflects their values and cultural traditions, was not created until the 1980s.[24] Appavoo and others who create folk-based music question earlier assumptions about the superiority of Western and elite Indian musical values by reviving pre-Christian village traditions, combining them with local hermeneutics perceived as parallel to early Christian or Jewish social contexts and Gospel ideologies. Activists and common people use Dalit Christian music to alleviate the religious stigma of pollution, to fight against the social and internal psychological oppression of discrimination, and to reconstruct their economic and political status. The following musical and linguistic analysis describes how Appavoo reclaims the content and form of folk culture as a powerful and valuable tool of Dalit liberation in Tamil Christian liturgy.

Liberative Indigenization through Folk Music in Appavoo's "Worship in Folk Music"

Appavoo's "Worship in Folk Music" (*girāmiya isai vari pād*) is one of several CSI Tamil music liturgies or *Tamil Isai Vari Pāṭṭu* (TIVP).[25] Since the 1950s, six of these fully sung liturgies have been composed in classical Carnatic style using Sanskritized or high literary Tamil. Appavoo composed his Tamil folk, spoken language version in 1994 in order to (re)indigenize the content and musical style of the TIVP to include metaphors, stylistic and performance devices, and cultural and religious values of rural Tamil life. Appavoo also intended to formally introduce folk music and spoken language into the CSI churches; thus he translated the language of the traditional CSI order from high literary written to pan-regional spoken Tamil.

Appavoo communicates his theology both in lyrical content and musical medium. While the transmission of the message through the lyrics is of primary importance, the values at the core of his theology, universal family, *oru olai*, and the strategy of reversal are contained within the system of folk music sound and performance. The corporate worship values of unity and sharing are encoded in call-and-response techniques, community participation in leading the service, and transformative empowerment through musical and theological recreation.

Appavoo seeks to create an unalienating participatory liturgical context, where the message is primarily communicated through the heart and emotions. This is signified musically through mood and rhythm, which he believes are the key structural elements to the transformative power of folk music. The lyrics help create the musical moods through painting nostalgic rural images and through emotional shock engendered by using "unrefined" language.[26] Appavoo also consciously draws on linguistic accents of spoken Tamil to create dramatic emotional responses in performance.

The three primary theological metaphors Appavoo constructs in his village liturgy are God as bigendered parent of one universal family, the Eucharist as *oru olai* (shared communal eating), and God as farmer (the strategy of reversal). They all address issues of unity as the means for a change in values and action against oppression. Appavoo believes that God has provided everything people need to live. He views the source of human problems as located not in God, but in the Church, the larger social structure, and Dalits themselves who do not worship as a unified group or universal family. According to Appavoo the essential action of being in one universal family is to share food communally; indeed he advocates this as the proper way of worshipping God.[27]

In the "universal family" all people are siblings born of the same parent's (*pettavarē*) womb.[28] There is no separation of people based on class, private ownership, or gender differences. Appavoo uses Galatians 3:28 as the biblical foundation for this tenet. He preaches that, "If you are in one family then [as in Christ] there is no difference between . . . man or woman, between slave and master."[29] There is no caste difference; no person is separated from the family table because he/she is considered unclean. There is also no separation between those who "have been saved" and those who have not nor between Christians and non-Christians.

Through exposure to the Dalit people's material reality, Appavoo realized that the Eucharist needs to be a daily living practice of communal eating and shared labor that liberates people from social and economic injustice. When discussing I Corinthians 10:22 in a rural theological education class ("We who are many are one body, for we all partake of the one bread"), a Dalit village girl asked Appavoo what he had eaten for breakfast. He replied "*idlies*"—a middle-class breakfast of steamed rice cakes and curry. She stated that she had had *kañji* the poor peoples' breakfast of rice gruel, and that her neighbor had had nothing (Appavoo 1992, 7). This encounter signified for Appavoo the reality that everyone does not literally partake in *one* food. Economic and social classes eat different foods, and some are not able to eat at all. Appavoo feels strongly that this analysis from the perspective of the most marginalized in Indian society, a Dalit girl, "questioned all the theological arguments over issues such as transubstantiation, consubstantiation, and memorable feast. Eucharist became *oru olai*, [the] common food of the Universal family" (Appavoo 1993, xxviii).

Appavoo advocates several "reversals": of values, of social hierarchy, of the paradigms with which hegemonic institutions interpret the Bible, of the concepts of inauspiciousness, cleanliness and purity, and of the metaphors used to understand Jesus and God. Appavoo's strategy of reversal is expressed most powerfully through reclaiming the use of folk music as a legitimate source for indigenized Christian liturgy in his *girāmiya isai varipāḍu*. He uses instruments such as the *parai*, vernacular language, melodies, rhythms and folk-music genres commonly thought of by middle-class pastoral and lay leaders as the degraded cultural antithesis of classical Carnatic music or Western hymnody.

Appavoo's biblical grounding for his theology of reversal lies in the metaphor of the kingdom of God. He follows Jesus' strategy of "using the language of paradox and reversal to shatter the conventional wisdom of his time" (Borg 1994, 80–81). The interpretation of Jesus' actions as efforts to benefit primarily the poor and oppressed challenge traditional Indian and Western interpretations that value private property and money over human relationships, and reverse the hierarchies of class, caste, and gender. Appavoo intends to reverse the metaphor of Jesus as *raja* (king), which has been common in Tamil liturgy for over 250 years. Instead, he portrays God as a farmer (*vevasāyi*) or a working-class political leader who rides a working animal, the donkey. Both reclaim a positive status for Dalit subjects. Appavoo also attempts to reverse the patriarchal ideology of Western Christianity by interpreting the qualities of God as both masculine and feminine.

Analysis of James Theophilus Appavoo's "Worship in Folk Music"

The invocation at the beginning of Appavoo's village music liturgy, *Girāmiya Isai Vaṛipāḍu*, mirrors the Tamil village religious tradition of invoking *sāmi* (God), announcing that all community disputes have been settled, and all the people have gathered in unity. The Adoration (Greetings and Praise) is extended to clearly define and reclaim God in the local agricultural and social context. The Repentance and Absolution draw on the folk lament style of *oppari*. Although the content and style have been redirected toward a village perspective, the Creed, Preparation of the Meal, Blessing the Meal, Lord's Prayer, and the Final Blessing all follow the CSI form very closely. All of the sections of the liturgy are usually sung except the Gospel readings and the sermon. However, Appavoo often replaces the formal spoken sermon with a street theater style skit that involves members of the congregation. Appavoo also consciously undermines the sanctioned priest/congregation hierarchy by involving the congregation in a call-and-response format with a rotating lead singer during the blessing of Communion traditionally sung only by the priest.

The penultimate section between Communion and the Final Blessing allows anyone from the congregation to pray publicly. It functions similarly to intercession prayers normally placed after the Creed and also provides an opportunity for community and individual expression typical of Dalit religions and many rural Christian congregations.

Greetings and Praise of God, *Sāmiya Vaṇaṅguṛadu*

Section 1
pettavaṛē olagattai paḍaiccavaṛē -ammayappā
O, parent who created the world, mamma/papa.
attaṇaikkum āṇḍavaṛē ompādam vaṇakkam
Lord of everything, we bow at your feet.
mūttavaṛē mīṭṭeḍukka vandavaṛē -kaṉṉimari
O, the eldest one who has come to redeem us.
petteḍutta pālagaṛē ompādam vaṇakkam
O, child of Virgin Mary, we bow at your feet.
suttattiru āviyaṛē sūriyaṛē -ottumaye
O, the Holy Spirit, the sun.
kattuttarum vāttiyāṛē ompādam vaṇakkam
The one who teaches us solidarity, we bow at your feet.

Section 2

āttukkuḷḷa ūttu taṇṇi sāmiyaruḷ nādā–pāva
You are the spring in the river, O divine one, gracious lord!
ūttai pōkkum jīvataṇṇi sāmiyaruḷ nāda.
The living water that cleans the filth of sin, O divine one, gracious lord!
sutta neyyi poṅga sōṟu sāmiyaruḷ nāda–pasiye
You are the pure *ghee pongal* rice, O divine one, gracious lord!
nittam pōkkum jīvasōṟu sāmiyaruḷ nāda.
The living rice that removes hunger every day, O divine one, gracious
    lord!
kāttula nī teṇṇaṅkāttu sāmiyaruḷ nāda–olaham
You are the breeze from the coconut grove, O divine one, gracious lord!
mottattukkum vīsum kāttu sāmiyaruḷ nāda.
That blows for all the world, O divine one, gracious lord!

Section 3

muttipōṉa sorakkā nāṅga sāmiyaruḷ nāda–oḍacci
We are the over-ripe vegetable, the *sorakkā*, O divine one, gracious
    lord!
vitteḍuttu vedappavaru nī sāmiyaruḷ nāda.
You are the one who breaks the gourd, removes the seeds and plants
    them!
neruñcimuḷḷu neṟañca nelam sāmiyaruḷ nāda–ēṅga
We are the land full of *nerinji* thorns, O divine one, gracious lord!
neñcaikkotti kaḷaiyeḍuppavar nīyē aruḷ nāda
You are the one who plows our hearts and removes the weeds, O
divine one, gracious lord!

Section 4

karugippōṉa kāṇappayiru sāmiyaruḷ nāda–adai
We are the wilted *kāṇai* plant, O divine one, gracious lord!
tuḷukkavaikkum vevasāyi nī sāmiyaruḷ nāda
You are the farmer who makes it sprout, O divine one, gracious lord!
viruttiyillā paruttikkāḍu sāmiyaruḷ nāda–adai
We are the cotton fields that do not yield, O divine one, gracious lord!
veḷaya vaikkum vevasāyi nī sāmiyaruḷ nāda.
You are the farmer who makes them grow, O divine one, gracious lord!
ēreḍuttu vantavarē sāmiyaruḷ nāda–oṅga
O you who took up the plow and came, O divine one, gracious lord!
pēreḍuttu pōtṟi seyyirōm sāmiyaruḷ nāda.
So we take your name and praise you, O divine one, gracious lord!

Interpretation of the Greetings and Praise:

The Greetings and Praise consists of four sections, each delineated by a change in musical mood, exploring joy and sadness, particularly through changes in tempo. Section one of the "Greetings and Praise" demonstrates how Appavoo uses music to articulate the core aspects of his indigenized theology. Using the same melody to describe the Holy Trinity (and their essential nature as equals or "three-in-one"), Appavoo outlines his theology of the universal family, characterizing God as the bigendered parent (*pettavarē*) and Jesus as the elder brother (*muttavar*) and son of Mary. Then, with a driving vocal and instrumental unity he describes the Holy Spirit, the sun, as a teacher of solidarity.

The second phrase of each melodic couplet musically defines the quality of each aspect of the Trinity by emphasizing the following words with *oṭṭuccol* syncopated accents at the end of the line: 1) *ammaiyappa*,[30] mother/father lord of everything; 2) *kaṉṉimari*, Virgin Mary; and 3) *ottumaya*, the one who gives and teaches solidarity. *Kaṉṉimari*, or Virgin Mary, is constructed from Appavoo's feminist standpoint as the independent bearer of salvation. Jesus was conceived independently of a male's help; furthermore, there would be no salvation without Mary's consent to the angel Gabriel's request and her willingness to risk social ostracism as an unmarried pregnant woman.[31] Rhyme patterns throughout become mnemonic devices in the folk transmission system that help people to remember the words and thus transmit the ideas easily.

Section two of the "Greetings and Praise" introduces a happy, excited mood both melodically and rhythmically. Its lyrics combine Christian, Tamil, Dalit, and rural metaphors to create a positive and hopeful indigenous perspective on the gracious gifts of *sāmi*, the divine one. In the first of three choruses, God is defined as "the spring in the river, the living water that washes off (or 'removes') the filth of sin."[32] Through rural symbols Appavoo calls on Christian Dalits to return to the life force of the land, to its rural simplicity and beauty, to wash off the filth of sins (like classism and internalized casteism), and to reclaim rural Dalit identity as clean. Appavoo attempts to reach the minds and hearts of the middle-class urban Dalit who has left behind the village and everything associated with it.

The second stanza continues this theme of rural purity, yet focuses more on culture. He presents the metaphor *sāmi* (or Christ), the living Eucharist, as "the pure *ghee pongal* rice, the living rice that removes hunger every day." *Pongal* is the Tamil harvest festival named for the sweet *pongal* rice that is cooked in a pot and boiled over to represent the promise of good fortune in the coming year. In a village context the *pongal* is cooked and shared communally.

This metaphor is the basis for Appavoo's understanding of Eucharist as *oru olai*. By describing the *pongal* rice as pure *ghee* [*nei*], Appavoo again attacks the myth of lower-caste culture as impure, replacing it with an emphasis on the rich delicacy and ritual purity of *ghee* (clarified butter).

In the Tamil context, the Western concept of the Eucharist as living bread is indigenized as the living rice that removes the daily hunger of poverty. Going beyond the simple cultural substitution of rice for bread to create an oppositional Dalit construction, Appavoo consciously uses the often denigrated vernacular term *sōru* for rice instead of the more literary or Brahmanic *sādam*. He reclaims the auspiciousness of Dalit culture and subverts the Brahmanic hegemony by fusing *sōru* with the more Sanskritic *jiva* (living) in a blasphemous marriage of the Brahmanical and Outcast as the primary Christian symbol of God: the Eucharist given with grace.

In this second section, the word *pōhhum* is used in two contexts: the daily removal of hunger, *pasiya nittam pōhhum*, and the removal or cleansing of the filth of sin, *pāva ūttai pōhhum*. The double use reinforced by their articulation with the same melody ties these two ideas together in the practice of *oru olai*. Appavoo advocates that if people of different communities eat together communally every day, no one will go hungry. Moreover, through this radical action they will undermine participation in the "sins" of caste separation and private property.

In the third stanza, Appavoo returns his congregation to a peaceful pastoral scene where they can feel the breeze from the coconut grove given freely as the grace of God and available for all to enjoy. He reminds us that God has already given people everything they need in nature, in contrast to the inequalities of modern urban life, with its material necessities like fans, which are available only to those who can afford electricity.[33] Section two of the "Greetings and Praise" focuses on "re-claiming" Appavoo's strategy of indigenization for the liberation of Dalits. God and God's grace are represented as rural beauty and natural auspiciousness in order to reassociate village life as positive. Appavoo's focus on food in this section represents the centrality of Jesus' radical action in table fellowship and highlights the perspectives and concerns of poor Dalit people.

In sections three and four of the "Greetings and Praise," rural hardships of rot, pain, heat, and infertility are not romanticized but in fact starkly spelled out as metaphors for humans who have made mistakes; this theme is encoded musically with melodic tension. Each couplet contrasts poignant rural images with positive images of God's grace as the nurturing *vevasāyi* (gender neutral "farmer") who plows, sows, and grows new life, bringing redemption and forgiveness for human mistakes and resolving the (social and musical) tension of painful misfortune. Appavoo reflected in a 1994 interview on the Dalit farmer as a metaphor for the divine: "I'm moved by that metaphor. I was really happy that I got that metaphor because we have only been thinking of God as father, the patriarchal father, only as king, the aggressive dominant king. *Vevasāyi* is a term that is used for both man and woman."[34]

The lyrics in section three ask the congregates to ponder their own sins. Accordingly, Appavoo slows the tempo back to the original and uses a 6/8 meter to express an interior "depressed mood," as one would reflect upon what has been left undone. The first couplet of section three reflects upon people's sins with the line "we are the overripe *sorakkā*." *Sorakkā* is a gourd-like vegetable that becomes inedible when overripe. It is also thought by some, particularly Brahmins, to be an inauspicious vegetable.[35] Farmers do not, however, waste or throw away the overripe *sorakkā*; they either dry its shell and use it to hold water, or break the shell to get seeds for the next generation of plants. The message of this metaphor is that, like the next generation of seeds, God sees our potential and has use for us even when we appear rotten to others or ourselves. Appavoo also described the overripe *sorakkā* as a symbol for the third and fourth generation of Christians who have left the village, and have become "soft" (passive, rotten, and corrupted by materialism, selfishness, and individuality) middle-class people. They have lost the taste for *sorakkā*, or village culture, and for liberating protest. In a tone of hopeful faith, the verse asks God to break our shells and "make us seeds to grow new *sorakkā*."[36]

The second couplet describes the land that grows *nerinji* (thorn weeds) because it lies fallow or is left uncultivated. If these thorns pierce the skin, they can be very painful. Furthermore, in Tamil literature this landscape carries negative symbolism. In Appavoo's liturgical context, God the farmer plows away the pain from our hearts, removing the harmful weeds. The phrase *karugippōṉa*, when applied to a plant, means that it has wilted or been burned by the sun. *Kāṉappayir* is a type of legume that needs very little water to grow, and thus does not wilt easily. If the *kāṉappayir* does wilt, as Appavoo describes in section four, the sun must be very hot. Such extreme heat is a metaphor for people's sins which lead to social oppression: people are hot with sin like the intense sun that wilts the *kāṉappayir* plant. But God, as farmer, gives grace to make the people sprout again.

The fifth and final couplet ends the "Greetings and Praise" section on a fully positive tone musically and lyrically. This time the two phrases do not contrast the sins of the people with the saving actions of God, but reverse the order of focus. The salvation of Jesus is described first by evoking the sacrifice of the Dalit farmer who takes up the plow (the cross) for all others. The people follow, taking up the name of Christ as liberator to praise him. The substitution of the Dalit plow for Jesus' cross, accompanied by powerful folk singing and playing in unison, fully indigenizes Christian faith and worship in the sacrifices and joy of Dalit culture. God is not only with Dalits, but *is* Dalit.

Indigenized Tamil Christianity, therefore, only becomes "Christian" if it is indigenized into a cultural medium that liberates the poor and oppressed (i.e., Dalits) through claiming them as valuable, auspicious, and worthy. In Tamil Nadu, in order for the Untouchables to be liberated, their cultural resources must also be liberated from hegemonic associations of inferiority, degradation, and inauspiciousness. Appavoo's *Girāmiya Isai Vaṛipāḍu* intends to induce spiritual, cultural, and psychological liberation in a Tamil Christian liturgical setting. This is achieved by drawing on the transformative aspects of folk culture including the transphysical power of *parai* drumming and rhythms, community participation, the emotional power invoked by folk language, metaphor and melodic devices, and a folk transmission system that allows for theological recomposition as indigenization.

Reception and Conclusion

The reception to Appavoo's "Worship in Folk Music" since its composition in 1994 has been positive, if slow. Several of his former students have adapted the liturgy to their own local contexts by making the language more regionally colloquial. As priests, a larger number of Appavoo's students have also been inspired to attempt an occasional practice of *oru olai* (communal eating) among their village congregations. By pooling financial and labor resources to share the ritual of eating in *oru olai,* many Dalit villagers have seen the possibility of unity, hope, and social change. Before Tamil Dalits can organize for structural, economic, and socio-political change, it is necessary to break the psychological barriers that prevent them from believing change is possible. The experience of *oru olai* in practice and as symbolized in the ritual and music of Appavoo's "Worship in Folk Music" appears to help inspire social change among these Dalit Christians who have been touched by his musical theology.

Since 1999 the Tamil Nadu Theological Seminary has been actively reviving rural congregations that have had little pastoral attention in years. To this end, they are introducing Appavoo's folk music liturgy and the practice of *oru olai* as the primary mode of worship instead of the orders of service in the CSI prayer book and hymnal.[37] The liturgy has thus gained official institutional sanction to be propagated among the rural people who may benefit from it the most.

The greatest challenge for Appavoo will be to reach middle-class and urban people, for folk music represents everything the lower-caste Christians in these communities have attempted to leave—poverty, caste identity, and an oppressive village context. Appavoo recognizes that social change for

Dalits requires a cultural reeducation process at all levels of the Protestant Churches in Tamil Nadu that positively revalues folk culture and recognizes its necessity as the foundation for indigenized music and theology. The tools for reclaiming, recreating, and transmitting Tamil folk music and theology are within this "Worship in Folk Music" (*Girāmiya Isai Varipāḍu*) liturgy. Appavoo's strategy is to begin by transmitting the liturgy to seminary students and rural people. If his musical theology is in fact liberating it will find meaning among the people who need to re/claim and transform their cultural esteem and value in the Church and in the greater Tamil society.

Notes

1. Dalit literally means broken or oppressed, taken from the Sanskrit root *dal*. It is the self-selected term that many people formerly called outcastes, Untouchables, or Harijans, call themselves particularly in the context of oppositional politics. It was first created in the early 1970s by the Dalit Panthers and other organizations based in Maharastra who claimed it as an expression of cultural pride and a rejection of oppression (Joshi 1986, 3).

2. These verses are from a larger liturgy called *girāmiya isai varipāḍu* (literally 'village music worship'). For a full analysis of Appavoo's songs, liturgy, and music history, see my dissertation in ethnomusicology entitled "The Indigenization of Tamil Christian Music: Folk Music as a Liberative Transmission System."

3. Dalit theology addresses the social and spiritual needs of Untouchables, as well as the lower castes, the economically disenfranchised, and women.

4. Untouchability was legally abolished in the Indian constitution in 1950. People from the Paraiyar community are categorized as a "scheduled caste," which allows for some compensatory rights through government quotas in jobs and education.

5. Since the early twentieth century, more Christian Dalits have become middle class, although the number is relatively small (20 percent of the population at the most).

6. Dalits make up 70 percent of the CSI and Lutheran churches in Tamil Nadu (Kambar Manickam personal communication, August 1994). Although 80 percent of this population still lives in rural settings, until recently the needs, values, and cultural perspectives of middle-class urbanites have dominated the focus of ministry, ministerial training, and liturgy.

7. Appavoo's conception of total liberation is articulated through his EPSIPEGS system. EPSIPEGS—*E*conomic, *P*olitical, *S*ocial, *I*deological, *P*sychological, *E*nvironmental, *G*ender-based, *S*piritual—is an acronym for a holistic analysis of oppression in India.

8. The idea of reversing the hegemonic dominance of Brahmanical cultural elements in Tamil music (as well as gender and caste inequity) occurred in The

Dravidian Movement between 1949 and 1972. Many Christians joined the Dravidian political parties, which had a significant influence on indigenized Christian music and literature. This movement articulated a positive Tamil identity through literary and linguistic study, Tamil Isai (music), and the de-Sanskritization of Tamil (Ryerson 1988, i). Although it contributed to self-respect among Dalits that had begun in the mass-conversion movements of the 1910s and continued under Ambedkar in the 1930s, it failed to speak to the economic grievances of the poor outcastes.

9. Appavoo (1993, 30), notes that 72 percent of total female agricultural labor in Tamil Nadu is Dalit, and 80 percent of Christian Dalits are landless. Furthermore, 80 percent of Dalits live below the poverty line.

10. Lower-caste scholars and activists have argued that Dalit religions are distinct from Hinduism. See Ilaiah 1994, and Appavoo 1994 in Massey.

11. The *parai* is a frame drum (small) played with the hands or (large) played with two thin sticks.

12. In the process of funeral performance, Paraiyar (pariah) drummers inherently repollute themselves by being associated with the pollution of the dead body and by having to touch the body in order to pick up coins thrown to them as payment.

13. Upper-caste elite and Westernized (neo-Victorian and popular) cultural values define cultural hegemony in the Protestant Tamil Christian Church today. In the greater Tamil culture the aesthetic values of upper-caste Brahmanical art forms devalue folk culture as *kōccai* (slang or vulgar), polluting, and not serious, but mere entertainment (see the theorist P. Sambamurthy 1984, 140–41, 105). Appavoo (1986, 13) challenges the discourse arguing for a lack of a purpose in folk music, insisting that its defining characteristic is purposeful adoption and dissemination connected with the social, economic, political, and cultural life of the folk.

14. Ethnomusicologists argue that social and musical structures are often homologous (Feld 1984, 383–409). By embracing upper-caste/class values that differentiate elite culture as pure and more refined than lower-caste folk culture, Dalits internalize this depravation.

15. J. T. Appavoo, speech given at the People's Music Festival, Tanjore, January 30, 1994.

16. I model my theories of indigenization in the Tamil context on Steven Kaplan's (1995) work on indigenized Christianity in Africa.

17. Christians make up approximately 2.5 percent of the total population of India today. Tamil Nadu is the state with the third largest percentage of Christians.

18. I have identified three major Tamil Protestant caste groups, Paraiyars, Nadars, and Vellalas, and several minor groups. See Sherinian (1998, 23–26) for a list of minor Christian castes. Also see Elder for an earlier list of Christian castes in Madurai.

19. When the Anglican Calvinist missionaries later attempted in the 1820s to eliminate the caste divisions that the Vellalas had incorporated in the eighteenth century as acceptable practice in Tamil Lutheran Protestantism, these new missionaries struck at the

heart of what Hudson (2000, 180) theorizes as an indigenous theology of pluralism. That is, all Christian people are unified by a common faith in Jesus expressed by the congregation as united prayer and love for each other; but they live, eat, and sit separately.

20. See letter from E. Webb (1853), ABCFM collection, Houghton Library, Harvard University and *The Missionary Herald,* 1854, New York: ABCFM. The Lutheran missionary C. F. Schwartz mentored Vedanayagam Sastriar from the time he was a boy (Sherinian 1998, 76–78).

21. Mid-nineteenth century American Congregational missionaries (ABCFM) required the new converts to give up their caste by participating in "love feasts." This meant a readiness to eat "under proper circumstances with any Christians of any caste, and to treat them with respect, hospitality, and other acts of kindness" (Chandler 1912, 141. Also see S. Manickam 1993 and J. C. B. Webster 1992).

22. *Kīrtanai* along with *pāmālai* continue to form the core of the Tamil hymnal.

23. This development within the Christian subculture reflected the larger regional Dravidian Tamil Isai (music) movement. It was also one of the earliest examples of a large body of indigenized repertoire having been composed without the influence or oversight of missionaries.

24. Christian castes defined today as Dalit in Tamil Nadu include Paraiyars, Pallars, and Chakliyars. The fishing communities like the Paravars and Mukkuvars are also considered by some to be Dalit; most of the Christians among them are Catholic.

25. Appavoo's liturgy uses spelling that reflects spoken Tamil pronunciation.

26. Nostalgia for rural landscape and village culture is aimed towards middle-class urban Dalits who have fled the village, and all its negative associations, physically and psychologically.

27. J. T. Appavoo, Interview, Madurai, July 1, 1994.

28. Appavoo understands the Christian God as both mother and father, feminine and masculine. Here *pettavarē,* literally means "parent who bore me," signifying the maternal womb.

29. J. T. Appavoo, Interview, Madurai, July 1, 1994.

30. Here *ammaiyappa (amma*—mother, *appa*—father, as one word) is separated from the other words with a syncopated rhythmic accent and articulated with a pulsating series of high melodic notes which then slide down into the beginning of the next line.

31. J. T. Appavoo, Lecture, Nagarcoil, September 20, 1994.

32. The word for sin in this passage is *ūttai,* which literally means foul-smelling (body) waste, (Kriya Dictionary 1992, 164). Thus the metaphor of cleaning the sin is appropriate here.

33. J. T. Appavoo, Interview, Madurai, August 18, 1994.

34. J. T. Appavoo, Interview, Madurai, August 18, 1994.

35. Paper given by Radhika Iyer, Conference on Religion in South India, Toronto, June 14, 1997.

36. J. T. Appavoo, Interview, Madurai, August 18, 1994.

37. D. Carr, Interview, Madurai.

References

Appavoo, James Theophilus. 1986. *Folk Lore for Change*. Madurai: Tamil Nadu Theological Seminary.

————. 1992. *"Oru Olai:* The Vision and Its Potential for Dalit Liberation." Unpublished paper.

————. 1993. "Communication for Dalit Liberation: A Search for an Appropriate Communication Model." Master of Theology thesis. University of Edinburgh.

————. 1994. "Dalit Religion." In *Indigenous People: Dalits. Dalit Issues in Today's Theological Debate,* ed. James Massey, 111–21. Delhi: ISPCK.

Borg, Marcus. 1994. *Meeting Jesus Again for the First Time: The Historical Jesus and the Heart of Contemporary Faith*. New York: Harper Collins.

Chandler, John S. 1912. *Seventy-Five Years in the Madura Mission: A History of the Mission in South India Under ABCFM*. Madurai: American Madura Mission.

Elder, Joseph Walter. 1954. "Caste in the Churches of South India in Madurai." Masters thesis proposal, Oberlin College.

Feld, Steven. 1984. "Sound Structure as Social Structure" *Ethnomusicology* 28, no. 3: 383–409.

Grafe, Hugald. 1990. *History of Christianity in India*. Vol. 4, part 2. *Tamilnadu in the Nineteenth and Twentieth Centuries*. Bangalore: Church History Association of India.

Hudson, D. Dennis. 2000. *Protestant Origins in India: Tamil Evangelical Christians, 1706–1835*. Grand Rapids, Mich.: William B. Erdsman Pub.

Ilaiah, Kancha. 1994. *Why I Am Not a Hindu: A Sudra Critique of Hindutva Philosophy, Culture and Political Economy*. Bombay: Samya.

Joshi, Barbara R., ed. 1986. *Untouchable!: Voices of the Dalit Liberation Movement*. London: Zed Books.

Kaplan, Steven, ed. 1995. *Indigenous Responses to Western Christianity*. New York: New York University Press.

Kriya Dictionary of Contemporary Tamil [Kriyāviṉ Taṟkālat Tamiḻ Akarāti]. 1992. ed. S. Ramakrishnan. Madras: Government of India, Department of Education.

Manickam, S. 1993. *Slavery in the Tamil Country*. 2nd edition. Madras: Christian Literature Society.

Massey, James. 1994. *Indigenous People: Dalits. Dalit Issues in Today's Theological Debate.* Delhi: ISPCK.

Nirmal, Arvind. P., ed. n.d. *Towards a Common Dalit Ideology.* Madras: Gurukul Lutheran Theological College.

Ryerson, Charles. 1988. *Regionalism and Religion: The Tamil Renaissance and Popular Hinduism.* Madras: Christian Literature Society.

Sambamurthy, P. 1984 [1952]. *A Dictionary of South Indian Music and Musicians.* 3 vols. Reprint. Madras: Indian Music Publishing House.

Sherinian, Zoe. 1998. "The Indigenization of Tamil Christian Music: Folk Music as a Liberative Transmission System." Ph.D. Dissertation. Wesleyan University.

Thangaraj, Thomas. 1990. "Toward a Singable Theology." In *Venturing Into Life: The Story of the Tamil Nadu Theological Seminary,* ed. Samuel Amirtham and C. R. W. David, 109–18. Madurai: Tamil Nadu Theological Seminary.

Thekkedath, Joseph. 1982. *History of Christianity in India.* Vol. 2. *From the Middle of the Sixteenth to the End of the Seventeenth Century (1542–1700).* Bangalore: The Church History Association of India.

Webb, Edward. 1853. Letter #440 from the Archives Collection of The American Board of Commissioners for Foreign Missions. Houghton Library, Harvard University, Cambridge, Mass.

———. 1854. Letter published in the *The Missionary Hearld.* New York: The American Board of Commissioners for Foreign Missions.

———. 1875. *Christian Lyrics for Public and Social Worship.* (5th Ed.) Revised by G. T. Washburn. Nagarcoil: Madras Tract and Book Society.

Webster, John C. B. 1992. *A History of the Dalit Christians in India.* San Francisco: Mellen Research University Press.

Wilson, Kottapalli. 1982. *The Twice Alienated Culture of Dalit Christians.* Hyderabad: Booklinks.

Interviews

Appavoo. J. T. Speech given at the People's Music Festival, Tanjore, January 30, 1994.

Appavoo, J. T. Interviews, Madurai, July 1 and August 18, 1994.

Appavoo, J. T. Lecture given to Catholic BCC workers, Nagarcoil, September 20, 1994.

Carr, D. Interview, Madurai, January 6, 2000.

Manickam, Kambar. Interview, Madurai, August, 1994.

CHAPTER 12

Afterword:
Diverse Hindu Responses to
Diverse Christianities in India

Vasudha Narayanan

Growing up Hindu in the sixties in south India, many of my Hindu friends and I attended a Catholic school. The Franciscan missionaries, the Anglo-Indian teachers, and students dressed and acted in a way that was quite different from us. These Christian teachers and missionaries spoke only English, and their clothes and food were vaguely "Western." Most of the students in school were Hindu—in the sixties, unlike now, parochial schools were considered to be the only good institutions where the medium of instruction was English. School began every morning with all the students assembling in the courtyard to sing a Christian hymn, say "Hail Mary" three times, the Lord's prayer, hear announcements, and in later years to round it off with the pledge [of allegiance] and the national anthem. The chapel upstairs was comparable to any one of the good ones I have seen in Europe, and the curriculum was good colonial fare of Shakespeare, Dickens, Wordsworth, Keats, Shelley, et al. There were no overt attempts to convert to Catholicism—indeed, Madras and all the major cities of India had dozens of Catholic schools and colleges that were populated with overwhelming numbers of Hindus. Nevertheless, we did leave the school with a good knowledge of the Bible, acted out little stories like the "good Samaritan" in our class drama hour, and certainly could sing most Christian hymns and say the prayers even in our sleep. These Anglo-Indian teachers and students in school were very different from not just the Hindus, but also from my *other* Christian friends. Sheela's family, for instance, was Protestant, and everyone dressed like my family. The women wore saris and on special occasions even sported a mark on their foreheads, which they interpreted in cosmetic terms. Sheela's mother wore a "thali," a gold wedding necklace around her neck, but we knew that instead of Vaishnava or Shaiva symbols, her chain had a little cross on it. She would ask her Hindu friends about "rahu kala"—the inauspicious hours during which south Indians do not undertake important or new ventures and made sure she worked around it. Sheela's mother, like Mrs. Verghese, our Roman Catholic friend originally from Kerala, reminded us frequently that they were of a high caste. Mrs. Verghese, in fact, told us that her ancestors were Brahmin, and when they arranged a marriage for their son, they looked in similar "high-" caste Christian families for a bride.

The essays in this volume are more about Sheela's family and the Verghese family than about the teachers in the "convent" schools I attended. For many decades after India's independence, families like these were politically and socially invisible, and there seemed to be very little pan-Indian Christian consciousness. When communal tensions were discussed socially or in newspapers, it was only in connection with Islam. In recent years, however, particularly in the post-Babri-Masjid period, there is a strong consciousness of the Christian minority and "conversion" activities. In hearing the political rhetoric and in having Christian and Muslim friends, one can immediately see at least two areas of potential discussion: first, the rising Hindu consciousness and perceptions about the benefits and special status enjoyed by the minority religions of India, including conversion activities; and second, the great intersecting ritual spaces between Indian Christians, Muslims, and Hindus. It is this second topic— the intersecting and shared spaces—between Hindus and Christians on the one hand and Indian Christians and Christians in other parts of the world, on the other—that is predominant in this volume.

While these essays showcase some of the heterogeneity of popular Christianity in India, most of them focus on south India, particularly, Tamil Nadu. As Selva Raj and Corinne Dempsey note in the introduction, there are many kinds of Christianity and many kinds of Christians in India. This has both scholarly and political implications. In terms of scholarship it means that we have moved beyond the time when the study of Indian Christianity was just a study of Indian missions or theology espoused by some of the Christian elite in India. With a few exceptions (Luke and Carman 1968) much of the scholarship on Christianity in India till recently has focused on the history of the missions or on theological issues (see especially Neill 1984; Appasamy 1926, et al.). Hudson's recent sensitive work focuses on the beginnings of Protestant missionary activity in India: the experiences of the early "high-caste" Vellala converts and caste regulations in the Church; the expression of Christian thought through Tamil literary genres and performing arts; and the complexities of people participating simultaneously in "elitist" and "popular" cultures. It is these complexities and phenomena that one cannot categorize simply as "popular" that we find in this volume. Theophilus Appavoo's folk songs valorize the Dalits; yet church music in south India is derived from a combination of Carnatic, film, folk, European, and American songs. Muttammal (in Kent's paper), an embarrassment to the Church hierarchy, nevertheless lashes out quotations in chaste Tamil from the Bible in her charismatic retellings, while the church pastor enunciates the Tamil creed with the speed of summer lightning and the intonation of Brahmin priests reciting the Vedas.

The complexities and heterogeneity of Christianity in India have to be stressed at a time when some Hindus perceive the Christians as "the other." Monolithic imaging is essential to stereotyping and the whipping up of emotions. There are Christians in every state; and they differ as starkly as the denominations to which they belong. There are, of course denominational differences between, for example, a Tamil CSI (Church of South India) member and a Roman Catholic from Goa—differences that can be attributed to the culture of the various Churches—as well as the differences that can be attributed to economic class (as in any society). In addition to these, there is a diversity based on many factors including language, caste, community, and political affiliation. There are Christians who are Brahmins, some from the Scheduled Caste (the administrative label for the Dalit), "high-" caste Vellala Christians, tribals; those who are pacifists; and others with strong political activist links–each with their own cultures and multiple identities. There are the contemplative monks who find affinities to Vedantic philosophy on the one hand and the radicals who, it is alleged, indulge in violent agitations and activities in Tripura and Nagaland, on the other. In short, we find in India the range of Christians that we find in the rest of the world. In this very volume we meet a host of people from very varied backgrounds and who have very different agendas. Can we then speak of anything monolithic as an "Indian Christianity"? Understanding and accepting the many kinds of Indian Christianities is the first step in the dismantling of political and social stereotypes and formulaic depictions of "the other."

Responses to the Christian Missions and Faith

Just as there are heterogenous Christianities in India, there are a variety of Hindu attitudes towards Christians. It is these attitudes that contextualize the phenomena we encounter in this volume. We can get an idea of the range of perceptions by looking at just three: the viewpoints of many gurus who preach "universal love" (a "spiritual" response); the RSS (Rashtriya Swayamsevak Sangh), which calls attention to and alerts the Hindus to conversion activities by Christian missions (one kind of socio-political response); and the hundreds of thousands of Hindus who (like some Christians) are multiritual and actively participate in selected Christian festivals (a multiritual/polytheological response). There are, of course, several other attitudes, including those of many traditional Hindu teachers who have only recently expressed concern at the growing numbers of Christians and Muslims in India.

Many of the dozens of charismatic gurus—men and women—in India advocate a generic message of love thy neighbor and say they are not trying to sway people's institutional affiliation to any religion or organization. A clear statement of this is enunciated by one of the most popular gurus in India, Sathya Sai Baba: "I have not come on behalf of any exclusive religion. I have not come . . . for any sect or creed nor have I come to collect followers for any doctrine. I have no plan to attract disciples or devotees into my fold or any fold." This declaration is found on the mission statement of the guru's web page (*http://www.sathyasai.org/*). The followers of Sathya Sai Baba express their faith in the "unitary" tradition, a tradition said to be that of love and their respect for all forms of religious expression. Sathya Sai Baba is quoted as saying: "Let the different faiths exist, let them flourish, and let the glory of God be sung in all the languages and in a variety of tunes. That should be the Ideal. Respect the differences between the faiths and recognize them as valid as long as they do not extinguish the flame of unity" (*http://www.sathyasai.org/logo/logo.htm*). The message about one god and several paths, a hallmark of modern Hinduism (Hatcher 1994, Bharati 1970) is stressed in many messages:

> Every religion teaches man to fill his being with the glory of God and to evict the pettiness of conceit. It trains him in the methods of unattachment and discernment, so that he may aim high and attain spiritual liberation. Believe that all hearts are motivated by the one and only God; that all faiths glorify the one and only God; that all names in all languages and all forms man can conceive denote the one and only God. His adoration is best done by means of love (*http://www.sathyasai.org/intro/message.htm#HisMessage*).

Indeed, their web pages contain devotional Hindu songs as well as several Christian hymns, including "Amazing Grace." The logo of this organization is said to contain symbols of five (presumably numerically) "major" world religions. Their explanation of the Christian cross is the exhortation that one should "cut the 'I' feeling clean across and let your ego die on the cross, to endow on you Eternity" (*http://www.sathyasai.org/logo/logo.htm*).

This kind of inclusivism is found in the teachings of many other gurus as well. Ammachi says that one can meditate on any mantra including the "names of Christ, Buddha, or Allah" (*http://www.ammachi.org/teachings/chanting-pujas.html*). Ma Karunamayi frequently alludes to Christ as a model of virtue: "Forbearance is the greatest virtue. Cover the blemishes, faults and weaknesses of others. Excuse their feelings, bury their weakness in silence . . . and forgive weak persons. Lord Jesus and Lord Buddha were the embodiments of forbearance and compassion. Follow their example and become divine" (*http://www.karunamayi.org/karun2ca.htm*).

This form of generic acceptance of the many traditions cast in a certain form of nineteenth to twentieth-century Hindu rhetoric is found in the statements of dozens of gurus and represents the attitude of one segment of the Hindu population to Christianity. While it is not relevant to the issue under discussion, one may also raise the question of whether these gurus "convert." Although they claim not to convert—indeed, they say that they do not represent any exclusive path or think of a particular belief structure as the only way to salvation—critics say that at the least it promotes allegiance to the guru figure.

Another viewpoint towards Christianity is that expressed by the Rashtriya Swayamsevak Sangh (RSS), an organization that is committed to the maintenance and propagation of Hindu dharma. The RSS has taken a strong line against conversion in India and believes that this activism, funded by an influx of foreign capital, should stop. While its resolutions say that ". . . We have nothing against our Christian brethren," they add that they are "totally against the vendors trading in wholesale evangelism" (*http://www.rss.org/march1999.htm*). Their resolution concerning the visit of the pope to India in 1999 expresses their perception of conversion activities:

> The Pope visit: This meeting of the ABPS [an inner group] of the RSS strongly condemns the averment of Pope John Paul the II that the Church would target the continent of Asia to convert it to Christianity in the third Christian millennium. That the Pope made his statement on the soil of Bharat, demonstrates that he has abused the hospitality that brought him to this land of tolerance and 'Sarva panthasamadar.' The ABPS calls upon all the people of Asia in general and those of Bharat in particular to be wary of the evil designs of the Church and thwart their attempts to denigrate and destroy our ancient religious (*sic*). Let it be clearly understood that the Church dare not touch the Muslim community and that all their proselytising machinations are directed only towards the Hindus including Jains, Bouddhas and Sikhs because the Church thinks that they are the soft target (*http://www.rss.org/march2000.htm*).

The RSS says that "as Hindus we are proud to have in our midst any number of faiths, beliefs, sects and religions. We do not only tolerate but also appreciate their existence" but contextualizes these statements in its criticism of evangelical activity which it says does not have "spiritual content." This activity, it alleges, is an "out and out imperialist conspiracy" and that by

converting "vulnerable sections of Hindu Society, by force, fraud, or allurement or by all of them put together, they are alienating our people from their
culture and tradition and thus, in effect denationalizing them." Finally, it
objects to what it calls the "exclusive, intolerant and fundamentalist doctrines" of the Church and says while they do not "object to their right to
profess and practice," they ask if "such faiths deserve to have a fundamental
right to propagate their intolerant creed? Is it consistent with our secular
democracy?" The resolution asks the RSS volunteers in particular to "reach
every nook and corner of our country and enlighten the people about the
imperialist designs of certain world powers that are financing the anti-national
progammes of mass conversion" *(http://www.rss.org/march1999.htm).*

These statements make many claims: that there are mass conversion
programs which are devoid of spiritual content and which in fact are effected
through "allurement" and even force; that these are financed by imperialist
powers and that they are creating antinationalistic individuals. The RSS asserts–and some of these sentiments are becoming increasingly diffused in
many segments of the population–that the Christian missionaries target only
Hindus and not the poor Muslims. It questions the morality of preaching an
exclusivist doctrine, a feature that I will discuss later. There has been a
growing awareness of these perceptions among Hindus in India and in other
parts of the world in the last decade; an awareness combined with frustration
that the Christians and Muslims are governed by separate family laws and are
not willing to accept a uniform civil code that is applicable to all citizens of
India.

A third attitude towards Christianity can be seen palpably in the participation of many Hindus in selective parts of Christian—notably Catholic—
devotional activity. While it is the doctrines and conversion policies of the
Catholic Church primarily (though not exclusively) that is of concern to the
RSS, it is ironic that there are literally hundreds of thousands of Hindus who
regularly or occasionally participate in devotional rites in Catholic shrines
and cathedrals. Such worship patterns suddenly become popular and increase
swiftly in renown following the release of a new film (as in Velankanni, as
Meibohm notes). The veneration of The Church of the Infant Jesus, for instance, in Bangalore, attracts hundreds and sometimes thousands of Hindus
every Thursday. Testaments to the popularity of the Infant Jesus can be seen
every Thursday in Bangalore area newspapers, where several paid messages
of thanksgiving or petition are posted by Hindus. In Corinne Dempsey's
fascinating chapter we hear many stories including Sr. Alphonsa's healing of
a Muslim boy. Sr. Alphonsa is extremely popular with Hindus in many parts
of south India. Indeed, as I was growing up, I would occasionally see someone I know go to her shrine at the end of Greenways Road in Madras to light
a candle. Apparently as early as 1944, Claire and Cissy Paul, friends of my

aunt Ranganayaki Sampathkumaran, gave my aunt a piece of cloth from Sr. Alphonsa's habit and said it had healing powers. I also knew Hindu friends who regularly went to Velankanni in Nagapattinam and later on, in the late nineteen seventies, to her shrine in Besantnagar (Madras). In Meibohm's essay we see Arya Nattu Chettiyars–a group of Hindus in Tamil Nadu– voluntarily and eagerly participating in the annual festival at Velankanni. While they are a high-profile and noticeable group, there are thousands of other Hindus (and hundreds of thousands during such festivals) who are involved in ritual participation of a "Christian" deity.

Shared ritual spaces and times abound in many parts of India with Hindus participating in Muslim or Catholic rituals. The boundaries between these traditions are fuzzy in some ritual spaces. The spaces, if they are a *dargah* or a Catholic shrine, are arguably Muslim or Christian in texture but what makes that place renowned is the interaction between the Muslim saint and the Hindu pilgrim or the Christian deity and the Hindu devotee. The Hindu pilgrim may go to Christian shrines and Muslim *dargah*s, where a Muslim saint is entombed; to enter these ritual spaces, one needs no special permission or visa. The Hindu's pilgrimage is based on a sacred (though frequently temporary) relationship between saint and pilgrim, deity and devotee, healer and patient.

Multiritualism, Exclusive Theologies, and Poly-Theologies

Selva Raj has argued that the Santals are multiritualistic, and their identity emerges as authentically tribal, fully Indian, and genuinely Christian. One may negotiate similar statements about the many Indian Christians–that they are multiritualistic in expressing their Christian devotion in the tradition of their forefathers and foremothers. It is a Christian faith that is expressed in the idiom of the larger culture that surrounds them spatially and that preceded them temporally. Selva Raj refers to the multiritualism of the Santals and describes it as "a religious performance in which the devotee observes more than one set of rituals, often drawn from diverse and disparate (sometimes even contrary) traditions, in order to obtain solutions to a single human or spiritual crisis." One may note that this is true of the Hindus in a different sense. Jude's objection to Sita (Schmalz) is that she is ritually promiscuous; hedging her bets and not putting all her faith in Christ. While there is no suggestion in Selva Raj's essay that the Santals are not completely faithful to Christianity, multiritualism may sometimes represent poly-theologies. It does not mean that a person is illogical or is inconsistent—it may simply refer to the participation in various worldviews for physical, aesthetic, emotional, intellectual, or spiritual reasons. Thus, a follower of the Ramakrishna Mission does not see anything incongruous in keeping pictures of Ramakrishna, Buddha, Vivekananda, and Christ side by side on the altar. A pilgrim to Velankanni in search of a cure may be a faithful Shaiva Hindu and for the duration of the healing accept the "shakti" or power of the Virgin Mary. In doing so, these Hindus are no different from the Chinese and Japanese who for centuries had flexible, opaque, and permeable boundaries between various traditions for the most part.

Many Hindu sampradayas or philosophical traditions have exclusive theologies. By this we mean that they believe in the rightness of their worldview and sole efficacy of their deity to enact liberation or salvation. One of the central tenets of the Sri Vaishnava community, for instance, is the notion of *ananyagatitvam*; that Vishnu alone can save, and some members of this community do not go to Shiva temples. Chaitanya and his followers taught that Krishna alone was supreme. Many Vaishnava and Shaiva traditions have similar viewpoints; the south Indian *nayanmar*s, the poet-saints who lived in the latter half of the first millennium CE, were devoted exclusively to Shiva and spoke of him as the only savior. However, while the enunciated doctrine is exclusive, in practice, most Hindus, by keeping pictures of many deities in their family shrines, going to St. Anthony's to light a candle or accepting the teachings of gurus like Sathya Sai Baba, are poly-theological in worldview. For miracles to occur, for healing to take place, there has to be faith; that faith in the revelation or perception of sacrality, however temporary, in select phenomena and personages and even if associated institutionally with another religious tradition is part of the poly-theological worldview and multiritualism of Hindus in India. It is primarily in this issue that many Hindus differ from the Christian and Muslim communities in India.

In keeping up caste distinctions Indian Christians are also multiritual, affirming simultaneously the equality of Church members in Christ and the social inequality in real life. Caste is an enduring factor of Indian Christianity; a look at the "Matrimonial" section of Sunday newspapers in south India (a section bigger than many real estate sections in the United States) will inform us of Nadar (CSI), Vellala, Scheduled Caste Christians, "Brahmin" Roman Catholics, and so on seeking partners from similar castes. The papers of Sherinian and Webster speak about the castes that are euphemistically called "scheduled" in India—the Dalits (Sherinian) who include the Chamars (Webster). Webster's paper in particular addresses the strategies of the Church in the conversion of these castes. Caste inequality is allegedly one reason why some Hindus convert to Christianity, and it is ironic that after conversion, the label persists. In Tanjavur observing caste segregation and purity in rituals and seating and refusing to give up caste awareness caused a schism in the nineteenth century and caused many major Vellala converts to form a separate congregation for a while. When the "new missionaries" who came to India in the eighteenth century—replacing the old Pietist evangelical—insisted that congregations sit and eat together without caste distinctions, Vedanayagam Sastriar responded with Paul's question, "Is the kingdom of God food and drink?" (Hudson 2000, 129–72).

Is caste Hindu or Indian? Obviously, anyone familiar with the history of the Hindu tradition and the Vedas would think of this as a strange question—the origin of the caste system, after all, is found in the Rig Veda. But over the centuries, caste has become a phenomena in other religions in South Asia but lost its punch when Hindus migrated overseas—thus we find very diluted and very different views of caste among Hindus in southeast Asia (Mabbett). If caste is present among the many religions of India but becomes diluted and weak among some (though not all) Hindu migrants, especially in later generations, can one describe it as Hindu in origin but South Asian in enduring practice?

We may raise this question of "Hindu" and "Indian" in several contexts. While the words were interchangeable in some contexts up to the nineteenth century, the two have been used with distinctive meanings for almost two centuries now. One may then ask: Is the use of chariots to process deities Indian or Hindu? Is the planting of little palms as thanksgiving for the gift of progeny (Raj) a Hindu or Tamil custom? In this liminal area falls a lot of phenomena discussed in this book—the music of Theophilus Appavoo (Sherinian), the healing of Jude (Schmalz), the stories from Kerala (Dempsey), the mediumship of Bernadette and Philomena Mary (MacPhail), the chariots of Avur (Waghorne), and the ten-day festivals of Velankanni (Meibohm).

Indian, Tamil, or Hindu?

Breaking coconuts as part of worship, processing deities in chariots, and other customs, it is argued, are largely Indian and not "Hindu." The planting of trees for the birth of a child may be localized Tamil (and Hindu) rather than pan-Indian Hindu. While many customs seen in popular Catholic festivals in India are part of regular Hindu practice and easily associated with them, one can point out that some of these practices are associated with other religious traditions in India as well. Local Christians frequently say that when one addresses these rituals to Christ, it becomes an act of Christian worship using the local Tamil, Malayalam, or Gujarati idiom. Many other rituals, practices, and customs may be seen in various religions, including Christianity, worldwide. Thus, fasting and feasting, pilgrimage and possession, singing and healing, and other phenomena are not the monopoly of any one religion. Thus, the healing work of Jude or even the Chariots of Avur have parallels in other places. And, indeed, one can find such chariots in the Japanese festival of Gion held every July in Kyoto in thanksgiving for relief from pestilence in the ninth century.

Nevertheless, it is hard to dissociate the customs from the larger Hindu population, and there can be problems on many fronts. Catholic hierarchy may condemn a particular ritual as non-Christian, and on the other hand, some Hindus may object to the "appropriation" of their customs by a faith perceived to be alien, say if it was done to lure unsuspecting people into the Christian tradition. While the Catholic churches in India have festivals in which Hindus participate—and many other rituals which in *form* (if not in content) are similar to those of the Hindus—Protestant churches in India have self-consciously stayed away from having implements or rituals that may either be similar to Catholicism or the Hindu tradition. One may raise yet another question: Do the Indian Catholic churches have rituals and phenomena which are structurally similar to the local population's—thus being *more* Indianized in some ways—than Protestant churches?

The answer is complex, and, as we see in this volume and other works (see for instance, Hudson), issues of local language, centrality of the Bible, and music come into play. While selective rituals and festivals of the Catholics may seem more Indianized and have greater participation of Hindu devotees—notice the cast of thousands in the Velankanni festival—the Protestant emphasis on the Book and its translation into local languages is very significant. So too is the presentation of Christian doctrine through Indian music and local literary genres by people like Vedanayagam Sastriar in the nineteenth century. Vedanayagam Sastriar composed Christian songs in traditional genres like *kuravanci* in exquisite Tamil, replacing the characters of the traditional heroine and the soothsayer with characters like the "virgin daughter of Zion" (representing the Church); a lady representing faith who foretells that the daughter of Zion will become the bride of Christ; and so on. We see shared ritual spaces between Hindus and Catholics in this volume; a next volume exploring shared literary spaces, languages, and music between Hindus and Indian Protestants is waiting to be written.

The focus on performing arts in Sherinian's essay is extremely important in this book. Hindus have traditionally transmitted their tradition through the performing arts for centuries. Their knowledge of the epic narratives and consciousness of the faith is largely informed by music and dance, appealing simultaneously on various levels: the intellect, the aesthetic, the emotional, and the spiritual. Webster's essay in this volume shows how open air services by the Chamar, involving lively singing and dancing, was far more influential and popular than the quiet Sunday services or the sermons. The use of traditional percussion instruments, lyrics, meters, and musical modes by Sastriar at an earlier time and Appavoo today is extremely important, making Christianity culturally and sociopolitically relevant. Thus the Lord's Prayer is movingly rendered by Appavoo in local idiom but with political connotations. The Christian devotees simply see their practice as worship in the mode of their ancestors, in musical strains and the ritual idiom they are used to, as natural as the language in which they express their faith. The Eucharist becomes the communal meal (*oru olai* in the language of Appavoo in Sherinian's essay) or *prasadam*, the deities ride like royalty on the chariots, and so on. It is in this mode that a unique form of Christianity emerges, one that is local. It is not just the ritual mode of worship that is "Indianized" or shared with Hindu practice–though that is stressed in many discussions in this book–but also the deities themselves. I would argue that Mary as Velankanni is not just a Christian deity but a Tamil and (more recently with her appeal to the Bombay pilgrims) an Indian deity because she is worshiped in her *particular* manifestation at Nagapattinam, and she favors all devotees, not just those who convert to Christianity or who are Christian by faith. One important feature of south Indian Hinduism is the association of a deity with a particular local land—thus Vishnu may be known as Venkateswara in Tirupati, Ranganatha in Srirangam, and so on. Each deity has a special iconography or style of dress and is recognized as such. Velankanni has thus emerged with her own distinctive appearance and cannot be confused with any generic Mary. More important, as we note in MacPhail's article, it is Velankanni who possesses the medium. He notes in an earlier version of his chapter that the medium displays pictures of Punti Mata ("Our Lady of Poondi near Tanjavur") and Ataikala Mata (Our Lady of Refuge) at Elakkuricci, Tamil Nadu; in other words these are not just pictures of a generic Mary. Just as a Hindu has pictures of Ranganayaki (Lakshmi's name in Srirangam) or Cen Kamalavalli ("She who is like the red lotus"—a name of Lakshmi in Terazhundur), Sagaya Mary has pictures of the various Marys distinctive from many Tamil places in her home. In becoming local, in inhabiting Nagapattinam, Tanjavur, and Elakuricci, and in using the physical space of Philomena Mary's body—the body of her Tamil devotee—Mary becomes *grounded* as it were in Indian soil, in Indian flesh and spirit.

The unique form of Velankanni is also taken by her Indian devotees wherever they go. Indian Christians also take their language of worship when they migrate, and language becomes an important identity marker. Indian Christians, when they come to America, do not always worship in any local Christian church. In 1998 devotees established an icon of Velankanni in the National Cathedral in Washington, D.C. Tamil Christians banding together in Atlanta under the leadership of Rev. Palmer Paramdhas established the Atlanta Tamil Church and hold their services in the local Korean church. Larger congregations of Malayalam-speaking Syrian Christians exist in Chicago and other areas. Minorities in India, the Indian Christians become minorities *twice over*—as Indians and as Indian Christians—in America.

The word "diaspora" is generally used more for ethnic rather than religious traditions, with the argument that religions tend to straddle many ethnic groups (Cohen 1997). Thus one does speak of a Jewish but not a Christian diaspora. Cohen recognizes that Judaism and Sikhism are exceptions. To this argument one may add that most people tend to think of Christians at home anywhere. Temporally, too, since, as Selva Raj and Corinne Dempsey state in the introduction, Indian Christianity is as old as Jesus Christ himself. Thus, one cannot really talk about Christianity being in diaspora in India. Although Cohen tends to restrict the term largely to ethnic groups, Vertovec has argued that Hinduism may be a case like Judaism and Sikhism. Vertovec makes his claim based on many factors. He talks about the close relationship between Hinduism and India and accepts the notion that this can make it an "ethnic" religion. In addition to the sacred geography, Vertovec says that the Hindus outside of India have "sentimental respect if not spiritual reverence for that place and its civilizational heritage remains exceptionally strong" (2000: 4). It is on this basis that he talks about a Hindu diaspora. If one takes the sacred geography of Velankanni, Pundi, and other places into account along with the distinctive nature of the manifestations there, along with the strong cultural and language ties, can we not then speak of the Indian Christian diaspora in America?

Amidst the predominantly Christian majority culture of America, the Indian Christians maintain their minority community by encouraging cultural shows in Indian languages. A typical example of such activity is an evening of Tamil music—similar to the kind that we find in Sherinian's paper—with performing artists from India. Tamil churches across America, for instance, sponsored the music of Vedanayagam Sastriar and Clement Vedanayagam Sastriar, descendants of the nineteenth-century Vedanayagam Sastriar of Tanjavur, who wrote over a hundred Tamil Christian works in Tamil literary genres.

Just as the doctrine of incarnation involved the resolution that Jesus was fully human and fully divine, the authors in this volume portray the people they write about in a manner best exemplified by Selva Raj in his essay: that the Santals are "authentically tribal, fully Indian, and genuinely Christian." Dempsey echoes this point: "although Indian, Kerala Christians consider themselves no less Christian than their European counterpoints and, although Christian, no less Indian than their Hindu neighbors." Straddling popular and elitist cultures; adapting and assimilating rituals that are called Hindu or Indian on the one hand and Catholic on the other; expressing faith in local language and above all local music; struggling with caste and class inequalities; balancing the many local Christianities with the doctrines of the Church; striving for social justice; and professing and propagating their faith, the people in this volume—Muttammal, Jude, Philomena Mary, the Santals, the

Chamars, the pilgrims at Oriyur, Avur, and Velankanni, Appavoo, Sr. Alphonsa, the healers and storytellers of Kerala—emerge as fully immersed in the local culture and multiple traditions. But there are others whose faith is not so well articulated; some who may participate in Hindu, Muslim, and Christian rituals; some who may have converted for reasons others than spiritual; and some whose faith is expressed through violence. These are hard areas to explore with tough questions to be asked of missions whose integrity is being questioned by many Hindus. The work is cut out for further scholarship on Indian religions.

References

Appasamy, Aiyadurai J. 1926. *Christianity as Bhakti Marga; A Study of the Johannine Doctrine of Love*. Madras: Christian Literature Society.

———. 1970. *A Theology of Hindu Bhakti*. Madras: Christian Literature Society.

Bharati, Agehananda. 1970. "The Hindu Renaissance and its Apologetic Patterns." *Journal of Asian Studies* 39, no. 2: 267–87.

Cohen, Robin. 1997. *Global Diasporas: An Introduction*. London: Routledge.

Hatcher, Brian. 1994. "The Cosmos Is One Family (Vasudhaiva Kutumbakam): Problematic Mantra of Hindu Humanism." *Contributions to Indian Sociology* 28, no. 1 (May): 149–62.

Hudson, D. Dennis. 2000. *Protestant Origins in India: Tamil Evangelical Christians, 1706–1835* . Grand Rapids, Mich.: William B. Eerdmans Publications.

Luke, P. Y., and John B. Carman. 1968. *Village Christians and Hindu Culture: Study of a Rural Church in Andhra Pradesh, South India*. London: Lutterworth.

Mabbett, I. W. 1977. "Varnas in Angkor and the Indian Caste System." *Journal of Asian Studies* 36, no. 3. (May): 429–442.

Neill, Stephen. 1984. *A History of Christianity in India: The Beginnings to A.D. 1707.* New York: Cambridge University Press.

Vertovec, Steven. 2000. *The Hindu Diaspora*. London: Routledge.

Contributors

CORINNE G. DEMPSEY received her Ph.D. from Syracuse University. She is assistant professor at the University of Wisconsin, Stevens Point, where she teaches courses on Asian religions, politics and religion, and popular Catholicism. Her recent book, *Kerala Christian Sainthood: Collisions of Culture and Worldview* (2001), explores how global, communal, gendered, and sacred identities are formed by saint devotion in south India. Her published articles reflect concerns with such issues as the de-centering of religious categories by Kerala's vampiric yakshi and the phenomenon of ethnography as pilgrimage in the field of religious studies. She is currently conducting fieldwork with a Sri Lankan Tamil temple located in the U.S.

WENDY DONIGER first trained as a dancer under George Balanchine and Martha Graham and then went on to complete two doctorates in Sanskrit and Indian Studies (from Harvard and Oxford). She has taught at Harvard, Oxford, the School of Oriental and African Studies at the University of London, and the University of California at Berkeley, and, since 1978, at the University of Chicago, where she is at present the Mircea Eliade Distinguished Service Professor of the History of Religions, in the Divinity School, the Department of South Asian Languages and Civilizations, and the Committee on Social Thought. She is the author of numerous books and articles (some under the name of Wendy Doniger O'Flaherty).

ELIZA F. KENT is an assistant professor at Central Washington University, with research interests in religion, gender studies, and cultural studies. She received her Ph.D. in History of Religions from the University of Chicago Divinity School in 1999. She has written several articles and a book manuscript on the encounter between Indian culture and religion and the nineteenth-century Protestant mission in India, including "Tamil Bible Women in the Zenana Missions of Colonial Tamil Nadu," *History of Religions* (November 1999).

269

RICHARD D. MACPHAIL is a consultant in Ottawa and teaches occasionally at Saint Paul University. Formerly chair of the department of religion and culture at the United Theological College in Bangalore, India, he holds an M.A. in Indian Philosophy from Madras University and a Ph.D. from McMaster University. His work includes a literary study of ethics and *apotheosis* in the Tamil epic *Cilappatikaram* and an ethnographic study of a miracle-healing cult associated with the Shrine of Our Lady of Good Health, Velankanni in Tamil Nadu. His interests include festival and pilgrimage, goddess traditions, the feminine in religion, and inter-religious dialogue.

MARGARET MEIBOHM is a Ph.D. candidate at the University of Pennsylvania. Her dissertation analyzes cultural complexity in relation to the cult of Our Lady of Velankanni in south India and the U.S. Her other interests include medical anthropology, diaspora, and the relation between religion and healing in India and the U.S.

VASUDHA NARAYANAN is a professor of Religion at the University of Florida. She is currently the president of the American Academy of Religion and the past president of the Society for Hindu-Christian Studies. She has written and edited five books, including *The Vernacular Veda: Revelation, Recitation and Ritual* (1994), and numerous articles. She has been the recipient of several grants and fellowships including a Guggenheim fellowship (1991–92) and an NEH fellowship (1998–99). Forthcoming books include "The Sacred Utterance: A Translation of a Ninth Century Poem" and "Hindu Traditions in the United States: Temple Space, Domestic Space and Cyberspace" (Columbia University Press).

SELVA J. RAJ, chair and associate professor of Religious Studies, is the Stanley S. Kresge Professor of Religious Studies at Albion College, where he also serves as co-chair of the Center for Interdisciplinary Studies in Meaning and Value. He received his Ph.D. in History of Religions from the University of Chicago in 1994. His research interests are popular Catholicism, ritual exchange between Hindus and Catholics, Indian Christian diaspora in the US, and female gurus. His recent publications include "Adapting Hindu Imagery: A Critical Look at Ritual Experiments in an Indian Catholic Ashram," *Journal of Ecumenical Studies* (2000) and "Ammachi: The Mother of Compassion" in *When the Goddess Comes to Life* edited by K. Pechilis-Prentiss (forthcoming). Currently he is co-editing a volume, "Dealing with Deities: Religious Vows in South Asia."

MATHEW N. SCHMALZ received his Ph.D. in History of Religions from the University of Chicago in 1998. He is presently an Edward Bennett Williams Fellow and assistant professor of Religious Studies at the College of the Holy Cross, where he also serves as director of Asian Studies. His most recent publications include: "Images of the Body in the Life and Death of a North Indian Catholic Catechist," *History of Religions* (November 1999) and "*Ad Experimentum*: Theology, Anthropology and the Paradoxes of Indian Catholic Inculturation," in *Theology and the Social Sciences*, edited by Michael Barnes (2001).

ZOE C. SHERINIAN is assistant professor of Music at the University of Oklahoma, where she teaches ethnomusicology. She is writing a book on Theophilus Appavoo and Indigenized Dalit Christian Music. Her research interests also include South Asian percussion and gender studies. Her publications include "K. D. Lang and Gender Performance" in *The Garland Encyclopedia of World Music*, vol. 3 edited by Ellen Koskoff, and "Tamil Christian Music" in *The Garland Encyclopedia of World Music*, vol. 9 edited by Allison Arnold.

JOANNE PUNZO WAGHORNE, who holds a Ph.D. from the University of Chicago, is a professor of religion at Syracuse University. Her current research interests are global and urban practices, new temples, and the transformation of rituals in contemporary Hinduism. Her theoretical/thematic interests include world systems analysis, public space, and visual culture. She is the author of *Images of Dharma: The Epic World of C. Rajagopalachari* (1985) and *The Raja's Magic Clothes: Re-visioning Kingship and Divinity in England's India* (1994) and coeditor of *Gods of Flesh/Gods of Stone* (1985). She is completing a new book, "The Diaspora of the Gods: Modern Hindu Temples and Their Middle-Class Patrons."

JOHN C. B. WEBSTER recently retired as a Diaconal Worker of the Worldwide Ministries Division of the Presbyterian Church (USA) on whose behalf he has served in India for many years. He has written extensively on the history of Christianity in India. His two major works in that field are: *The Christian Community and Change in Nineteenth Century North India* (1976) and *The Dalit Christians: A History* (1992, 1994).

Index

accommodation, 17, 18, 19, 33; at Velankanni festival, 77
acculturation, 41
Achan, 122–28, 129, 133, 134
Agatha, Saint, 128
Agra, 213
A.I.A.D.M.K. (All India Anna Dravida Munnetra Kazhagam), 31
Akbar, xvii
Albuquerque, Teresa, 73, 74
Ali, Theophilus Qasim, 220
Alphonsa, Sister, 128–33, 260–61
Alter, James, 228
Amaladoss, Michael, 2
ammans, 154
animal sacrifices, 43, 45; in ordination rite, 53; at Oriyur, 89–94; slaughtering methods, 44; at St. John de Britto shrine, 87, 88
Annunciation of Mary, 196
Anthony, Saint, 151
Anthony of Padua, Saint, 66
anti-Catholic bias, xi, xiv
anti-Christian sentiments, xvii
Antony, Saint, 107–8n. 4
Apollonia, Saint, 128
apparitions, 62, 71; Marttasmuni's, 120–22
Appavoo, James Theophilus, 233–52
architecture, 22–23, 29
Ariya Nattu Chettiyars, 62, 64, 65, 70, 71, 76, 77, 261
Arokkiya Mata, 141
Arupadaividu Temple, 27

Asad, Talal, 116, 134, 135
Assam, 1
assimilation, xvii, xviii
authority, 204; of Bible women, 206; of Catholic Church, 157–58; *cepakulam* and, 156; church, 207, 226; and CSI, 193, 195–97; ecclesiastical, 16–21, 104–5, 158; of missionaries, 194; religious, 2, 204
avi kattu, 145–49, 155–56
Avur: chariot, *12;* chariot procession at, 12–13, 16, 17, 18, 21–26, 33–34; church at, 22–23; mission, 16; missionaries in, 12
ayurvedic medicine, 166, 168, 169, 180
Azariah, Bishop M., 234

Baba, Sathya Sai, 258, 262
bahre bonga (outskirts spirits), 58n. 16. See also *bonga* (spirits)
baptism, 54, 213, 216, 220, 222, 224
Baptista, Elsie W., 72, 74
Baptist Missionary Society, 212, 213–20
Baptists, 225, 226–27, 228; converts, 213, 214, 217, 226–27
Bartholomew, 79n. 14
Basilica of Our Lady of Health, 27
Bayly, Susan, 17–18, 18–19, 31, 86
Bell, Catherine, 76, 192, 207
Besant, Annie, 27
Besant Nagar: processions in, 12, 13; Virgin Mary birthday festival at, 26–31

273

Printed in the United States
118967LV00003B/103-105/A